The Manufacturing of a President

The CIA's Insertion of Barack H. Obama, Jr. into the White House

Wayne Madsen

Copyright ©2012 by Wayne Madsen

All rights reserved. No part of this publication may be reproduced, stored in a retrieval system, or transmitted in any form or by any means, electronic, mechanical, photocopying, recording, or otherwise, without the prior permission of the author.

ISBN: 978-1478260646
ISBN: 1478260645

To my late parents, Charles Viggo Axel and Betty
Madsen

iv

Contents

Acknowledgements	vii
Preface	ix
1 Barack Senior, Out of Africa via the CIA	1
2 Pay No Attention to the Furniture Store, It's Not There	23
3 Stanley Ann Dunham and the Years of Living Dangerously	41
4 East and West of Krakatoa: CIA anthropologist spies	93
5 Mother and Son: CIA "Flexible Cover" Agents	125
6 The Spy Who Loved Him: Obama's Mother's Classified Mission in Indonesia	161
7 MK-ULTRA Hawaiian Style	169
8 New York, New York and the CIA	199
9 A Star Is Born	225
10 Stanley Ann Dunham and the Misery Industrial Complex	253
11 The Captain America Recruiting Program	269
12 Chicago: The CIA's Kind of Town	283
13 Back to the Future with Obama and the CIA	299
Afterword	317
Appendix	323
Index	353

vi

Acknowledgements

There are so many people to whom I am grateful for their support – moral, financial, and professional – in taking on the endeavor of writing this heretofore secret history of Barack H. Obama, Jr. and his family.

I want to especially thank my support lifeline Tassi McKee, without whose support I could not have completed the task of writing this book.

I also want to acknowledge my mother, who, after coming out of a coma in the intensive care unit of Tampa General Hospital, told me she was proud of my bravery in writing about subjects that others avoid. After her passing, those words have kept me going in investigating the high and mighty and their crimes against the poor and downtrodden.

To my friends and colleagues over the years – they have my everlasting thanks for keeping the support, reference material, and contact information for sources flowing. If there was an "Oscar" trophy for assisting authors over the years, then such a trophy would assuredly be awarded to Steve Conn, Andrew Kreig, Len Bracken, John Edward Hurley, Jeff Stanton, Joe Lauria, Yoichi Shimatsu, Robert Finnegan, Sam Smith, Ernie Fitzgerald, Kenichi Komatsu, Jim Bamford, and Mike Springmann.

Thanks also to Dana Jill Simpson for filling in many blank pages from Barack Obama's past.

And to my friends from careers past, Vern and Gwen Smith, Ron and Nancy Lauzon, John and Bev Keith, Dave Harmon, John and Patricia Hamlet, Duane Fagg, Tom Znidar, the late Lynn McNulty, and the many others who continue to honor me with their friendship, a heartfelt thank you.

Apologies, if I omitted anyone. It was not purposeful but a memory lapse that, unfortunately, comes with the inevitable aging process. Others who I wanted to thank publicly are omitted to protect them from the inevitable retribution for which the Obama administration has become infamous. Those in this category know who they are and I thank them wholeheartedly for their assistance. Thanks also go to the thousands of subscribers to WayneMadsenReport.com. Their support has kept the spirit of journalistic muckraking alive in Washington, DC and around the United States and the world.

Preface

During the middle of the 2008 Democratic primary campaign between Hillary Clinton, who was then considered the presumptive candidate by a raft of Washington pundits and politicos, and her challenger, Barack Obama, Jr., I spoke to a friend who was a top Clinton supporter and adviser. He berated me about my support for Obama over Clinton. In response, I defended my support for the junior senator from Illinois by stressing that a Hillary Clinton presidency would raise all the old scandals from her husband's administration. "We need a change," I said, reiterating Obama's "hope and change" message. The Clinton supporter then said something that still echoes in my ears today, "You have no fucking idea who Obama is and what he represents!"

I would have chalked up the attack on Obama as merely the emotional stance of an ardent Hillary Clinton supporter. The warning, however, about Obama came not from a Democratic Party Clinton hack but an individual who had worked with the Central Intelligence Agency for decades in the world's major hot spots.

It was only after Obama became President of the United States that the warning about the "hope and change" candidate came into focus. My CIA friend had been correct -- neither I nor many others, supporters and opponents of Obama alike -- had any idea who this political upstart really was and what he actually represented.

My friend from the CIA obviously knew something about Obama during the campaign that he did not want to reveal publicly, not even to me. Obama and his family were longtime CIA operatives. In fact, Obama's CIA pedigree dated back to the beginning of the CIA's existence, when the World War II forerunner of the agency, the Office of Strategic Services (OSS), transitioned to the CIA. The enactment of the National Security Act of 1947 ushered into being the "national security state," a parallel government that operated in the shadows and largely outside the U.S. Constitution. It is important to note that Obama's grandparents, Stanley Armour and Madelyn Dunham, were key covert elements in the transition of America into a national security state.

Following one of the most mercurial rises in the history of American politics, Barack Hussein Obama, Jr. took the oath of office as President of the United States on January 20, 2009. Amid hopes that Obama would offer a new style of presidential leadership to a nation weary of eight long years of the Bush administration's contrived wars, domestic fears of another 9/11 terrorist attack, and a collapsing economy, the nation was ready for the "hope and change" message that was a hallmark of Obama's presidential campaign sloganeering.

Soon, the American people would realize that their hopes for Obama were misplaced. Illinois's junior senator, who had only served a mere four years in the U.S. Senate, would prove to be no Abraham Lincoln, the other Illinoisan who served as President. Lincoln also had a sparse political resumé and was catapulted into the White House with only a single term as a member of the U.S. House of Representatives under his belt. Obama continued many of George W. Bush's national security policies, even continuing the service of Bush's Defense Secretary, Robert Gates, a scandal-plagued former director of the Central Intelligence Agency, at the Pentagon. Many Americans, including those who supported Obama in his primary race against Hillary Clinton and his general election race against Republican candidate, Senator John McCain of Arizona, began to suffer from acute buyer's remorse.

What did the country really know about Obama? Why were there so many inexplicable gaps in his background? And his family, including his mother, Stanley Ann Dunham; maternal grandparents; Kenyan-born father; and Indonesian step-father, had huge holes in their own biographies and curricula vitae.

Uncovering formerly classified documents in the U.S. National Archives that pointed to the CIA's heavy use of anthropologists during the time frame that Obama's mother ventured off to Indonesia, it was clear I had stumbled upon something that was missing from the official Obama history. The document trail eventually led me to Indonesia where many of my suspicions about the past of Ann Dunham and her Indonesian husband, Barry Obama's stepfather, were confirmed. Further investigations into the past of Obama's maternal grandparents yielded numerous additional links to the CIA and OSS.

Obama's entire career was a mirage. The 44th President of the United States, the son and grandson of CIA operatives, was, in essence, a "Manchurian candidate" groomed from an early age to be inserted into the White House at the proper time. In Obama's case, "Manchuria" was located in the bowels of the CIA in Langley, Virginia. The records of Obama and his family's intelligence activities are, in themselves, shocking. However, what is more astounding is that little to nothing about Obama's actual past has been investigated by the corporate news media.

The news blackout on Obama's true past inspired me to write this book. The following pages will peel back intelligence agency-manufactured biographies of Obama and his family, onion layer by onion layer. You, the reader, will discover that President Obama serves not the interests of the American people but those of a small wealthy elite who have instructed him on how to carry out his major and even minor duties.

You will discover why Obama took no action to discipline CIA officials for torture and kidnappings during his predecessor's term; why Obama authorized the assassination of U.S. citizens abroad believed by a White House "star chamber" to be plotting terrorist attacks; why Obama launched bloody civil wars, under the umbrella of NATO, against Libya and Syria; and why Obama stepped up already draconian surveillance operations against the American public.

Just a few months into his presidential term, Obama visited CIA headquarters to a raucous welcome. Obama praised CIA veteran officer John O. Brennan, the man whose contractor firm, The Analysis Corporation, examined Obama's State Department passport records at the outset of the 2008 presidential campaign. Obama selected Brennan, one of the main architects of the CIA's extraordinary rendition kidnapping and torture program, as his adviser on counterterrorism and homeland security. Obama praised former CIA director Robert Gates and his work for the CIA. Gates was kept on as Obama's defense secretary as a holdover from the Bush administration.

In praising Gates's directorship of the CIA, Obama seemed to have forgotten that the Senate rejected Gates' nomination by President Ronald Reagan to be CIA director in 1987. Gates's role in the Iran-contra affair was the major reason for the Senate's rejection. Obama's deferential treatment of Gates was almost as if Obama was in awe of an old boss. Considering Obama's work for a CIA front company after graduating from Columbia University in 1983, there may be a reason for Obama's favorable attitude toward Gates. When George H. W. Bush re-nominated Gates for CIA director in

1991, he was confirmed but 31 Democrats, including Obama's Vice President, Joe Biden, voted no. Also voting no were some of Obama's future Senate colleagues, including Edward Kennedy, John Kerry, Max Baucus, Jay Rockefeller, Frank Lautenberg, and Carl Levin. Also voting no were Al Gore; Obama's Middle East envoy George Mitchell; Obama confidante Tom Daschle; Bill Bradley; and Paul Wellstone. Obama apparently respected Gates more than the opinions of his fellow Democratic senators and party elders.

Obama told the CIA audience that the agency was more important in the 21st century than ever before, even at the height of the Cold War. Obama assuaged anxieties at the CIA about investigations by the Justice Department of the CIA's involvement with torture. Obama put to rest those fears. There would be no further investigations and no prosecutions. Obama agreed with some in the CIA who believed that it was naïve for the CIA to operate at a much higher standard. The President of the United States gave the CIA a presidential pardon without even signing one.

Obama also, in an unprecedented move for an American president, charged six individuals working within the national security establishment for violating the arcane 1917 Espionage Act. The charge was that the six passed classified information to members of the press. No other president, including former CIA director George H. W. Bush, had used the Espionage Act to deter whistleblowers from informing the Fourth Estate of high crimes by intelligence and law enforcement officials, crimes that included torture and fraud.

The "Obama Six" included:

> John Kiriakou, a former CIA officer, who allegedly passed information on water boarding torture tactics and the identity of a CIA torturer

to someone identified by the government as "Journalist A."

Jeffrey Sterling, former CIA, charged with providing *The New York Times'* James Risen with classified information on Iran's nuclear program.

Army Private First Class Bradley Manning, who was charged with providing over a quarter million State Department classified and unclassified cables from the Secret Internet Protocol Router Network (SIPRnet) communication system to WikiLeaks.

Thomas Drake, a former NSA senior official, who was charged with providing classified information to journalists, including former *Baltimore Sun* reporter Siobhan Gorman. The charges against Drake were later reduced.

Stephen Kim, a former State Department contractor, charged with leaking classified information about North Korea to Fox News' James Rosen.

Shamai Leibowitz, former FBI Hebrew translator, convicted of leaking classified FBI wiretaps to a blogger on Israeli intelligence activities in the United States that were directed at stirring up war fever against Iran.

I know of at least a half dozen other U.S. intelligence agency employees who have not been indicted but who have faced administrative reprisals and loss of their security clearances and jobs as a result of bringing violations of federal law and massive corruption to the attention of their superiors. Moreover, federal indictments and secret grand juries still hang over their heads.

Compounding the Obama administration's war on the press, in June 2012, the Justice Department announced yet another investigation of leaks to *The New York Times* about CIA malware programs called "Flame" ans "Stuxnet" and a classified program called OLYMPIC GAMES that used the malicious software program to spy on Iranian computers. *New York Times* reporter James Risen continued to face a grand jury subpoena to give up his sources on the CIA's Operation MERLIN, a nuclear material spiking program directed at Iran during the Clinton administration!

The Justice Department secretly subpoenaed the phone call records of the workplace and personal phones of Associated Press reporters and editors, used by over 100 journalists, for the months of April and May 2012. The Obama administration was looking for leaks about a covert CIA operation in Yemen.

The probes blasted a new chill through the Fourth Estate.

Potential intelligence agency and military whistleblowers live in fear of being seen or heard talking to the press. The climate of fear in the government had not been seen since the "witch hunt" days of Senator Joseph McCarthy.

Obama and former President George H. W. Bush maintained a rather unusual relationship. In January 2010, Bush and his son, former Florida governor Jeb Bush, paid a surprise call on Obama in the Oval Office during a heavy snow storm. The meeting was termed a "social call." Obama invited Jeb Bush to a Miami speech on education reform in March 2011. Obama cited Bush's championing of education reform. Of course, nothing was mentioned about Jeb Bush and his father's CIA-connected illegal operations, much of which were based in Miami, on behalf of the Nicaraguan contras in the 1980s. On January 27, 2012, George H. W. and Jeb Bush again paid Obama a visit at the White House. Obama and the Bushes would spend the following evening together at the annual Alfalfa Club Dinner, a gathering of Washington's super-elite.

Even when it comes to Obama's personal tastes, he has a fascination for the spy world and spy craft not even evidenced by former CIA director George H. W. Bush during his one-term presidency. In July 2010, Obama and First Lady Michelle and daughter Sasha paid an impromptu visit to the campy International Spy Museum in downtown Washington. A museum official confided that he was taken surprise by the visit, so much so that he sped to the museum from his home in northern Virginia after being told the President of the United States would be paying a surprise visit in a half hour. The museum, a commercial venture, extols the tradecraft of the CIA but ignores the decades of illegal assassinations and weapons and drug smuggling, coups, and other violations of U.S. law by an out-of-control intelligence agency. On January 26, 2012, *The Hollywood Reporter* revealed that Obama had ordered at least four sets of DVDs of the jingoistic Showtime cable television series *Homeland*, which features a team of CIA agents battling terrorists.

The more the United States and the rest of the world saw of Barack Obama as President the more it appeared that the Obama administration was merely the continuation of the Bush I and II administrations – a virtual fourth Bush administration. The continuation of the gulag detention facility in Guantanamo Bay, the failure to bring American torturers and kidnappers to justice, the continuation of the militarization of civilian law enforcement – including the power for the U.S. military to indefinitely detain American citizens and legal residents, the expansion of U.S. military and CIA bases around the world – from Colombia to Australia and the Seychelles to the Cocos (Keeling) Islands -- all pointed to a President who was more beholden to the whims of the Pentagon and CIA than to the Constitution of the United States and the needs of the American people.

I have attempted to be as accurate as possible in describing Obama's and his family's CIA links. Because of the similarity in some names, for example, Barack H. Obama, Sr. and Barack H. Obama, Jr.; Lolo Soetoro, Ann Soetoro, and Barry Soetoro; and Stanley Ann Dunham and Stanley Armour Dunham, these names are often referred to in their entirety to avoid confusion.

To sum up Obama and his astounding and rapid rise from Illinois state senator to the White House in a mere five years, one should recall the words of Edward L. Bernays, the "father of modern public relations," in his seminal work on managing public opinion, *Propaganda*: "A presidential candidate may be 'drafted' in response to 'overwhelming popular demand,' but it is well known that his name may be decided upon by half a dozen men sitting around a table in a hotel room."[1]

In the case of Obama, it was not a half dozen men sitting around a hotel room table but a series of shadowy manipulators who had, over decades, crafted the insertion of a President of the United States while nested in secure rooms at the CIA headquarters in Langley, Virginia.

---

[1] Edward L. Bernays, *Propaganda*, New York: Horace Liveright, 1928.

Chapter One – Barack Senior, Out of Africa via the CIA

The CIA is made up of boys whose families sent them to Princeton but wouldn't let them into the family brokerage business – President Lyndon Baines Johnson.

This chapter will show Obama, Sr., was sent by the CIA to the United States, where he was met by President Obama's grandfather, who was, himself, a CIA agent. Using reliable press articles and formerly classified CIA documents, this chapter proves these early CIA connections were real but yet they somehow remained invisible to the mainstream media during the 2008 presidential campaign.

The connections of Obama's family to the CIA and the OSS run deep. The Obama story begins in Kenya, in former British East Africa.

Propelling Africa into a major front for U.S.-Soviet rivalry during the 1950s and the Cold War was a major initiative of Vice President Richard Nixon, who, upon returning from a 1957 trip to Africa, said the decolonization of Africa presented a wonderful opportunity for U.S. penetration of the continent as the European powers, "tarred by their colonial past," departed.[2]

The CIA understood Nixon's belief that it was incumbent on America to penetrate Africa. The OSS had only a major presence in Egypt and Libya. When the CIA was created in 1947, the agency's coverage of Africa remained as sparse as that of its predecessor. In

---

[2] George Morris, "Meany, Brown, the CIA and Africa," *Daily World*, May 23, 1973.

the 1950s, the CIA expanded its coverage of the continent by establishing stations and intelligence networks in the Belgian Congo, French West Africa, French Equatorial Africa, the Portuguese colonies of Angola and Mozambique, South Africa, Ethiopia, British East Africa, and Algeria.

Harry Rositzke was the CIA's point man for operations directed against foreign communist parties. In 1977, after he retired from the CIA, Rositzke wrote, "In Africa, an area of primitive, unstable states, Soviet influence is substantial in Somalia, Guinea, Nigeria, and Angola. The support of black independence movements against the Rhodesian and South African governments may extend that influence. The training of five thousand African students each year in the Soviet and East European universities is a direct investment in the future leadership of a largely illiterate continent."[3]

Obama's Kenyan-born father, Barack Obama, Sr., reportedly met President Obama's mother, Stanley Ann Dunham, in 1960, in a Russian language class at the University of Hawaii. Much will be said about the covert nature of this university in later chapters. For now it suffices to point out that the Kenyan had been brought to Hawaii in an airlift of east African students that was sponsored by the CIA.

According to a Reuters report from London, the airlift of 280 East African students to the United States to attend various colleges was "aided" by a grant from the Joseph P. Kennedy Foundation.[4] The airlift was integral to a CIA operation to train and indoctrinate future agents of influence in Africa, which was fast

---

[3] Harry Rositzke, The *CIA's Secret Operations – Espionage, Counterespionage and Covert Action*, New York: Reader's Digest Press, 1977, p. 254.
[4] Reuters, Radioteletype in English, September 12, 1960.

becoming a battleground among the United States, the Soviet Union, and China for influence among newly-independent and soon-to-be independent countries on the continent.

The airlift, which saw 23-year old Obama, Sr. flown to college in Hawaii, was condemned by the deputy leader of the opposition Kenyan African Democratic Union (KADU) as favoring certain tribes -- the majority Kikuyu and minority Luo -- over other tribes to support the Kenyan African National Union (KANU).

KANU's leader was Tom Mboya, the Kenyan nationalist and labor leader who selected Obama, Sr. for a scholarship at the University of Hawaii. Obama, Sr., who was already married with an infant son and pregnant wife in Kenya, married Dunham on Maui on February 2, 1961. He was also the university's first African student. Dunham was three month's pregnant with Barack Obama, Jr. at the time of her marriage to Obama, Sr.

KADU deputy leader Masinda Muliro, according to Reuters, said KADU would send a delegation to the United States to investigate Kenyan students who received "gifts" from the Americans and "ensure that further gifts to Kenyan students are administered by people genuinely interested in Kenya's development.'" There is no record of KADU or Muliro having conducted an investigation of Obama, Sr., or other Kenyans airlifted to the United States under the auspices of the CIA.[5]

Mboya received a $100,000 grant for the airlift from the Kennedy Foundation after he turned down the same offer from the U.S. State Department. Mboya was concerned that direct U.S. assistance would look

---

[5] *Ibid.*

suspicious to pro-Communist Kenyan politicians who suspected Mboya of CIA ties. The Airlift Africa project was underwritten by the Kennedy Foundation and the African-American Students Foundation. Obama, Sr. was not on the first but on a subsequent airlift. The airlift, first organized by Mboya in 1959, included students from Kenya, Northern Rhodesia, Nyasaland, Southern Rhodesia, Tanganyika, Uganda, and Zanzibar.

Obama, Sr. arrived in New York City on August 3, 1959, aboard a British Overseas Airways Corporation (BOAC) flight from London. From there, he traveled to Hawaii and was enrolled at the University of Hawaii for the fall semester while back home the airlift engendered considerable controversy and for good reason.

Reuters also reported that Muliro charged that Africans were "disturbed and embittered" by the airlift of the selected students. Muliro stated that "preferences were shown to two major tribes [Kikuyu and Luo] and many U.S.-bound students had failed preliminary and common entrance examinations, while some of those left behind held first-class certificates."[6]

Obama, Sr. was a friend of Mboya, who was a fellow Luo. After Mboya was assassinated in 1969, Obama, Sr. testified at the trial of his alleged assassin. Obama, Sr. claimed he was the target of a hit-and-run assassination attempt after his testimony.

Talent spotted early on by his U.S. and Kenyan handlers, Obama. Sr. was a key part of the development of the CIA's Africa Intelligence division. The Ford Foundation, which would figure so prominently in Ann Dunham's CIA career, selected a "Committee of Africanists" in August 1958, following discussions with the CIA about its need for African specialists. In a report, the Ford Foundation concluded the CIA would

---

[6] *Ibid.*

need "a constant staff level of something like 70 people specializing in the African area."[7]

In addition, "those with training in economics, geography, or political science" and, in some cases, those who could be trained in such areas, were to be recruited by the CIA. While the State Department saw a need for only fifty Africa specialist diplomats over a ten-year period, from 1958 to 1968, the CIA saw a clear need for more. In 1961, State Department adviser Vernon McKay stated, "the professional staff of the Africa office declined from twenty-three to fifteen when certain long-range activities were transferred to the Central Intelligence Agency. The CIA coordinated all U.S. government research on Africa through its participation in the Foreign Area Coordination Group and the State Department's Bureau of Intelligence and Research.[8]

Obama, Sr. left Hawaii for Harvard in 1962 and divorced Dunham in 1964. After moving back to Kenya, Obama, Sr. worked for the Kenyan Finance and Transport ministries as well as an oil firm. Information on Obama's oil company employer is sketchy, but Esso Kenya, which was later sold to Mobil, was the most active U.S. oil company in Kenya in the 1960s. Standard Vacuum (STANVAC), a joint operation of Standard Oil of California and Socony [Standard Oil of New York] Mobil, also operated in Kenya.

Obama, Sr. died in a 1982 car crash and his funeral was attended by leading Kenyan politicians, including future Foreign Minister Robert Ouko, who was assassinated in 1990.

---

[7] Africa Research Group, African Studies in America, the Extended Family, October 1970.
[8] *Ibid.*

CIA files indicate that Mboya was an important agent-of-influence for the CIA, not only in Kenya but in all of Africa. A formerly SECRET CIA "Current Intelligence Weekly Summary," dated November 19, 1959, states that Mboya served as a check on extremists at the second All-African People's Conference (AAPC) in Tunis. The report states that "serious friction developed between Ghana's Prime Minister Kwame Nkrumah and Kenyan nationalist Tom Mboya who cooperated effectively [emphasis added] last December to check extremists at the AAPC's first meeting in Accra."[9] The term "cooperated effectively" appears to indicate that Mboya was cooperating with the CIA, which filed the report from field operatives in Accra and Tunis. While "cooperating" with the CIA in Accra and Tunis, Mboya selected the father of the president of the United States to receive a scholarship and be airlifted to the University of Hawaii where he met and married President Obama's mother.

An earlier CIA Current Intelligence Weekly Summary, Secret, and dated April 3, 1958, states that Mboya "still appears to be the most promising of the African leaders." Another CIA weekly summary, Secret and dated December 18, 1958, calls Mboya the Kenyan nationalist an "able and dynamic young chairman" of the People's Convention party who was viewed as an opponent of "extremists" like Nkrumah, who was supported by "Sino-Soviet representatives."

In a formerly Secret CIA report on the All-Africa Peoples Conference in 1961, dated November 1, 1961, Mboya's conservatism, along with that of Taleb Slim of Tunisia, is contrasted to the leftist policies of Nkrumah and others. Pro-communists who were elected to the AAPC's steering committee at the March 1961 Cairo

---

[9] Current Intelligence Weekly Summary, CIA, November 19, 1959.

conference, which was attended by Mboya, are identified in the report as Abdoulaye Diallo, AAPC Secretary General, of Senegal; Ahmed Bourmendjel of Algeria; Mario de Andrade of Angola; Ntau Mokhele of Basutoland; Kingue Abel of Cameroun; Antoine Kiwewa of Congo (Leopoldville); Kojo Botsio of Ghana; Ismail Toure of Guinea; T. O. Dosomu Johnson of Liberia; Modibo Diallo of Mali; Mahjoub Ben Seddik of Morocco; Djibo Bakari of Niger; Tunji Otegbeya of Nigeria; Kanyama Chiume of Nyasaland; Ali Abdullahi of Somalia; Tennyson Makiwane of South Africa, and Mohamed Fouad Galal of the United Arab Republic.[10]

The only attendees in Cairo who were given a clean bill of health by the CIA were Mboya, who was certainly a snitch for the agency; Joshua Nkomo of Southern Rhodesia; B. Munanka of Tanganyika; Abdel Magid Shaker of Tunisia; and John Kakonge of Uganda.

Nkrumah would eventually be overthrown in a 1966 CIA-backed coup while he was on a state visit to China and North Vietnam. The CIA's overthrow of Nkrumah followed by one year the agency's overthrow of Sukarno, another coup that was connected to President Obama's family on his mother's side. There are suspicions that Mboya was assassinated in 1969 by Chinese agents working with anti-Mboya factions in the government of Kenyan President Jomo Kenyatta in order to eliminate a pro-U.S. leading political leader in Africa. Upon Mboya's death, every embassy in Nairobi flew its flag at half-mast except for one, the embassy of the People's Republic of China. However, blaming the Communists for Mboya's assassination may have been another CIA propaganda ruse, as it was in Indonesia

---

[10] CIA, All-Africa Peoples Conference report, November 1, 1961.

with blaming the PKI for the assassination of the six generals in 1965.

The following is what the CIA reported on Mboya's assassination: "The government announced in 21 July the arrest of Nahashon Njenga on suspicion of assassinating Tom Mboya. [REDACTED] In 1965, Njenga was arrested for the murder of opposition leader Oginga Odinga's principal adviser, but was never tried. The government may attempt to counteract any charges that it is involved in the assassination of Mboya by implicating the Communists." [REDACTED][11]

Mboya's influence in the Kenyatta government would continue long after his death and while Obama, Sr. was still alive. In 1975, after the assassination of KANU politician Josiah Kariuki, a socialist who helped start KANU along with Mboya and Obama, Sr., Kenyatta dismissed three rebellious cabinet ministers who "all had personal ties to either Kariuki or Tom Mboya." This information is contained in the CIA Staff Notes on the Middle East, Africa, and South Asia, formerly Top Secret Umbra, Handle via COMINT Channels, dated June 24, 1975. [Appendix 1]. [12]

The intelligence in the report, based on its classification, indicates the information was derived from National Security Agency (NSA) intercepts in Kenya. No one was ever charged in the assassination of Kariuki.

The intercepts of the phone calls of Mboya's and Kariuki's associates are an indication that the NSA and CIA also maintain intercepts on Barack Obama, Sr., who, as a non-U.S. person, would have been lawfully

---

[11] Director of Intelligence, *Central Intelligence Bulletin,* July 23, 1969.
[12] CIA Staff Notes on the Middle East, Africa, and South Asia, June 24, 1975.

subject at the time to intercepts carried out by NSA and Britain's Government Communications Headquarters (GCHQ).

British Colonial Office files declassified in April 2012 show the name "Barack H. Obama" on a list of Kenyan students studying at American universities. British colonial officials in Kenya agreed with KADU deputy leader Muliro that the Kenyans selected for scholarships in the United States were "academically inferior" to other Kenyan students who remained in Kenya for their studies. Obama's name appeared on the following list of Kenyans receiving American scholarships:

OBAMA, Barrack [sic] H. Univ. of Hawaii, Honolulu, Business Administration[13]

Obama's class (level), such as graduate student or senior level, was left blank, as well as his home town.

Other Kenyan students are listed as receiving scholarships at other U.S. colleges and universities, including the University of Chicago, Harvard, Cornell, Columbia, Purdue, Stanford, University of Illinois, San Francisco State College, Ohio State, Indiana University, St. Mary's University of San Antonio, Howard University, University of Washington, Morehouse College in Atlanta, Tuskegee Institute, DePauw University in Indiana, Berea College in Kentucky, Clemson Agricultural College in South Carolina, and Dunbarton College of the Holy Cross in Washington, DC.

---

[13] Richard Norton-Taylor, "Barack Obama's father on colonial list of Kenyan students in U.S.," *The Guardian*, April 18, 2012.

In addition to Business Administration, other students' fields of study were listed as Natural Science, International Relations, Sociology, Labor Sciences, Economics, Journalism, Geography, Home Economics, Agriculture, Plant Pathology, Structural Engineering, Engineering, Education, Political Science, and Pre-medicine.

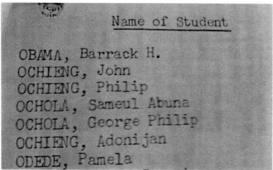

Partial list of Kenyan students released by the National Archives of the UK.

CIA Investment in Mboya and allies

Mboya was, undoubtedly, the mentor of Barack Obama, Sr. It was Mboya who arranged for President Obama's father to be selected over more qualified candidates to be sent to the University of Hawaii as part of the CIA-linked Airlift Africa project to groom future pro-U.S. leaders of newly-independent English-speaking African states.

The main objective of the CIA, according to a formerly Secret CIA "Current Intelligence Weekly Summary," dated February 8, 1962, [Appendix 2], was to isolate Kenya's main leftist leader Oginga Odinga from the post-independence government of Kenya. Odinga's son, Raila Odinga, became Prime Minister of Kenya, some nine months before Obama was sworn in as President of the United States. Odinga was aided in his ascension to power by the input of financial support for his "Orange" movement's election victory from George Soros. Soros was also a major donor to Obama's presidential campaign. Unlike their fathers, President Obama and Raila Odinga maintain a very cordial relationship. Leftist Oginga Odinga, although an ethnic Luo like Mboya and Barack Obama, Sr., was a political adversary of both.[14]

In 1962, Obama, Sr. participated in what can only be called a CIA "sheep dipping" program at the University of Hawaii. While married to President Obama's mother, Ann Dunham, the CIA ensured that Obama's connections to Airlift Africa were tightly masked. A *Honolulu Star-Bulletin* report on September 19, 1959, stated that Obama Sr. worked as a "clerk" in Nairobi for "several years" to earn enough money to attend the University of Hawaii, chosen for what he read in *The Saturday Evening Post* about its "racial tolerance." [15] [16] The article said nothing about Mboya pushing Obama, Sr. to the front of the line for the Airlift Africa scholarship. The article also claims Obama had run out of money and was planning to get a job and "possibly apply for s scholarship."[17] However, he was already on a scholarship, courtesy of the CIA. Barack Obama, Sr. was also friends with Neil Abercrombie, Hawaii's future member of the U.S. House of Representatives and governor.[18] After he became governor in 2011, Abercrombie sought to dispel

---

[14]CIA, "Current Intelligence Weekly Summary," February 8, 1962.

[15] Shurei Hirozawa, "Young Men from Kenya and Iran here to study," *Honolulu Star-Bulletin*, September 19, 1959.

[16] Janny Scott, *A Singular Woman: The Untold Story of Barack Obama's Mother*, New York: Riverhead Books, 2011. p. 82.

[17] *Ibid.*

[18] Janny Scott, *op. cit.,* p. 82.

questions about the authenticity of Obama's birth certificate in Hawaii.

Stanley Armour Dunham [third from right, second row] with Barack Obama, Sr. [fourth from right] at welcoming ceremony to Hawaii in 1959.

     The CIA was heavily involved with a number of African scholars at American universities and colleges. Most of these connections were maintained through the State Department and "close and overlapping ties with such agencies as the Ford Foundation and its academic front committees."[19]

     The President of the African Studies Association from 1969 to 1970, L. Gray Cowan, had ties to Willard Matthias, a CIA agent and visiting fellow specializing in Africa at Harvard's Center of International Affairs (sometimes, also referred to as the "CIA"). Cowan was the director and founder of the Institute of African

---

[19] Africa Research Group, *op. cit.*

Affairs at Columbia University and an expert on privatization in the developing world. From 1950 to 1973, Matthias was on the CIA's Board of National Estimates. Matthias became a critic of the CIA's overestimation of the Soviet "threat" that became "self-fulfilling prophecies" and the short-sighted belief that a loss of U.S. influence in one arena was an automatic gain for the USSR, China, or another competitor.

In his memoirs, *The Reds and Blacks*, one-time U.S. ambassador to Guinea and Kenya, *Look* magazine editor William Attwood, summed up the CIA's attractiveness to academic scholars. Upon returning to the United States, Attwood wrote, "I put in long hours answering questions for roomfuls of people at CIA (pipes, casual sports jackets, and yellow pads) and State (cigarettes, dark suits, and white notebooks). It appeared that academics preferred pipes and yellow pads every time."[20]

However, not all CIA efforts were directed against Africa's leftists. Right-wing elements accused the CIA of trying to co-opt some leftist African movements. In 1974, a Monaco-based newsletter edited by Hilaire du Berrier irritated CIA officials, including Deputy Director of the CIA General Vernon Walters, by suggesting that the CIA infiltrated Angola's nascent pro-independence movement when it sent Frank Montero and William Scheiman to Angola in March 1960 to advance an Algerian-type revolt against the Portuguese colonialists.[21] Born Hal du Berrier in North Dakota, du Berrier moved to Paris and took the name Hilaire. Du Berrier flew mercenary missions for Ethiopia's Haile Selassie after the Italian invasion of the African country and later joined the Republican side in the Spanish Civil

---

[20] Cited in *Ibid.*
[21] CIA Official Routing Slip, November 20, 1974.

War. During World War II, du Berrier worked for the OSS and later became a journalist who covered the Vietnam War.

The American Committee on Africa, with the support of Eleanor Roosevelt, Adlai Stevenson, baseball great Jackie Robinson, and Hubert Humphrey, was said to be behind the establishment of the Union of the Angola People in Leopoldville to recruit leaders for the Angolan independence movement and start up a four-language newspaper, Voice of the Angolan People, and a radio station. The Monaco group also stated the CIA started the Union of Angola Workers in 1961. This, the newsletter charged, was followed by the CIA co-opting a Syracuse University professor, Eduardo Mondlane, to begin the revolt in Mozambique against Portugal by his Mozambique Liberation Front (FRELIMO) with money from the Ford Foundation-financed Mozambique Institute. In a routing sheet attached to the newsletter, General Walters simply said the "newsletter, at quick glance . . . looks like a far right-wing outlet."[22] However, it had also been reported from left-of-center groups that the CIA channeled money to various southern African liberation movement in order to mold them in pro-western directions.[23]

Robinson, along with singer Harry Belafonte and actor Sidney Poitier, were supporters of the CIA-linked African American Students Foundation that financially backed Obama Sr.'s scholarship in Hawaii.[24]

Obama, Sr. left Hawaii for Harvard in the fall of 1962 and Obama, Jr. and Ann briefly joined him there before they moved to Mercer Island, Washington before ultimately moving back to Hawaii. The Obamas

---

[22] *Ibid.*

[23] Africa Research Group, 'The CIA in Africa, June-October 1970.

[24] Norton-Taylor, *op. cit.*

divorced in 1964. In 1965, Obama, Sr. moved back to Kenya with his new Jewish-American wife, Ruth Beatrice Baker Obama (her last name later became Nidesand, also known as Ndesandjo, after her re-marriage to a Tanzanian after divorcing Obama, Sr). One of Ruth's sons by her second marriage, David Ndesandjo, a half-brother of Barack Obama, Jr., died in a motorcycle accident in 1987

Obama joined Mboya's political movement that pitched him against Odinga, the pro-Soviet Bloc leftist, and President Jomo Kenyatta, an ethic Kikuyu nationalist who was a leader of the Mau Mau rebellion against the British. In the early- and mid-1960s, Kenyatta's anti-European sentiments made the CIA uncomfortable about his leanings, especially at the height of the Cold War.

The 1962 CIA document indicated the CIA wanted moderates to emerge as a single bloc in 1962, prior to independence. [Appendix 3][25] The bloc favored by the CIA was the KANU, but the agency noted with alarm that KANU was divided over three issues: "the cleavage between the Kikuyu and the Luo, the two main tribes which support the party; the activities of its left wing, which unites former Mau Mau 'old guard' Kikuyu leaders with Oginga Odinga, a Luo extremist [REDACTED] party secretary general Tom Mboya, also a Luo." The CIA's redaction appears to be an attempt to cover up the CIA's support for Mboya.[26]

A formerly Secret CIA Special Report titled "Leftist Activity in Kenya," dated July 31, 1964, [Appendix 4] describes the CIA's fear of Odinga and his recruitment of students to study in the Soviet Bloc: ". . .

---

[25] "Current Intelligence Weekly Summary," February 8, 1962, *op. cit.*

[26] *Ibid.*

the 51-year-old Odinga has nevertheless established his power base largely through his astute dispensing of Communist funds and scholarships supplied by both Moscow and Peiping. It has been estimated that at least 1,000 men in reasonably important positions in the government, civil service, and trade unions owe personal allegiance to Odinga, who has either sent them to study in Communist countries or supplied them with regular financial aid. Several members of Parliament almost certainly owe their election to financial support from Odinga."[27]

The CIA Special Report also states that Odinga, not the CIA's man Mboya, was "the undisputed leader of the Luo tribe, second only in members and influence to Kenyatta's Kikuyu with whom it shares power in a sort of uneasy tribal coalition"[28]

Ignoring the fact that Mboya personally selected students like Barack Obama, Sr. to study in the United States as part of Airlift Africa, the Special Report states: "On more than one occasion Odinga has personally selected students to go to Communist countries, bypassing both the minister of education and the KANU selection committee . . . The Kenyan ambassador to the UN and US is an Odinga partisan, as is the minister of information, Achieng Oneko. As vice president of KANU, Odinga organized a KANU 'Friendship Delegation' which left Nairobi in June for visits to the USSR, North Korea, and Communist China. . . He also selected the Kenyan representative to the 26 July celebration in Havana. . . [REDACTED] [perhaps signals intelligence intercepts revealed] in March a chartered Czechoslovak aircraft left Nairobi with 50

---

[27] CIA Special Report , "Leftist Activity in Kenya," July 31, 1964.
[28] *Ibid.*

Kenyan students, mostly Luos, for an unknown destination . . .Some Kenyan 'students' in Communist countries are receiving paramilitary training. A group of five, selected by Odinga, reportedly returned in June from several months of such training in Bulgaria . . . Almost immediately after independence, the state controlled Kenya News Agency (KNA) began using Soviet-installed radio receivers and teleprinters flown in from the USSR, while Kenyans trained in Czechoslovakia and the USSR arrived to work in the agency. Others have reportedly arrived since, and in June the Czechoslovak News Agency representative in Nairobi was quietly appointed by Oneko [the pro-Odinga Information Minister] as 'informal' adviser and editorial and training expert for KNA, although the previous month Oneko had shown some enthusiasm for the suggestion of naming an American adviser . . . the Soviets plan to build a powerful radio station in Kenya."[29]

The Special Report also refers to Odinga's foreign connections:"An extreme left-wing Goan journalist P. G. Pinto, long resident in Kenya -- and the only Asian detained during the Mau Mau emergency -- is a close associate of Odinga and Oneko, and appears to be lurking in the background of KNA, as well as engaging in clandestine political activity on their behalf. The editor of KNA, considered 'politically reliable' by Odinga and Oneko, lives in Pinto's home, and Pinto's wife is Oneko's secretary. She has a reputation for losing letters, shifting appointments, and otherwise sabotaging -- without his knowledge -- Western efforts to get to Oneko. The Nairobi papers somewhat belatedly raised a hue and cry over the case of the Kenyan students recently arrested following a fight with some

---

[29] *Ibid.*

New York policemen. The US Embassy believes that instructions to run this story came directly from Oneko and that he was responding to Soviet and Chinese pressure to keep the case alive . . . Kenyatta and his moderate associates -- Murumbi, Finance Minister Gichuru, Minister of Commerce and Industry Kiano, and even Tom Mboya, minister of justice and constitutional affairs and a Luo -- are more or less painfully aware of Odinga's operations. Odinga's suspected involvement in the Zanzibar coup, and the ease with which a small band of leftists overthrew the Sultan, opened Kenyatta's eyes to the personal and national danger represented by Odinga and his followers. Although Odinga's actual involvement in the coup has never been established, he did, as minister of home affairs, hide 'Field Marshal' Okello when the latter fled from Zanzibar. He apparently supplied him with money and a car, while professing complete ignorance of his whereabouts." John Okello was a Ugandan who led the Zanzibari revolution in 1964. It has been reported that Ugandan dictator Idi Amin had Okello murdered in Uganda in 1971."[30]

The 1962 CIA report states that Kenyatta had "gravitated into the [REDACTED} company of Odinga and the hard-line extremists." The document also states that Mboya had indicated to the CIA that the Kenyan constitutional conference might be able to "isolate the extremists and form a 'national government' of moderate elements from both KANU and the governing party, the Kenya African Democratic Union -- with himself, by implication, in a leading position."[31] Mboya never achieved the top leadership position in post-

---

[30] *Ibid.*

[31] CIA, Current Intelligence Weekly Summary," February 8, 1962.

independence Kenya but it is certain had he done so, Barack Obama, Sr. would have been ready to assume a major position in the government, perhaps Finance Minister with a PhD in economics under his belt from Harvard. It is interesting to note how history might have changed had Obama, Sr. become a major political figure in Kenya under a CIA-backed President Mboya. Certainly, Obama, Jr. may have been tempted to live in luxury in Kenya and, instead of now being President of the United States, may have very well ended up as the President of Kenya.

Obama, Sr. met his old friend Mboya, the Kenyan Minister of Economic Planning and Development, shortly before Mboya was gunned down by an assassin in Nairobi in 1969. Kenya's autocratic president, Kenyatta, was viewed as being behind the assassination of Mboya, a would-be rival for the presidency. Mboya was 39 when he was assassinated. Shortly after Obama, Sr. testified at the trial of Mboya's accused assassin, Obama, Sr. was the target of an attempted hit-and-run assassination attempt.

As fate would have it, with Mboya's assassination in 1969, Obama, Sr., no longer had a political mentor and he never achieved a major Cabinet post under Kenyatta, who distrusted the Luos. Obama, Sr. began drinking heavily and was killed in an automobile accident in Kenya in 1982, blamed on drunk driving.

The anti-Soviet program of the CIA in Africa also saw the agency's station in Leopoldville, Congo assisting in the assassination by Joseph Mobutu's government, installed by a CIA coup, of Congolese nationalist leader and former Prime Minister Patrice Lumumba in 1961. The Airlift Africa project of the CIA was a direct response to the establishment in Moscow of the People's Friendship University, renamed Patrice

Lumumba University in 1961, to train African leaders... The CIA document indicates that Congolese Premier Cyrille Adoula, who was a client of the CIA, and Katangan secessionist leader Moise Tshombe were used by the CIA to stymie support for Lumumba's leftist successor, Antoine Gizenga. The CIA document states that officials in Leopoldville told the CIA that Gizenga's "removal from the capital to a small island off the Congo coast on 3 February was at *his own request" [emphasis added]* .The suppression of Gizenga's support in Kivu Province was a main element of CIA policy, with the document stating that "In conversation with U.S. officials, the president of Kivu Province stated in early February that there is still the lack of security which enabled Stanleyville troops [Gizenga loyalists] last December to kidnap him and his ministers." [32]

Tshombe's Katanga was highly-prized by the CIA because of its natural resources, particularly gold, uranium, and diamonds, and the CIA saw Tshombe as a foil against the Soviet Bloc obtaining access to the Katangan resources. However, the CIA was acting against the wishes of President Kennedy who wanted to see a quick end to the Katangan secession from Congo. Gizenga, after years of exile, became Prime Minister of the Democratic Republic of Congo from 2006 to 2008.

The CIA document provides a window into the inner workings of the CIA to stem actual and imagined Communist influence around the world in 1962.

The political beliefs of President Obama's CIA-connected mother, father, and maternal grandparents were fashioned in this CIA environment. The idea of a Communist monolithic threat to the United States fashioned U.S. intelligence and foreign policy. The

---

[32] *Ibid.*

above referenced CIA report states the United States rebuffed an attempt by communist Mongolia to establish diplomatic relations with Washington in 1962. The all-powerful Taiwan Lobby and its allies at the East-West Center in Hawaii would not entertain the establishment of relations with Ulan Bator.

The CIA report states: "Mongolia, seeking wider recognition outside the Communist bloc, apparently feels sufficiently encouraged by its winning UN membership last fall to renew its approaches to free world countries. Two members of its UN delegation told an American official on 30 January of their country's desire to establish relations with the US and 'as many other non-Communist nations as possible.' Mongolia was disappointed over its failure last summer to secure U.S. recognition, which it considers would prompt other Western countries to follow suit. Ulan Bator, more successful than other Asian satellites in gaining recognition, has been recognized by 12 non-bloc nations -- most recently by Iraq, Afghanistan, and Ceylon . . . In his conversation with the American official, one of the Mongolian UN delegates intimated that the position of his country's remoteness was compounded by the "rather overpowering pressures of living between the USSR and Communist China."[33]

In 1962, the CIA was more interested in propping up corrupt Asian regimes rather than reach out to North Vietnam and North Korea, which were also trying to establish diplomatic relations with the West.

In Laos, the CIA was violating the terms of the International Control Commission (ICC) and providing covert assistance, paid for by illicit opium smuggling, to the anti-Communist right-wing forces of Prince Boun

---

[33] *Ibid.*

Oum and General Phoumi Nosavan against the neutralist forces of Prince Souvanna Phouma and communist Pathet Lao forces and against the orders of President John F. Kennedy. The East-West Center and the affiliated Asia Society both colluded to provide propaganda and other assistance to the anti-Communists in Laos.

Ironically, the onset of the CIA affiliations of President Obama's family came at a time when the agency had adopted one of its most aggressive stances during the Cold War, even disregarding the orders of President Kennedy, whose one-time office Obama now occupies.

On June 27, 2010, the Obama administration, in a surprise move that upset President Obama's "reset" relations with Russia and after a well-publicized "hamburger and beer" summit with President Dmitry Medvedev in Arlington, Virginia, announced that ten Russians in New York and Washington, DC had been arrested for espionage.

The leader of the alleged spy ring, Anna Kushchyenko Chapman, who was found guilty of failing to register as a lobbying agent for a foreign government and was later swapped, along with her colleagues, in a prisoner exchange, had an interesting link to Kenya. Her father, Vasily Kushchyenko, was a former diplomat and suspected KGB officer assigned to the Soviet embassy in Nairobi. What information had Vasily possibly shared with his daughter about the Russian-speaking Barack Obama, Sr.'s activities on behalf of the CIA and Britain's MI-6 in Kenya? And was Anna digging up additional details on Barack Obama, Jr.'s CIA activities in New York while she was posted there? One former U.S. military intelligence officer told the author, "If Obama's father was working for the CIA, the KGB's Nairobi station would not have missed it."

Chapter Two – Pay No Attention to the Furniture Store, It's Not There

It is the function of the CIA to keep the world unstable – John Stockwell, former CIA agent.

Relatively little is known about Obama's grandfather, Stanley Armour Dunham, who Obama mistakenly referred to as "his father" in two speeches, one to a convention of the Disabled American Veterans. This chapter uncovers the actual biography of Mr. Dunham whose background strongly suggests that he was

anything but a vagabond furniture salesman.

What is officially known about Stanley Armour Dunham is that he served with the 9th Air Force in Britain and France prior to and after the D-Day invasion. After the war, Dunham and his wife, Madelyn and his daughter Stanley Ann – Obama's mother – moved to Berkeley, California; El Dorado, Kansas; Seattle; and Honolulu. Armour Dunham is said to have worked for a series of furniture stores.

Obama maintains that his mother and father first met in a Russian-language class at the University of Hawaii in 1959. However, a photograph has emerged of Stanley Armour welcoming Barack Obama, Sr., complete with traditional Hawaiian welcoming leis, from Kenya. (see Page 12). Obama, Sr. was the only Kenyan student airlifted to Hawaii as part of the CIA-inspired Airlift Africa project that saw Obama and 279 other students from British eastern and southern African colonies brought to the United States for college degrees prior to their homelands gaining independence from Britain.

The photograph of Armour Dunham with Barack Obama, Sr., indicates that the "furniture salesman" in Hawaii was, in fact, working with a CIA-funded project to rapidly educate aspiring politicians to serve in post-independence African governments to counter Soviet- and Chinese-backed political leaders in the region.

There is a strong reason to believe that Armour Dunham worked in the 1950s for the CIA in the Middle East. An FBI file on Armour Dunham existed but the bureau claimed it destroyed the file on May 1, 1997. Considering the sour relations between the FBI and CIA during the Cold War, it is likely that Armour Dunham was being monitored by FBI director J. Edgar Hoover in the same manner as a number of other CIA officials and agents were placed under surveillance. Similarly, the pre-1968 passport records of Obama's mother, Stanley Ann Dunham, were destroyed by the State Department.

There is a photographic clue that the Dunhams may have been assigned by the CIA to Beirut, Lebanon in the early 1950s. A photograph of Obama's mother and grandparents has emerged that shows Ann Dunham wearing what may be a school uniform with the insignia of "NdJ," which stands for the College Notre-Dame de Jamhour, a private Jesuit Catholic French language school in Beirut, Lebanon. Graduates of the school include three former presidents of Lebanon, Amine Gemayel, Bashir Gemayel, and Charles Helou, all of whom maintained close relations with Washington.

Beirut sources revealed that NdJ was a male-only school until 1975 but there is also information that NdJ had a previous sponsorship arrangement with Catholic educational institutions in Lyon, France. Armour

Dunham had been assigned by the Army to duty in France.

Did Obama's mother [left] go to a private school in Lebanon in the early 1950s while her father [middle] worked for the CIA in Beirut?

The importance of the December 19, 1971, article in the *Boston Globe* by Dan Pinck, [a historian and former OSS officer] titled "Is everyone in the CIA?" is germane. The article alleged that identifying U.S. Agency for International Development (USAID) officers as CIA agents was a "reasonably accurate accounting of certain leading operatives and associates of the CIA." President Obama's mother, Ann Soetoro, worked for USAID in rural Java in Indonesia. Pinck's article was a review of a 1968 book, *Who's Who in the CIA* published in Berlin.

The book, published in West Berlin in 1968, lists some 3,000 CIA agents and agents-of-influence around the world.

The book also contains a reference to one CIA operative whose area of primary place of operation was Mercer Island, Washington. He is Air Force General Don Zabriskie Zimmermann, who was the Chief Engineer for the Boeing Company in Seattle. Before retiring from the Air Force, Zimmermann was the Air Force Assistant Deputy Chief of Staff for Development in Foreign Countries. Ann Dunham reportedly graduated from Mercer Island High School in 1960 and met Obama later that year in a Russian language class after her parents moved to Hawaii. Ann's mother, Madelyn Dunham, worked at a Boeing plant in Wichita, Kansas during World War II.

The book lists the number of CIA agents in countries during the 1950s and 60s where Obama's father, mother, step-father Lolo Soetoro, and allegedly, his grandmother and grandfather worked:

Indonesia

Jakarta   64

Surabaya   12

Medan   8

Hollandia   1

Kenya

Nairobi   19

Mombasa   2

Lebanon

Beirut 61   (including one agent also assigned to Jakarta, Lahore, and Karachi and another assigned to Lahore)

Hawaii

Honolulu   6 (one agent also assigned to Canton Island and another was fluent in French, Ann Dunham spoke French, Urdu, Bahasa Indonesian, Dutch, and she studied Javanese at the University of Hawaii, in addition to Russian).

A close examination of the rare *Who's Who in CIA*, published by Julius Mader in West Berlin, provides a fascinating insight into the CIA world in which the family of President Obama operated in the 1960s.

Most of the 3,000 CIA agents named in the book operated under various State Department "Official Cover" occupations as diplomats, as well as USAID, USIA, and military attaché officials.

U.S. diplomatic posts with a heavy CIA presence included the U.S. embassies in Jakarta, Indonesia; Vientiane, Laos; Saigon, South Vietnam; Karachi, Pakistan; Ankara, Turkey; Leopoldville, Congo; Rio de Janeiro, Brazil; Tehran, Iran; Bangkok, Thailand; Manila, Philippines; Beirut, Lebanon; London, UK; Athens, Greece; Baghdad, Iraq; Bonn, West Germany; Brussels, Belgium; The Hague, Netherlands; Vienna, Austria; Paris, France; Tokyo, Japan; Santo Domingo, Dominican Republic; Warsaw, Poland; Kabul, Afghanistan; Cairo, Egypt; Singapore; Rangoon, Burma; Rome, Italy; Taipei, Taiwan; Kathmandu, Nepal; Mexico City; Phnom Penh, Cambodia; Geneva,

Switzerland; Seoul. South Korea; New Delhi, India; and Moscow, USSR.

Busy CIA stations also existed at the U.S. Consulates General in Hong Kong, Frankfurt, Hamburg, and Munich, West Germany; Lahore, Pakistan; Trieste, Italy; Bombay, India; Casablanca, Morocco; Tangier, Morocco; Dacca, East Pakistan; Istanbul, Turkey; the U.S. Consulates in Isfahan, Iran; Port Said, Egypt; and Chiang Mai, Thailand; and the U.S. mission in West Berlin.

A number of companies provided cover for CIA operatives, including Litton Industries, Boeing Corp., Hughes Aircraft, Rand Corporation. Marconi Telegraph-Cable Company; General Electric; Eastman Kodak; and RCA.

U.S. corporations also provided directors for the CIA proprietary airline Air America and its subsidiary Air Asia. These firms included Seattle First National Bank, Cheeseborough Ponds, William C. Walker's Son, Equitable Life Assurance Society, Simpson Timber Company, General Insurance Company, and Northern Pacific Railroad.[34] The New York-based publisher, Frederick A. Praeger, Inc., was also known to be a major conduit for CIA-endorsed books.

The CIA's relationship with United Fruit was so close that "United Fruit" was synonymous with "United States." The government of democratically-elected Carlos Arbenz was considered such a threat to United Fruit, the CIA engineered a 1954 coup against him, an operation code named PBSUCCESS. The coup came at a height of CIA covert actions around the world, with the *Saturday Evening Post*, NBC News, *Reader's*

---

[34] John Burgess, 'Air America: Flying for U.S. and Profit in Asia," *Washington Star*, December 13, 1972.

Digest, and *Chicago Tribune* all hyping the "Red Menace" in Guatemala to justify the military coup that installed Colonel Castillo Armas as dictator.[35] It was a time frame, at the height of Senator Joseph McCarthy's red-baiting, when the Dunhams' could be assured of a maximum degree of assurance that their classified cover would not be blown from within the ranks of the U.S. government.

There is another curious connection of young Barack Obama and his grandfather to the CIA. In his book *Dreams From My Father*, Obama writes about "Gramps" taking him "downtown to one of his favorite bars, in Honolulu's red light district."[36] Jerome Corsi, writing for the conservative website *World Net Daily*, stated the bar in question was Bill Lederer's Bar on Hotel Street in Honolulu's Chinatown district.[37] In a commentary written in the *Grenada* (Mississippi) *Star* on February 2, 2010, Arnold Dyre revealed that Bill Lederer's Bar was owned by famed author William (Bill) Lederer, Jr., co-author of The *Ugly American* and author of *A Nation of Sheep*, the latter on U.S. intelligence failures in Asia. Lederer was also a retired U.S. Navy Captain, a U.S. intelligence liaison to a "Mr. Nguyen" in China (later identified as Ho Chi Minh), and an OSS/CIA active agent in Hawaii. One can only wonder, from a fly on the wall perspective, what OSS and CIA tales young Barry Obama heard at Bill Lederer's Bar. Bill Lederer lived to see Barry become

---

[35] John DiJoseph, *Noble Cause Corruption, The Banality of Evil, and the Threat to American Democracy*, 1950-2008, Lanham, Maryland: University, p. 61.
[36] Barack Obama, *Dreams From My Father*, New York: Crown Publishing, 1995, p. 78.
[37] Jerome Corsi, "Does WND's reporting rule out an Obama Kenya birth?" *World Net Daily*, June 27, 2011.

President of the United States, dying in Baltimore on December 5, 2009, at the age of 97.

An interesting postscript is the fact that one of the CIA's main agents in Jakarta during the Cold War was Lewis H. Lederer. It is not known whether Lewis and Bill were related but like Bill, who worked in Navy public affairs, Lewis was a veteran of the U.S. propaganda operations, joining the CIA from the U.S. Information Agency in 1956.[38]

Bill Lederer's co-author of *The Ugly American*, Eugene Burdick, testified before Representative Dante Fascell's Subcommittee on International Organizations and Movements on September 11, 1963. The subject was "Winning the Cold War: The U.S. Ideological Offensive." Burdick, along with CBS News correspondent Eric Sevareid and actors Theodore Bikel and Hal Holbrooke, testified on the need to increase the U.S. ideological offensive in the Cold War. Lederer's and Burdick's *The Ugly American* was one of the volumes found in the CIA's training library.[39] However, although a number of old OSS and CIA hands appreciated the message in *The Ugly American*, the book did not sit well with Allen Dulles, who believed books like it and Graham Greene's *The Quiet American*, promoted "mischief-creating" prejudices about Americans and the United States. In what reflected Dulles's belief on where the CIA should recruit its agents, he believed that the agency should be "taking the raw material which we find in America – naïve, homegrown, even homespun – and training such a man

---

[38]Julius Mader, *Who's Who in the CIA: A Biographical Reference Work of the Officers of the Civil and Military Branches of the Secret Services of the USA in 120 Countries*, Berlin: Julius Mader, 1968, p. 303.

[39] CIA Deputy Chief, Plans, Research and Administration, Weekly Activities Report, October 9, 1958.

to be a good intelligence officer, however long the process lasts."[40]

Individuals familiar with Barack Obama, Jr. at Harvard and in the city of Chicago speak quite openly about the hidden history of the 44th President of the United States. Combined, these individuals who researched Obama during his early lawyer and political years, paint a very different portrait of Obama and his mother and maternal grandparents.

It is evident, from information gleaned from African-American associates of Obama's in Chicago in the mid-1980s, that Stanley Armour and Madelyn Dunham, like their daughter Stanley Ann Dunham, have fabricated personal histories.

From an African-American political activist in Chicago, who knew Barack Obama, Jr. in Chicago, the author was told that Obama's mother was not born in Wichita, Kansas but was born in Beirut, Lebanon while her parents were serving with the wartime OSS. Ann Dunham's birth date is reported to have been November 29, 1942. This was during the time after which Lebanon's Vichy-led government collapsed – July 14, 1941 – and when the leader of the Free French, General Charles de Gaulle, proclaimed Lebanon nominally independent. After Lebanon's nominal independence was declared on November 26, 1941, the United States opened an embassy in Beirut at ambassadorial level. Soon, the U.S. embassy in Beirut became one of the top OSS listening in the Middle East and U.S. Army personnel, seconded to the OSS, arrived in the city.

---

[40] George Harmon, "Fiction: An ex-CIA man's disputed thriller," Book Review of *Company Man* by Joe Maggio, *Chicago Daily News*, September 23-24, 1972.

Stanley Armour Dunham reportedly enlisted in the U.S. Army on January 18, 1942, a few months after Lebanon's nominal independence was granted under French domination. It is not certain when Mr. Dunham actually joined the Army because his service records in the military have been curiously sealed. It has been reported that Dunham served in England with the 1830th Ordnance Supply and Maintenance Company, Aviation in support of the 9th Air Force in the lead up to the June 6, 1944 Allied invasion of Normandy. However, from 1942 to 1944, little is known of Dunham's military service.

Dunham's wife, who supposedly worked at a Boeing B-29 assembly plant in the Dunhams' hometown of Wichita, reportedly gave birth to Ann Dunham on November 29, 1942. However, we have now learned that Mrs. Dunham was, in fact, posted to Beirut with her OSS husband in 1942 when she gave birth to Obama's mother.

The Dunhams would not have been the only couple working together for the OSS. Famed chef Julia Child met her husband Paul Child during their joint service for the OSS during World War II. Julia Child served in Ceylon and China during the war and she met Paul during her OSS service abroad. They married in 1946. Before joining the OSS, Julia Child worked for a furniture store in New York City, W. & J. Sloane. The fascination of retail store people for OSS, and later, CIA work is uncanny. One of the OSS's and Britain's Secret Intelligence Service's (SIS) top "archaeologist" spies in Peru, Cuba, and Chile during World War II was William J. Clothier II, grandson of the co-founder of the Strawbridge & Clothier Department Store chain based in Philadelphia.

Clothier's continued interest in the CIA was evident in his attendance at a dinner of the Philadelphia Committee on Foreign Relations, the Philadelphia chapter of the Council on Foreign Relations, on January 18, 1979. The dinner's guest speaker was Frank Carlucci, the deputy director of the CIA. In 1974, Clothier invited CIA director William Colby to address the same group's dinner in Philadelphia.

Another archaeologist who was a spy for the United States in both World Wars I and II was Samuel Lothrop, who, according to David H. Price in his book "Anthropological Intelligence: The Deployment and Neglect of American Anthropology in the Second World War," was not only from a wealthy New England family but was friends with New York socialite and one of Franklin Roosevelt's intelligence advisers, Vincent Astor. Lothrop was kin to Alvin Lothrop of Chelsea, Massachusetts, who, with Samuel Woodward founded the Woodward and Lothrop department store chain in Washington, DC.

Anthropologist spies would not have been unknown to the Dunhams in Beirut. According to Price in his book, one of the OSS's leading anthropologist spies, Derwood Lockard, served in Beirut toward the end of World War II after having served in Kenya from 1943 to 1944.

U.S. intelligence sources have questioned whether Stanley Armour Dunham actually worked as a manager for a furniture store in Honolulu after moving there from Seattle. There is a strong belief among U.S. intelligence veterans that Dunham held non –official CIA cover status with the Honolulu "furniture store," which was actually a CIA shell company cover.

33

Dunham officially worked as a manager for the Pratt furniture store in Honolulu. The official biography indicates that Dunham sought a better furniture store opportunity after working at Doces Majestic Furniture Company and Standard-Grunbaum Furniture store in Seattle. Previously, Dunham had worked at J.G. Paris furniture store in Ponca City, Oklahoma.

However, there are no records that Pratt Furniture was an actual legitimate "brick and mortar" retail outlet in Honolulu. Dunham's wife, Madelyn, who Barack Obama called "Toot," handled escrow accounts for CIA operations at the Bank of Hawaii in Honolulu while Stanley Dunham was involved in the CIA's Airlift Africa project that saw Barack Obama, Sr. brought to the University of Hawaii and the CIA-linked East-West Center to be "sheep dipped" by the CIA into future service.

What is officially known about Stanley Armour Dunham is that he served with the 9th Air Force in Britain and France prior to and after the D-Day invasion. After the war, Dunham and his wife, Madelyn and his daughter Stanley Ann – Obama's mother – moved to Berkeley, California; El Dorado, Kansas; Seattle; and Honolulu. Armour Dunham is said to have worked for a series of furniture stores.

There was a "Pratt's" in Kailua Kona on the island of Hawaii that sold furniture and kitchenware but the store listed as Dunham's employer is "Pratt Furniture Company" in Honolulu. There was also a Pratt Furniture store in Pratt, Kansas. Dunham lived in Wichita, Kansas before shipping out to Europe in World War II. Ann Dunham was born in Wichita in 1942. Madelyn Dunham worked at a Boeing B-29 plant in Wichita while her husband was in Europe. Pratt Furniture in Pratt, Kansas was not a chain and did not

34

have a branch in Honolulu. However, Pratt, Kansas is about 75 miles due west of Wichita on U.S. Highway 54.

The CIA has a history of using retail store front operations as cover. The CIA and National Security Agency once operated a super-secret Special Collection Service (SCS) facility out of a strip mall in College Park, Maryland. The two spy agencies operated in the back of a restaurant and dry-cleaning store. The stores operated as legitimate retail operations with the secret operations being carried out in the back rooms.[41] For many years a furniture store in Arlington, Virginia operated with the popular suspicion that it, too, is a front operation for the CIA.

The photograph of Armour Dunham with Barack Obama, Sr., indicated that the 'furniture salesman' in Hawaii was, in fact, working with a CIA-funded project to rapidly educate aspiring politicians to serve in post-independence African governments to counter Soviet- and Chinese-backed political leaders in the region. There is a strong reason to believe that Armour Dunham worked in the 1950s for the CIA in the Middle East. An FBI file on Armour Dunham existed but the bureau claimed it destroyed the file on May 1, 1997. Considering the sour relations between the FBI and CIA during the Cold War, it is likely that Armour Dunham was being monitored by FBI director J. Edgar Hoover in the same manner as a number of other CIA officials and agents were under surveillance. Similarly, the pre-1968 passport records of Obama's mother were destroyed by the State Department.

---

[41] Mike Frost, *Spyworld: Inside the Canadian and American Intelligence Establishments*, Toronto: Doubleday Canada, 1994, p. 205.

There is another possible reason for the FBI to have maintained a file on Dunham. In the years in which "Ozzie and Harriett" and the "Cleavers" represented the typical American family on television, Ann Dunham's marriage to a black African when she was 17 may have resulted in a report being filed by the FBI from Honolulu. Although Hawaii was much more tolerant of mixed race marriages in the early 1960s then the mainland, Hoover frowned on such marriages, especially one involving the daughter of a CIA operative.

Ann's taking a Russian-language class at the University of Hawaii, where she allegedly first met Barack Obama, Sr., was the sort of thing the local FBI office would have noted. Armour Dunham's FBI file may have grown a bit larger after his daughter moved with Barack Obama. Jr. to Jakarta, where young Barry Soetoro was partly raised by a transsexual nanny named "Turdi." Hoover, himself a homosexual, was keen on identifying and keeping files on any other homosexuals connected in any way to the government, especially the CIA.

Turdi tended to Barry by day and frolicked at night with a dance group called the "Fantastic Dolls." Obama lived with his step-father, Lolo Soetoro, and mother in the Menteng-Dalam district of Jakarta from 1967 to 1971. There is a strong reason to believe that Obama's mother sent her son back to live with her parents in Honolulu because of a physically-abusive behavior by Obama's step-father Lolo Soetoro.

Stanley Armour Dunham supposedly was discharged from the Army on August 30, 1945, but because his military records are sealed, this cannot be verified. In the post-war years, the Dunhams were said to have moved to Berkeley, California; Ponca City,

Oklahoma; Vernon, Texas; El Dorado, Kansas; and Mercer Island in Seattle, Washington before moving to Honolulu, Hawaii in 1960. Stanley Armour Dunham, according to what is now appears to be a biography concocted by the CIA, for whom Dunham began working for in 1947 after the transition from the OSS. Mr. Dunham supposedly worked for a chain of furniture stores. Not much is known about Ann until she was enrolled in Mercer Island High School in 1956.

However, if the Dunhams were stationed in Beirut up until the time Ann was enrolled in Mercer Island High School in 1956, all the furniture store jobs held down by Stanley Armour and all the restaurant waitress jobs held by his wife were clever ruses devised by the CIA to mask their actual war-time work in the Middle East. From Oklahoma to Washington state and finally to Hawaii, Stanley Dunham reportedly worked for four furniture stores: J. G. Paris in Ponca City, Doces Majestic and Standard-Grunbaum in Seattle, and Pratt Furniture in Honolulu. There is no documentation to show that Pratt in Honolulu existed beyond a Hawaii-registered shell company. In addition, Madelyn Dunham's wartime OSS work with her husband in Lebanon would explain why she became one of the first female vice presidents at the Bank of Hawaii in Honolulu and was trusted to handle the escrow accounts used to bribe CIA-financed leaders in Indonesia, South Korea, Taiwan, Japan, and the Philippines. Madelyn was enrolled at the University of Washington before moving to Hawaii but she never obtained her degree.

Evacuating Madelyn Dunham and her daughter from Lebanon in 1956 would have made sense for the CIA. In 1956, what had been a peaceful country conducive to a CIA family posting became embroiled in conflict between the Christian Maronite President

Camille Chamoun on one side and Sunni Muslim Lebanese Prime Minister Rashid Karami and Egypt's President Gamal Abdel Nasser on the other side. The UK, French, and Israeli invasion of Suez, although not supported by President Dwight Eisenhower, caused problems for the Americans in Lebanon. The pro-U.S. Chamoun was accused by Karami and Nasser of not taking stronger action against London and Paris, including severing diplomatic relations, for their attack on Egypt. The creation of the United Arab Republic (UAR) by Egypt and Syria in 1958, the calls by Lebanese Sunnis for Lebanese accession to the UAR, and the overthrow of the Hashemite monarchy in Iraq the same year, promoted Eisenhower to land U.S. Marines in Lebanon in 1958 in response to a request from Chamoun. By that time, the Dunham mother and daughter had been safely inserted into Mercer Island, which had a heavy concentration of CIA and Pentagon personnel. It is quite possible that Stanley Armor Dunham's "furniture store" cover in Seattle was used to mask his actual continued work in Lebanon for Eisenhower's OPERATION BLUE BAT Marine landing in Beirut.

In her book, *A Singular Woman*, Janny Scott wrote, "Stanley's [Armor's] work selling furniture in Seattle had dried up. Hawaii, in its newness, was courting transplants. The mayor of Honolulu and a delegation of Hawaii businessmen had been at the Seattle Chamber of Commerce in October [1959], talking up business opportunities. Madelyn would have been happy to stay put, her brother Charles remembered. Her career in banking was flourishing. Stanley Ann had no interest in moving, either. Some said she wanted to attend the University of Washington, where many of her

38

friends were headed. Or, she may have wanted to go east to the University of Chicago."[42]

The above paragraph from Scott's book shows some major inconsistencies in Stanley Armour's resumé from 1959. Standard Grunbaum Furniture store, where he worked, was far from being on the financial ropes and Stanley Armour's photograph welcoming Barack Obama, Sr. to Honolulu International Airport in September 1959, was months before Stanley Armour's supposed move to Hawaii from Seattle in 1960. There is every indication that Stanley Armour was working for the CIA in Hawaii months before his family arrived in the U.S. territory from Washington state.

---

[42] Janny Scott, *op. cit.*, pp. 70-71.

40

Chapter Three – Stanley Ann Dunham and the Years of Living Dangerously

You are never to tell anyone what it is that I do! – Edward Wilson character in the movie, "The Good Shepherd."

This chapter will describe the Obama and his family's early years in volatile Indonesia. In 1965, a bloody CIA-engineered coup ousted the nationalist leader Sukarno. It was in an environment of genocidal reprisals against communists and ethnic Chinese that Obama had his first taste of life in a foreign country. The experience helps to explain Obama's interventionist foreign policy and utter disdain for human rights.

An example of his continuance of his mother's subservience to the Indonesian military elite is the fact that President Obama reversed Clinton and George W. Bush administration policies by lifting a ban on U.S. military support for the Indonesian Red Beret (KOPASSUS) special operations forces. The ban was imposed after the unit committed human rights abuses in East Timor in the late 1990s. Although human rights groups condemned Obama's reversal of policy, the criticisms fell on deaf ears at the White House.

Barack Obama's mother, Stanley Ann Dunham, has been painted by mainstream biographers as a combination of Mother Teresa – a woman trying to help impoverished women in the Third World – and Margaret Mead, the famed anthropologist. Neither is the case. Stanley Ann, like her parents, was rooted deeply in the U.S. intelligence infrastructure, especially in Indonesia, where she served in the front lines of Cold War rivalry.

The State Department revealed in July 2010, in a response to a Freedom of Information Act request, that the pre-1965 passport files of Obama's mother, Ann Dunham Soetoro, were destroyed in the 1980s. The FOIA request was filed by Christopher Strunk of New York. The admission about the destruction of the passport files re-ignited suspicions that Obama's mother worked for the CIA under non-official cover (NOC) in Indonesia while married to Lolo Soetoro Mangunharjo, a lieutenant colonel in General Suharto's CIA-backed ranks. Soetoro and Dunham married in 1965 after meeting at the University of Hawaii. That same year, the CIA-backed Suharto launched an anti-Communist coup that saw leftist President Sukarno eventually ousted from power and up to one million suspected communists, including many ethnic Chinese Indonesians, massacred by government troops.

The CIA believed the ethnic Chinese in Indonesia were strongly connected to what the agency then referred to as "Communist China" and even the wealthy ethnic Chinese merchant class, mostly committed capitalists, was also suspect. The Bank of China branches in Jakarta, Medan, and Surabaya were identified as Chinese intelligence operations by the CIA as early as 1959. [43]

In 1967, Dunham moved with six-year old Barack Obama to Jakarta. In 1966, as Suharto consolidated his power, Lieutenant Colonel Soetoro was battling Communist rebels in the country's hinterlands. Ann Dunham moved back to Hawaii in 1972, a year after Obama left Indonesia to attend school in Hawaii. Dunham divorced Soetoro in 1980. Soetoro was hired

---

[43] CIA, "Chinese Communist International Activities and Contacts," Second Edition, March 1959, pp. 20-21.

by Mobil to be a liaison officer with Suharto's dictatorship.

Soetoro died in 1987 at the age of 52. Ann Dunham died in 1995, also at the age of 52. Obama, Sr. died in an automobile accident in Kenya in 1982 at the age of 46. Barack Obama, Jr., one of America's youngest elected presidents, was, ironically and unlike many other young presidents, bereft of any living close relatives, except for a half-sister.

Files released by the State Department on Dunham's name-change passport application lists two dates and places of marriage to Soetoro: March 5, 1964, in Maui and March 15, 1965, in Molokai -- almost a year's difference. In her 1968 passport renewal application, Barack Obama's name is listed as Barack Hussein Obama (Soebarkah). In passport renewal and amendment applications filed from Jakarta, Dunham uses two different names: Stanley Ann Dunham Soetoro and Stanley Ann Soetoro.

Dunham again applied for a passport from Jakarta in 1981 while working for the Ford Foundation. Her New York-based boss at the time was Peter Geithner, the father of President Obama's Treasury Secretary Timothy Geithner. Dunham also worked in rural villages in Java for the U.S. Agency for International Development (USAID), which was and remains notorious for conducting covert CIA operations around the world.

Timothy Geithner, like Barack Obama, Jr., experienced an amazing ascension in the power structures of the United States. At the age of forty-two, Geithner became the Chairman of the Federal Reserve Bank of New York, the most powerful of the twelve regional "Feds." After Obama's election, Geithner became the favorite of the Goldman Sachs crowd to become Secretary of the Treasury, edging out the experienced former Federal Reserve Bank chairman Paul Volcker.[44]

It is significant that Ann Dunham and President Obama's father, Barack Obama, Sr. met in a Russian class at the University of Hawaii in 1960. The teaching of Russian in Hawaii, which hosted a number of U.S. military bases and intelligence operations, is noteworthy since a Russian language class during the height of the Cold War would normally attract a majority of U.S. military and civilian intelligence professionals. The CIA continued to maintain a CIA-linked interest in Soviet affairs. A letter dated August 19, 1981, from University of Hawaii history professor John A. White to CIA headquarters asks the agency for a panel speaker at a March 18-21, 1982 Western Slavic conference titled, "Soviet Muslims and their Middle Eastern neighbors." White wrote that he discussed the CIA's participation with "Mr. [name redacted] in the CIA's Honolulu office."[45]

At the time Dunham met Obama, Sr. in the Russian class, the CIA was engaged in major covert operations in Asia, including attempted assassinations of Asian leaders. An August 1975 article in *Penthouse* by former *New York Times* reporter Tad Szulc reported on two high-level planned CIA assassinations that were turned down by the "highest levels" at the White House in the late 1950s: ". . . senior CIA officials proposed the assassination of Indonesian President Sukarno as part of a broader plot to overthrow his left-leaning government. At least one American pilot, employed by the CIA, was captured by Sukarno's forces during the coup attempt.

---

[44] Ron Suskind, *Confidence Men,* New York: Harper Collins, 2011, pp. 146-147.
[45] Letter from John A. White, University of Hawaii at Manoa, to CIA Office of Public Affairs, dated August 19, 1981.

To kill Sukarno, the CIA, according to intelligence sources, planned to fire a shell from a ceremonial 105-mm cannon in front of the presidential palace while Sukarno spoke from a balcony."[46] The CIA finally succeeded in ousting Sukarno in 1965, with the help of Barack Obama's step father.

Szulc also wrote: "In 1958, a plot was concocted to kill China's Premier Chou En-lai during a visit to Rangoon, Burma. This was at the beginning of the Soviet-Chinese split, and apparently the CIA reasoned that Chou's death would aggravate the developing split. The notion was that Chou was a moderate and thus posed an obstacle to a possible Soviet-Chinese confrontation.

Furthermore, intelligence sources said, the CIA planned, by the dissemination of "disinformation" through intelligence channels, to lead the Chinese to believe that Chou was killed by the Russian KGB. This murder plot, which was also stopped, provided for a Burmese CIA agent to place untraceable poison in a rice bowl from which Chou was expected to be eating at a government dinner in his honor. This particular kind of poison, intelligence sources said, would have acted within forty-eight hours and there would be no trace of it if an autopsy were performed. The plan was countermanded at the last moment."[47]

Another CIA plan, quickly aborted, was to distribute a hard-core pornographic film that showed a performer who was supposed to be Sukarno engaging in sexual acts with a tawdry-looking female. However, the close-up genital action in the grainy production was

---

[46] Tad Szulc, "Murder by Proxy," *Penthouse*, August 1975.
[47] *Ibid.*

totally unbelievable since the male actor looked like a Mexican rather than an Indonesian.[48]

The East-West Center and the CIA

The East-West Center at the University of Hawaii, where Dunham met Soetoro, had long been affiliated with CIA activities in the Asia-Pacific region. Partly the brainchild of then-Senate Majority Leader Lyndon B. Johnson, the center, with five buildings designed by architect I.M. Pei, became a nexus for America's power projection into the Asia-Pacific region during the Cold War. In addition, the University of Hawaii was the CIA's favored center for teaching CIA agents Korean, Hindi, Urdu, and Marathi.[49] The East-West Center's Institute for Technical Interchange (ITI) was also used to train Asian-Pacific "middle-men" in personnel administration. Students from the Republic of China, Cambodia, India, Indonesia, Nepal, Philippines, Thailand, Korea, Vietnam, and the Ryukus were trained by the Institute.[50] The center's first team of recruiters landed in Bangkok, Saigon, Calcutta, Rangoon, Dacca, Kathmandu, Colombo, Karachi, and other Asian cities looking for prospective students to attend campus courses.[51]

The East-West Center would be a "kinder and gentler" version of the infamous "School of the Americas" at Fort Benning, Georgia, a training center since 1946 for some of Latin America's most brutal

---

[48] Brian Toohey and William Pinwill, *Oyster: The Story of the Australian Secret Intelligence Service*, Port Melbourne, Victoria: William Heinemann Australia, 1989, p. 93.
[49] CIA, Office of Training (OTR) Bulletin. CIA Internal Use Only, January-February 1964.
[50] *Ibid.*
[51] Janny Scott, *op. cit.,* p. 77.

military dictators and death squad commanders. Before the East-West Center was established, there was some interest in establishing a "School of the Americas" for Asia at an Australian university.[52]

The fact that Ann Dunham married two East-West Center students across racial lines points to one of the key elements in the operation of the facility: American influence-peddling abroad through marriage. Statistics showed that over thirty-three percent of students who married after arriving at the center did so across ethnic or national lines.[53] Later, a close friend of Ann Soetoro's told author Janny Scott about Ann's marriage to Lolo Soetoro: "it wasn't like a real marriage . . . It was just kind of a marriage in name."[54]

In 1965, the year that Dunham met and married Soetoro, the center saw a new chancellor take over. He was Howard P. Jones who served a record seven years, from 1958 to 1965, as U.S. ambassador to Indonesia. Jones was present in Jakarta as Suharto and his CIA-backed military officers planned the 1965 overthrow of Sukarno. The co-founder of independent Indonesia, Sukarno was seen, along with the Indonesian Communist Party (PKI), as allies of China.

When Jones was chancellor of the East-West Center, he wrote an article for the *Washington Post*, dated October 10, 1965, in which he defended Suharto's overthrow of Sukarno. Jones was "invited" by the *Post* to comment on the Suharto coup, described as a "counter-coup" against the Communists. Jones charged that Suharto was merely responding to an earlier attempted Communist-led coup against Sukarno

---

[52]Toohey and Pinwill, *op. cit.*, p. 74.

[53] Janny Scott., *op. cit.,* p. 101.

[54] *Ibid.,* p. 214.

launched by Lt. Col. Untung, "a relatively unknown battalion commander in the palace guard."[55]

Jones's article, which mirrored CIA situation reports from the U.S. embassy in Jakarta, continued by stating that the alleged leftist coup on September 30, "came within an inch of succeeding through the assassination of six of the top military command. It might well have succeeded had not Defense Minister Nasution and a number of other senior generals also marked for assassination acted fast in a dramatic counter-coup."[56] Of course, Jones did not inform the *Post's* readers that the Suharto "counter-coup" had been assisted with major assistance from the CIA. Jones left as East-West Center chancellor in 1968.

Sukarno never blamed the Communists for the assassination of the army generals nor did the Indonesian Cabinet, where the second- and third-ranking leaders of the PKI were present. The possibility that the assassination of the generals was a CIA/Suharto "false flag" operation to affix blame on the PKI is a more likely scenario. Two days after Suharto's coup, a CIA "rent-a-mob" burned down the PKI headquarters in Jakarta. As they marched past the U.S. Embassy, which was also the site of the CIA station, they yelled out, "Long live America!"

Untung later said that when he became aware that Suharto and the CIA were planning a coup on October 5, 1965 -- Indonesian Armed Forces Day -- forces loyal to him and Sukarno moved first. Jones described this as "typical Communist propaganda." Suharto moved against Sukarno on October 1. Jones iterated that "there was not an iota of truth . . . in the

---

[55] Howard P. Jones, "Indonesian Coup was a Red Bobble," *The Washington Post*, October 10, 1965.
[56] *Ibid.*

accusation that the CIA was working against Sukarno."[57] History has proven otherwise. Jones accused the Communists of taking advantage of Sukarno's failing health to beat out the other candidates to succeed him. The goal, according to Jones, was to have PKI boss D.N. Aidit succeed Sukarno.[58] Sukarno did not die until 1970, while under house arrest.

A CIA paper, formerly classified Secret and undated, states "Sukarno would like to return to the status quo ante-coup. He has refused to condemn the PKI or the 30th September Movement [of Lt. Col. Untung]; instead, he calls for unity of Indonesia and asks that no vengeance be taken by one group against the other. But, he has not succeeded in forcing the Army to abandon its anti-PKI activities and, on the other hand, he has bowed to their demand by appointing its single candidate General Suharto as head of the Army." [59]Suharto and Barry Obama Soetoro's step-father Lolo Soetoro would ignore Sukarno's call for no vengeance, as hundreds of thousands of Indonesians would soon discover.

The mass murder by Suharto of Indonesian Chinese is seen in the CIA paper's description of the Baperki Party: "the leftist Baperki Party, with its major strength in rural areas, is largely Chinese-Indonesian in membership." [60]A CIA Intelligence Memorandum, dated October 6, 1966, formerly classified Secret, shows the extent of the CIA's monitoring of the anti-Sukarno coup from various CIA agents assigned as liaisons to Suharto's army units surrounding the Presidential Palace in Bogor and at various diplomatic posts around the

---

[57] *Ibid.*

[58] *Ibid.*

[59] CIA paper, undated.

[60] *Ibid.*

country, including the U.S. Consulate in Medan, which was keeping track of leftists in that Sumatran city[61] and, which, in an October 2, 1965, Intelligence Memo, reported to the CIA that the "Soviet consul-general in Medan has a plane standing by that could be used for evacuation of Soviet citizens from Sumatra."[62] The October 6 memo also warns against allowing Untung from developing a following in Central Java.[63]

A CIA formerly Secret "Weekly Summary Special Report" on Indonesia, dated August 11, 1967, and titled "The New Order in Indonesia," [Appendix 5] reports that in 1966, Indonesia re-aligned its economy in order to receive International Monetary Fund (IMF) assistance. The CIA reports it was happy with the new triumvirate ruling Indonesia in 1967: Suharto, Foreign Minister Adam Malik, and the Sultan of Jogjakarta, who served as minister for economics and finance. The report also rejoices in the outlawing of the PKI, but states it "retains a significant following in East and Central Java."[64] It was in those areas of Java where Ann Dunham Soetoro would largely concentrate her later efforts on behalf of USAID, the World Bank, and the Ford Foundation, all front activities for the CIA to "win the hearts and minds" of the Javanese farmers and artisans.

A CIA Intelligence Memorandum, formerly Secret, dated July 23, 1966, clearly saw the Muslim Nahdatul Ulama party (NU), the largest party in Indonesia and Muslim, as a natural ally of the United States and the Suharto regime. The report states that

---

[61] CIA Intelligence Memorandum, October 6, 1966.

[62] CIA Intelligence Memo, October 2, 1965.

[63] CIA Intelligence Memorandum, October 6, 1966.

[64] CIA, "Weekly Summary Special Report" on Indonesia," "The New Order in Indonesia," August 11, 1967.

helped Suharto put down the Communists in the post-coup time frame, especially where the NU was strongest: East Java.[65] It was in East Java, especially Surabaya, where Obama's mother would concentrate some of her activities, as well as in North Sumatra and parts of Borneo. An April 29, 1966, formerly Secret CIA Intelligence Memorandum on the PKI, states: "Moslem extremists in many instances outdid the army in hunting down and murdering members of the party [PKI] and its front groups."[66] It was the CIA that nurtured the Muslim gangs to carry out the genocide against PKI members and ethnic Chinese.

In fact, one of Ann Dunham's closest colleagues in Indonesia was Adi Sasono, who has been a leader of Muslim students during the overthrow of Sukarno. Sasono was one of several Muslim activists against Sukarno who became champions of Islamic reform movements in the decades after the coup.[67]

One of President Obama's chief campaign promises was to run the most transparent administration in history. Considering the fact that his own personal history is one of the most opaque of any past president, there is little wonder why Obama's administration is the least transparent in recent history. Attempts to pry open classified CIA files pursuant to the Freedom of Information Act have met with strenuous opposition from the Obama White House.

Meet the Soetoros

Lolo Soetoro, who Dunham married in March 1965, departed Hawaii for Indonesia on July 20, 1965, some

---

[65] CIA Intelligence Memorandum, July 23, 1966.
[66] CIA Intelligence Memorandum, July 23, 1966.
[67] Janny Scott, *op. cit.*, p. 235.

three months prior to the CIA's coup against Sukarno. Soetoro, who, according to Indonesian sources close to the government of President Susilo Bambang Yudhoyono, served Suharto as an Army lieutenant colonel.

Soetoro was one of 4000 Indonesian army officers trained by the United States, a number that represented half of the total officer corps and one-third of the general staff. The importance of the recruitment of Indonesian army officers for future service to the United States was stressed by U.S. intelligence analyst Dr. Guy Pauker of the Rand Corporation in 1962. Pauker stated, "Many responsible elements in Indonesia are convinced that if the officer corps appreciated its historic role, it could be the nation's salvation."[68]

Lieutenant Colonel Soetoro was clearly called back from the CIA-connected East-West Center to assist in the coup against Sukarno. It is a history of his family that President Obama would like the press to ignore. And ignore is exactly what he press did during the 2008 primary and general election campaign.

In fact, in his book *The Audacity of Hope*, Obama wrote that Soetoro's student visa had been revoked while at the University of Hawaii and he was conscripted as an enlisted man into the Indonesian army a few months before Ann Dunham and young Obama moved to Jakarta.[69] Soetoro was placed into active duty status in the Indonesian army as a senior officer, not as an enlisted man as maintained by Obama, upon his return to Indonesia in July 1965.

Obama was being fast and loose with the truth with his allegation that Soetoro's student visa had been

---

[68] Toohey and Pinwill, op. cit., pp. 93-94.
[69] Barack Obama, *The Audacity of Hope*, New York: Crown Publishers, 2006, p. 273.

revoked by the United States. According to high-level sources with connections to the Indonesian government of President Yudhoyono, Lieutenant Colonel Soetoro was in Hawaii as part of a Pentagon- and CIA-funded training program. Obama also contends that the massacre of Indonesians by the Suharto regime was unknown to his mother: ". . . my mother would insist that had she known what had transpired in the preceding months, we would have never made the trip. But she didn't know – the full story of the coup and the purge was slow to appear in American newspapers." [70]

Obama recalled how his step-father "refused to talk politics with my mother, advising her that some things were best forgotten."[71] In fact, the Indonesian coup and massacre were reported by U.S. newspapers and Ann Dunham would have certainly known about the environment to which she was moving from her father's own CIA contacts. The CIA, as the major perpetrator of the coup and massacre, knew all the sordid details of Soetoro's "clean-up" operations in the rural hinterlands.

The official histories of Indonesia and the Obama administration would have everyone believe that in 1965, Indonesian Army General Suharto put down an attempted Communist Party of Indonesia (PKI) coup attempt that saw six senior Indonesian military officers, plus a first lieutenant mistaken for General Nasution, brutally shot by PKI partisans and dumped down a dry well. The official time line continues by suggesting that a lowly enlisted man, Lolo Soetoro, re-called from a scholarship at the University of Hawaii and drafted into the Indonesian army some three months before the PKI coup attempt, was sent into the field to fight anti-

---

[70] *Ibid.*
[71] *Ibid.*

government guerrillas. Two years later, in 1967, along came Soetoro's American wife, Ann, along with her six year-old mulatto child by a Kenyan father, to take on a series of odd jobs and helped raise her son in practical poverty. Ann, an alleged free-spirited hippie type, eventually used her anthropology degree to assist Javanese villagers in marketing their batik textiles and to become entrepreneurs by taking out micro-loans. Or so we are told.

Sukarno seemed to predict the near future when, in an August 17, 1964, speech, he said the next twelve months would be "A Year of Living Dangerously." The CIA had been preparing for such a dangerous year for over a decade. Sukarno's description of the twelve-month period would serve as the inspiration for the title of the 1982 movie about the Indonesian coup, which starred Mel Gibson and Sigourney Weaver, "The Year of Living Dangerously."

A January 31, 1958, heavily-redacted formerly Secret NOFORN [no foreign dissemination] memorandum for CIA Director Allen Dulles from the Deputy Assistant Director of the CIA for Research and Reports [name redacted] reports on a fact-finding mission to the Far East, Southeast Asia, and the Middle East from November 17 through December 21, 1957.

The CIA Office of Research and Reports (ORR) chief reports a meeting with the staff of retired Army General Jesmond Balmer, a senior CIA official in Hawaii, about requests by the Commander-in-Chief Pacific (CINCPAC) for "a number of detailed, time-consuming research studies." The ORR chief then reports about a CIA "survey of students at the University of Hawaii who have both Chinese language and research ability." The ORR chief also reports that at a South-East Asia Treaty Organization (SEATO) Counter Subversion Seminar at Baguio, Philippines held from November 26-29, 1957, the Economic Subcommittee discussed an "economic development fund" to combat "Sino-Soviet Bloc subversive activities in the area and a consideration of possible counter-measures which might be employed." [72]

Indonesian Foreign Minister Subandrio accused a number of Jakarta newspapers that agitated against Sukarno shortly after the coup of being financed by the CIA.[73]

The Thailand and Philippines SEATO delegations were pushing hard for U.S. funding for an economic development fund, which may have provided the impetus for later USAID projects in the region, including those with which Peter Geithner and Obama's mother were intimately involved.

The actual historical record of Indonesia confirms that General Suharto, the head of the army under President Sukarno, conspired with the CIA to topple the nationalistic Sukarno, who was opposed to the World Bank, International Monetary Fund, United Nations, U.S. Agency for International Development (USAID), and U.S. Peace Corps presence in Indonesia. The abduction and execution of the six top Indonesian military officers was carried out by Suharto's men and then blamed on the PKI as a reason to carry out a coup against Sukarno and a bloody pogrom against the PKI, an operation that saw between 800,000 and 1 million Indonesians killed by Indonesian military and intelligence officers over a period of time that included Dunham and her son's arrival and residency in Indonesia.

---

[72] Memorandum for DCI from Deputy Director, Intelligence, dated January 31, 1958.
[73] "A Challenge to Subandrio," *New York Herald Tribune*, October 30, 1965.

In the months following the CIA coup, Sukarno accused the CIA of trying to kill him. "They [the CIA] have been trying to overthrow Sukarno, destroy his dignity and even kill him. I have proof," declared Sukarno in a speech to veterans of the Independence War," adding, "In some places now there are snipers to kill Sukarno."[74]

Lolo Soetoro, the reserve Indonesian army officer called back into service in the army in 1965 from his CIA-supplied scholarship that began in 1962 at the East-West Center, was, in fact, a foot soldier in the putschist cabal of Suharto, the man who the CIA designated as the leader of the 1965 coup. Some 4000 Indonesian army officers were trained in the United States between 1958 and 1965 and the CIA and Pentagon ensured that these officers would be available for the long-planned overthrow of Sukarno.

In 1967, Ann Dunham was dispatched from Hawaii, where she had lived with her son at her parents' house at 2234 University Avenue in Honolulu, to Indonesia to infiltrate villages in Java to carry out a CIA survey of political leanings among the Javanese population. Those unfortunate enough to be tagged as Communists or Sukarno supporters were targeted for elimination by the CIA, which turned the target lists over to Suharto's army officers, including Lolo Soetoro. During the Cold War, the use of anthropologists like Dunham by the CIA and Defense Department in the collection of ethnographic and cultural intelligence was commonplace. In Indonesia, the CIA/Pentagon program to infiltrate villages and report on political allegiances was called Project PROSYMS.

---

[74] "CIA accused of trying to kill Sukarno," *Pakistan Observer* (Dacca), September 8, 1966.

Project PROSYMS was a reference listed in the CIA's Intelligence Handbook for Eastern Indonesia, dated December 1966. The references states: "American University, Special Operations Research Office, Project PROSYMS, Psychological Operations Indonesia, June 1961 (CONFIDENTIAL)."[75]

The Suharto government, taking its cues from the CIA, carefully re-wrote Indonesian history. The official history of Indonesia has been directly and effectively used by Barack Obama and his handlers to avoid Obama having to admit the role of his mother and Indonesian step-father in one of the bloodiest chapters in the history of modern Asia. It is very apparent that a "cargo cult" personality has been built up around Barack Obama in Indonesia, one that has been exported to an unknowing American public.

The Indonesian museum located at the former air base at Halim, outside of Jakarta, where the bodies of seven Indonesian military officers were dumped into a dry well, allegedly by the PKI, is now a showcase for the CIA-contrived history of Indonesia. Various displays at the museum push the CIA/Suharto time line. For example the infamous "Gilchrist memo" is referred to as a forgery.

In July 1965, a few months after Lolo Soetoro arrived from Hawaii, a mysterious letter surfaced in Indonesia, purportedly sent by British ambassador in Jakarta Andrew Gilchrist to the British Foreign Office in London. The memo referred to "our local army friends" in the Indonesian army. Gilchrist, in the months leading up to the coup, told London that regime change in Jakarta would entail "more than a little shooting."

---

[75] Directorate of Intelligence, CIA, Intelligence Handbook Eastern Indonesia, SECRET, December 1966.

57

Before being posted to Jakarta, Gilchrist was British Consul General in Chicago.

The University of Chicago's "New Nations Project," a suspected CIA-linked research project that examined nationalist movements around the world during the 1960s, involved none other than Ann Soetoro's colleague in Indonesia, Dr. Clifford Geertz, who will be discussed later in greater detail.

In March 1965, Sukarno infuriated the West by taking over the operations of western oil companies, including Shell, Caltex, and Stanvac, the latter owned by Mobil. In 1970, after leaving the army, Lolo Soetoro went to work for Mobil, which was assured of no interference from the pro-U.S. Suharto government. Lolo Soetoro also worked for Union Oil of California (UNOCAL)

The CIA was also concerned in early 1965 that Sukarno might try to seize U.S.-owned rubber estates in Indonesia. In a January 1965 Intelligence Brief, the CIA wrote, "President Sukarno allegedly has approved a plan for takeover of U.S. and Belgian rubber estates . . . The takeover presumably would follow the lines taken against the Dutch estates (in 1957-58), the Belgian states (in 1961 – Indonesian 'protective custody' over the Belgian estates ended in May 1963), and the British estates (in 1964)."[76]

However, even the CIA's brief conceded that the rubber concessions to the U.S. Rubber Company, Hawaiian Sumatra Plantations, and Goodyear Tire and Rubber were due to expire in 1965 and that the Indonesian government made it clear as early as

---

[76] CIA Directorate of Intelligence, Office of Research and Reports, Intelligence Brief, CONFIDENTIAL, "Impending Takeover of U.S. Rubber Estates in Indonesia," January 1965.

September 1960 that when the concessions expired five years later, they would revert to government control."[77]

The sources for the rubber estate nationalization report were CIA sources in Jakarta (Djakarta) and Medan in Sumatra, where the U.S. rubber estates were located.[78]

In April 1965, Sukarno expelled the Peace Corps from Indonesia as he grew more and more suspicious of American covert activities in his country. The next month, Sukarno accused the United States and Britain of planning a coup against him with the aid of the Indonesian army. Army forces began to call back Indonesian army reserve officers who were studying abroad in order to supplement their ranks for the planned coup against Sukarno. On July 20, 1965, Lolo Soetoro, who had been in the United States receiving CIA- and Pentagon-funded training since September 18, 1962, quickly left Hawaii for Indonesia. Ann Soetoro received her U.S. passport on July 19, 1965, the day before Lolo Soetoro left for Indonesia and just as events were heating up in Indonesia.

Suspiciously, Lolo Soetoro's Wikipedia entry was altered to reflect his departure from Hawaii to Indonesia in 1966, the year following the coup. It appeared that certain interests wanted to cover up Lolo Soetoro's involvement in the 1965 CIA coup.

In August, Sukarno committed the arch sin, as viewed by the West and quasi-CIA support organizations like the Ford Foundation. Sukarno withdrew Indonesia from the World Bank, the International Monetary Fund, and INTERPOL. In August, while receiving a foreign delegation, Sukarno

---

[77] *Ibid.*
[78] *Ibid.*

began to vomit uncontrollably and he collapsed. This was during the height of the CIA's assassination program led by the "Black Sorcerer," Dr. Sidney Gottlieb, the head of MK-ULTRA, who had previously attempted the poisonings of Fidel Castro, Iraqi leader Abdul Karim Qassem, and Congo's Prime Minister Patrice Lumumba.

On September 30, 1965, what unfolded in Indonesia was a classic CIA disinformation and "false flag" operation. Low-ranking army officers, said to be part of an attempted PKI takeover and calling themselves the "30 September Movement," attempted to kidnap seven anti-PKI army generals, however, oddly, General Suharto, the CIA's point man for the coup, was not among the kidnapping targets. Generals Yani, Haryono, and Panjaitan were killed at their homes "while resisting arrest," while Generals Soeprapto, Parman, and Sutoyo were taken alive and shot later by the coup plotters. The bodies of the six generals were dumped into a well.

The Minister of Defense and Security, General Nasution, managed to escape alive from his home and received asylum at the Iraqi embassy, although his five year-old daughter was killed in the attack. The coup was launched from the Halim airbase outside Jakarta. However, for a coup attempt blamed on the PKI, which was used to launch a bloody massacre of PKI members and their sympathizers and force Sukarno from power, it was amazing that most of the PKI leaders were not in Jakarta and were not in contact with the low-ranking accused coup leaders. Aidit, one of the PKI Politburo members, was present at the Halim base but Politburo members Njoto, Lukman, Subandrio, Chaerul Saleh and Sastroamidjojo were away from Jakarta. There is no conclusive evidence that the PKI staged the murders of the six generals but there is ample evidence that given the CIA's and MI-6's pre-coup operations, that it was they and Suharto that staged the massacre to provide a reason to oust Sukarno and begin the systematic massacres of PKI members.

It was also odd that given General Yani's soft approach to the PKI, that he was marked for assassination by alleged PKI cadres. However, General Nasution, who was known to be extremely anti-Communist and who was counted in the pro-U.S. camp, was able to escape assassination and hide out in the Iraqi embassy. Although Nasution swore Suharto in as the new president after the formal ousting of Sukarno, Nasution later broke with Suharto.

The anti-PKI museum states the following in one of its displays about the time frame leading up to the September 1965 coup: "The campaign against ABRI [the Armed Forces of the Republic of Indonesia], and in particular against the Army, had as its background the jealousy of the PKI amongst the people. Various kinds of anti ABRI Campaigns were carried out by the PKI such as changes, issues, Provocations, political slander which were launched to the public by PKI mass media and propaganda bodies. Since 1964 this campaign increased as a 'revolutionary offensive.' Unilateral acts of violence, demands for the dissolution of the teritorial [sic] instrumentalities, the issue of the influence of 'Nasakom' (Nationalist, Religious, Communist) on ABRI, the issue of the 'Fifth Force' i.e., Peasements [sic] and workers, and the false Gilchrist document were all manifestations of their actions. A climax of the campaign was the issue of the Council of Generals in 1965, which led to the attempted communist coup of 30th September 1965 (G.30 S/PKI).

One of the covert actions of the campaign was conveyed to the Congress of the Association of Indonesian Village Administration (PPDI), a PKI Mass organization, on 3rd August 1964 at the Railway Workers Union Building Manggarai, Jakarta."

From another anti-PKI museum display appears further targets for the Indonesian army and CIA: all believed to be hot-beds for PKI activity and all of which figured prominently in Ann Soetoro's Vietnam Operation PHOENIX-like pacification work. PKI targets included farmers who were members of the "Indonesian Farmers Front (BTI), People's Youth (PR), and Indonesian Communist Women's Movement (Gerwani)." The groups were targeted after the Bandar Betsy Incident, in which peasants were accused of "stealing" land at the State Rubber Plantation No. IX at Bandar Betsy, Pematang Slantar.

Former CIA agent Ralph McGehee documented the CIA's role in altering the official history of the Indonesian coup in his book *Deadly Deceits: My 25 Years in the CIA*. McGehee wrote, with redactions ordered by the CIA:

"In Indonesia in 1965, a group of young military officers attempted a coup against the U.S.-backed military establishment and murdered six of seven top military officers. The Agency seized the opportunity to overthrow Sukarno and to destroy the Communist Party of Indonesia . . . Estimates of the number of deaths that occurred as a result of this CIA [one word deleted] operation run from one half million to more than one million people.

Initially, the Indonesian Army left the PKI alone, since it had not been involved in the coup attempt. [Eight sentences deleted] Subsequently, however, Indonesian military leaders [seven words deleted] began a bloody extermination campaign. Media fabrications played a key role in stirring up popular resentment against the PKI. Photographs of the bodies of the dead generals – badly decomposed – were featured in all the newspapers and on television. Stories accompanying the pictures falsely claimed that the generals had been castrated and their eyes gouged out by Communist women. This cynically manufactured campaign was designed to foment public anger against the Communists and set the stage for a massacre . . . To conceal its role in the massacre of these innocent people the CIA in 1968 concocted a false account of what happened (later published by the Agency as a book – *Indonesia 1965: The Coup that Backfired*). At the same time that the Agency wrote the book, it also composed a secret study of what happened. [One sentenced deleted]. The Agency was extremely proud of its successful [one word deleted] and recommended it as a model for future operations [one-half sentence deleted].[79]

The official Indonesian history of the pre-coup events illustrates that it was the very Indonesian village administration, later targeted by Ann Soetoro, which was considered by Suharto to be a hot-bed of PKI activity and sympathizers. USAID, a pass-through for CIA work with anthropologists like Dunham, along with the CIA-linked Ford Foundation, provided Dunham's "pacification" project with tons of cash through programs like PROSYMS.

Jakarta, Indonesia is where young Barack Obama grew up with his CIA-connected mother and his Indonesian army officer step-father. Obama's attendance at two schools that from 1967 to 1971 required the student to be an Indonesian citizen – a time frame when Indonesian law did not permit dual citizenship – means that the so-called "birthers," those who claim that Barack Obama was not born in Honolulu, Hawaii but in

---

[79] Ralph W. McGehee, *Deadly Deceits: My 25 Years in the CIA*, New York: Sheridan Square, 1983, pp. 57-58.

another country, have been on a dead-end wild goose chase. The answers to Obama's eligibility to serve as President of the United States were not found in Hawaii or Kenya, but in the narrow alleyways of the sprawling Indonesian capital city.

It was the renouncement of Obama's U.S. citizenship by his step-father that permitted Obama to be enrolled in two schools in Jakarta – the Santo Fransiskus Assisi Catholic parochial school from the first to third grades, and the Menteng State Elementary School from the fourth to the fifth grades. While attending the Menteng School, Ann Soetoro was employed as a department head and a director of the Institute of Management Education and Development in Jakarta. Lolo, after his time in the field with the Indonesian army following the 1965 CIA-inspired coup against Sukarno, worked in the Director General's office of the Indonesian Army's Topography division of the Indonesian Army. Ann Soetoro's covert work for the CIA's and Pentagon's Project PROSYMS, the ethnographic political mapping of pro- and anti-government tribes and villages in Java, was complemented by Lolo's access to topographic maps of Java and other islands.

One of Lolo Soetoro's missions took him to the Indonesian-occupied former Dutch New Guinea, where he was involved in mapping the easternmost claimed Indonesian border with Australian-controlled Papua New Guinea. The mission was code named Operation Cenderawasih, Border Survey Team.[80] After the incorporation of Dutch New Guinea (now known as West Papua by secessionists) by Indonesia, Papuan nationalists waged a rebellion against the Indonesian forces, a conflict that remains to the present day.

---

[80] Janny Scott, *op. cit.,* p. 112.

Even Lolo Soetoro's "official cover" work in topography for the Indonesian Army had a classified component. In March 1965, a few months before Lolo Soetoro was called back to pre-coup duty in Indonesia, the U.S. Army's Image Interpretation and Transmission Technical Area, Combat Surveillance and Target Acquisition Laboratory, U.S. Army Electronics Laboratory, Fort Monmouth, New Jersey, was working with the CIA on Project ART (Aerial Reconnaissance in the Tropics). The liaison with the CIA was through the Counterinsurgency Information Analysis Center (COIN) at the Special Operations Research Office (SORO) at American University. SORO was the initial funding organization behind Projects CAMELOT in LatinAmerica and PROSYMS in Indonesia. COIN, which was also called CINFAC, worked with Battelle Memorial Institute, which ran the Remote Area Conflict Information Center (RACIC) and conducted studies and developed plans for covert operations in countries like Laos, Cambodia, Thailand, and Indonesia.[81]

The CIA's Geography Division routinely produced reports on geographic intelligence. The reports contained detailed data on remote ethnic groups, such as those in northern Thailand and the Thai-Malay border that was directed at enlisting ethnic group participation in insurgency/counter-insurgency activities.[82]

For a step-father of a future President of the United States, it is amazing that so little is known about Lolo Soetoro.

Lolo Soetoro joined the Indonesian Petroleum Club in Jakarta, a meeting place for oil company

---

[81] CIA, Chief of Intelligence School, Weekly Activities Report, No. 33. October, 1965.
[82] CIA, Project Proposal, Research Activity Notice, January 30, 1968.

executives, expatriates and Indonesians, alike. It was never certain what Lolo Soetoro did for the U.S. oil companies but he was generally thought to have been involved in "government relations," a fancy title for a go-between with the Suharto dictatorship and back-slapping oil executives from Texas and Louisiana.[83] Petroleum clubs were also known to be hangouts for intelligence agents, including those from the CIA. The Houston Petroleum Club remains famous for hosting more than one secret rendezvous where the overthrows of some Latin American or Caribbean dictator, including a planned 1963 coup against Haitian dictator Francois "Papa Doc" Duvalier, were discussed. More infamously, the Dallas Petroleum Club was a magnet for several ne'er-do-wells who were later associated with the plot to assassinate President John F. Kennedy.

---

[83] Janny Scott, *op. cit.*, p. 123.

Barry Soetoro, his mother, and step-father would not have lived in such an expensive house in an upscale neighborhood in Menteng, the diplomatic quarter of Jakarta, had Lolo been a lowly enlisted man and Ann Soetoro been a free-spirited hippie from Hawaii.

    Indonesians who knew Lolo Soetoro at the time he and Ann and Barack lived in Jakarta told the author in August 2011 that there was a widespread belief among many Indonesians that Lolo was trained for the coup and follow-on assignments by the CIA while at the East-West Center. Ann's employment by Indonesian and international non-governmental organizations like the Ford Foundation, as well as the U.S. Agency for International Development (USAID) is contrasted by general Indonesian suspicion of white foreigners, known as "bule" in Bahasa Indonesian. For Ann Soetoro to have been propelled into the inner workings of Indonesian and foreign NGOs, so soon after Sukarno's anti-foreign influence campaign and the 1965 coup that ousted him, suggests that Ann had powerful benefactors and handlers in the U.S. and Suharto governments.

There was also the odd situation of Lolo moving from a house that he owned near the St. Fransiskus school, where Obama attended grades one through three, to a smaller rental home in Menteng, where Obama lived while attending the Menteng Elementary School and where he attended grades four and five. There was some evidence that the CIA moved Lolo to a house they owned to provide better security for Lolo and Ann, both of whom were important in the post-coup village and rural area "pacification" program to root out Communist cadres, Project PROSYMS, which had a now-infamous counterpart in South Vietnam called PHOENIX.

The house near the Catholic school, while surrounded by a wall, offered limited security and abutted other houses. However, the detached house in Menteng Dalam, where the Soetoros moved, permitted enhanced security, including a fence line and gate where security guards could be stationed with an adequate security perimeter to the residence.

There has been a major effort in Indonesia to mask and alter the history of Obama, who is ineligible to serve as President because of the break in his "natural born" status from Hawaii after he was adopted by Lolo Soetoro and became an Indonesian citizen. At the very least, since the United States has never had to contend with a president who had broken natural born citizenship status, the Obama situation appears to be a U.S. Supreme Court case made-to-order for constitutional lawyers.

Combine two bogus histories, one of 1960s Indonesia and the other of Obama's globalized family background, and the result is a cargo cult of personality, complete with a statue of a young Obama at the Menteng State Elementary school, featuring an outstretched hand holding a butterfly. A false history has been developed around the President of the United States.

Only Indonesian citizens could attend the Menteng Elementary School at the time Obama attended and, at the time, Indonesia did not permit dual citizenship. Lolo Soetoro would have been required, according to the 1958 law in force at the time, to have formally renounced Obama's American citizenship for Obama to have attended either the Menteng School or the Catholic Fransiskus Assisi School in Jakarta. There is a major constitutional question as to whether a natural born U.S. citizen, having broken the natural born status by swearing or having sworn for him by a legal guardian, fealty to a foreign sovereign, is eligible to serve as President of the United States. In having his status changed from "natural born" to "native born," Obama could no longer claim the status required by the Constitution to serve as president.

Obama's registration card at St. Fransiskus Assisi school in Jakarta, listing his citizenship as "Indonesian." [Bangsa: Warga Negara: nation of citizenship].

There was very visible secrecy and a fear by those Indonesians who remember Obama and his family to talk to foreigners who inquire about the past of

Obama and his family in post-1965 coup Jakarta. Compare Jakarta to other presidential hometowns like Hope Arkansas; Plains, Georgia; Abilene, Kansas; Hyannisport, Massachusetts; Dixon, Illinois; Yorba Linda, California; and Independence, Missouri and the "creepiness" associated with Obama's upbringing in Jakarta literally reaches out and smacks one upside the head. The fear to talk critically about Obama is pervasive in Jakarta. In any other presidential hometown, the older folks who remember their respective presidential native sons are more than happy to reminisce with anecdotes. That has not been the case in Jakarta with Obama and his family.

It is clear that the U.S. embassy in Jakarta, working through local agents, was working overtime to scuttle any unofficial contact between Americans interested in Obama's past and Indonesians who recalled Obama and his family in the late 1960s and early 1970s. During the author's month-long investigation of Obama/Soetoro in Indonesia in August 2011, there was a long list of suddenly cancelled meetings with those in positions to shed light on the past of Obama, his mother, and step-father.

For Obama and his handlers, Jakarta is an insurance policy on keeping secrets. The bitter taste of decades of the dictatorship of General Suharto has left many Indonesians wary of talking to foreigners, especially journalists.

Obama's classroom at St. Fransiskus Assisi school in Jakarta.

Coupled with the largely invented "cargo cult of personality" that has been built up around Obama in Jakarta is the odd situation that, aside from his Indonesian-born step-sister Maya Soetoro-Ng, Obama has no living close relatives. Ann Dunham, who changed the spelling of her last name while married to her Indonesian husband from "Soetoro" to Sutoro," died of cancer in Hawaii on November 7, 1995, at the age of 52. On March 2, 1987, Lolo Soetoro Mangunharjo died of liver failure at the age of 52 in Jakarta. Obama's maternal grandmother, Madelyn Dunham, died of cancer, at the age of 86 on November 2, 2008 (Hawaii time, it was November 3 in the continental United States), mere hours before Obama was elected president. Madelyn Dunham's death followed months of her refusing to grant interviews about her and her famous grandson to the media. Obama's maternal grandfather, Stanley Armour Dunham, who was associated with OSS and CIA activities in France, Lebanon, Cuba, and

Hawaii, died in Hawaii on February 8, 1992 at the age of 73. Obama's purported father, Barack H. Obama, Sr., died in a car crash in Nairobi, Kenya on November 1982 at the age of 46.

One Obama relative who was virtually disowned and ignored by the Obama family was Lia Soetoro, who was informally adopted by Lolo and Ann Soetoro while Barry Soetoro lived in Jakarta. Lia was only a few years older than Obama when she suddenly died in February 2010 in Indonesia.

Lia was invited to Obama's inauguration on January 20, 2009, according to the following press release in Indonesian issued by the Indonesian government. Lia was so poor, collecting grass to make ends meet, she could not afford to attend the inauguration.

DIRECTORATE of INFORMATION and MEDIA
PRESS CABLE
number: 005/09012009
DAY: Friday 9 January 2009
IV. Other:
1. Invited by Obama, Lia Soetoro, with many memories, was surprised, sad, and proud. All these feelings were in the mind of Lia Soetoro, 51, since her adoptive brother, Barack Hussein Obama, was elected President of the United States (US). After decades of separation, the two planned to meet again in a different atmosphere and occasion. Barring any constraints, Lia will attend the inauguration of Barack Obama as US President in Washington DC, January 20, at the invitation of her adoptive brother. Knowing him as a young Barack Obama, he has now become the number one in the US. While Lia still remains in her village, the young Barack Obama has now become number one in the U.S. In

addition to being a homemaker, the wife of Ibn Sobah, 58, also collects grass for their goats.

In Indonesian:
DIREKTORAT INFORMASI DAN MEDIA
PRESS CABLE
NOMOR : 005/09012009HARI : JUMAT
TANGGAL : 9 JANUARI 2009
IV. LAIN-LAIN :

1. Diundang Obama, Lia Soetoro Bawa Boneka Kenangan Terkejut, haru, sedih, dan bangga. Perasaan itu kini berkecamuk dalam benak Lia Soetoro, 51, kakak angkat Barack Hussein Obama, presiden terpilih Amerika Serikat (AS). Setelah puluhan tahun berpisah, keduanya direncanakan bertemu kembali dalam suasana dan kesempatan yang berbeda.

Jika tidak ada kendala, Lia akan menghadiri pelantikan Barack Obama sebagai Presiden AS di Washington DC, 20 Januari mendatang atas undangan khusus dari saudara angkatnya itu.

Jika Barry, sapaan kecil Barack Obama, kini menjadi orang nomor satu di AS, Lia masih tetap tinggal di kampung. Selain sebagai ibu rumah tangga, istri Ibnu Sobah, 58, ini juga punya kesibukan sehari-hari mencari rumput untuk kambing.

On February 25, 2010, Lia died suddenly from a heart attack at the age of 53 after suffering from headaches. The following is an Antara News Agency report, in English, on Lia's death. The dateline is Lia's hometown of Sukabumi:

Obama's Adopted Sister Died

Friday, February 26, 2010
Sukabumi, (ANTARA News) – Adopted sister of the U.S.
President Barack Obama, Holiah (53) alias Lia Soetoro
who lived in Babakan Banten Village, RT 03/ RW 09
Sukasirna, Sukabumi, West Java, dies last Thursday
afternoon (February 25).

Lia, whom Obama called "Mbak Non" was
buried nearby her residence on Friday morning around
9:00 a.m. [West Indonesian Time Zone]. Lia died
Thursday at 17:45 p.m. from a heart attack.

Before her passing, she was scheduled to meet
with Obama who will visit Indonesian this coming
March.

"My wife should have been in Jakarta that
Thursday to meet with Barry (Obama's nickname) at
LCC Menteng Dalem, Central Jakarta." Said her
husband, Edi Sobah (60) in Sukabumi, Friday.

Edi said that before her passing, Lia had just
been interviewed by one of the radio stations in Jakarta.
Not too long after that, she had a headache. "She even
vomited and based on doctor's exam, she broke blood
vessels in her brain so needed to be taken to the
hospital." Her husband said in watery eyes.

But she died on the way to the hospital.
According to him, his wife had been complaining about
her health condition for a while, and based on the
examination by Puskesmas (local government Clinic) of
Bukit Duri, Jakarta, she had high blood pressure and
high cholesterol.

"Before she died, she hoped to meet with the
U.S. President Barack Obama, but she died before it
happens." Edi have said.

Edi wishes that during Obama's visit in
Indonesia, he would collect himself the mementos of his
wife and Barry when they were children which consist of
two glass cups, a bed sheet and a monkey doll.

"It is her wish and mine that Barry would see those mementos himself."

One of Lia's grandchildren, Yudha said that his grandmother had told him to be a smart and good person like Barack Obama who now becomes the President of the United States. His grandmother has also told him that now Barack Obama has become a President as he wished," he has said.

Lia was the daughter of the Obama household maid. Indonesian families often unofficially "adopt" the children of their house maids as their own, sometimes providing them with money for education and other necessities, such as clothing. Maya Soetoro-Ng, Obama's half-sister, criticized Lia as a charlatan trying to gain fame by claiming a relationship with Obama.

In 1967, after arriving in Indonesia with Obama, Jr., Ann began teaching English at the American embassy in Jakarta, which also housed one of the largest CIA stations in Asia and had significant satellite stations in Surabaya in eastern Java and Medan in Sumatra.

The Soetoros lived in what amounted to Jakarta's center of military, intelligence, and foreign diplomatic power – the Menteng district of central Jakarta. Most of Indonesia's political and military elite lived in Menteng when Barack Obama and his mother and step-father lived there. In addition, during the 1960s, Menteng was the home to all the major embassies, including those belonging to countries that supported the coup against Sukarno – the United States, Britain, and Australia, embassies that opposed the coup – the People's Republic of China, North Vietnam, and Yugoslavia, and those embassies that were neutral – the Soviet Union, India, and Japan. Housed within the embassies were the foreign intelligence agents, who, along with the diplomats, mostly all lived in Menteng.

In fact, Obama's mother was teaching English for USAID, which was a major cover for CIA activities in Indonesia and throughout Southeast Asia, especially in Laos, South Vietnam, and Thailand. The USAID program, which was co-sponsored by the spooked-up U.S. Information Agency, was known as *Lembaga Pendidikan Pembinaan Manajemen* - Indonesia-America Friendship Institute. Even Ann Soetoro, in a letter to a friend in Mercer Island, tipped her hand about some of the so-called diplomats at the U.S. embassy: "careerists in the State Department, the occasional economist or journalist who would mysteriously disappear for months at a time, their affiliation or function at the embassy never quite clear."[84] Eventually, a number of observers would make the same claim about Ann Soetoro and her travels and affiliations, which were "never quite clear."

Obama's mother, painted as a free spirit and a "sixties child" by President Obama and people who claimed they knew Ann in Hawaii and Indonesia, had a curriculum vitae in Indonesia that contradicts the perception that she was a "hippie" from the flower power generation.

There has been a major effort by the U.S. embassy in Jakarta and the CIA station there to re-write Obama's and his family's history in Indonesia. Scheduled for President Obama's first state visit to Indonesia in 2010 was the Indonesian film *Obama Anak Menteng* (Young Obama), which features actors playing Obama's mother, Ann Soetoro, and his transvestite nanny, Turdi.

During the author's August 2011 investigation in Jakarta, several Indonesians were queried about their

---

[84] Janny Scott, *op. cit.*, p. 116.

familiarity with the film "Young Obama." Almost everyone polled replied that they had never heard of the film, which was particularly hyped by the two English-language newspapers in Jakarta, the *Jakarta Post* and the *Jakarta Globe*. The intended primary audiences for the film were the bi-lingual and English-speaking communities in Indonesia. The film's release was originally planned for June 17, 2010, coinciding with President Obama's state visit to Jakarta. However, the visit was postponed at the last minute and the film was released on July 1, 2010. It took only five weeks to film the movie in Bandung, because of that city's resemblance to the Menteng neighborhood in Jakarta where Obama grew up. The film's premier in Jakarta was attended by U.S. ambassador to Indonesia Cameron Hume, a sign of U.S. government approval. A rave review of "Young Obama" was carried by the heavily CIA-linked Voice of America.

There were charges from political circles in Indonesia that the film was rushed to production as a propaganda vehicle for Obama's state visit. In fact, the trailer shows a scene where an eight-year old Obama is poring over photographs of important black leaders and a photograph of Martin Luther King, Jr. appears alongside a photograph of a very old Archbishop Desmond Tutu, a feat that could only have been accomplished if Tutu traveled back into time into the 1960s.

Later, President Obama viewed in the White House the low-budget, fast-tracked production. The film was due for general release in the United States in 2012, just in time for the presidential campaign.

During a pre-screening of "Young Obama" at the U.S. embassy, Hume, CIA, and other embassy officials objected to two scenes. One showed a young Obama saluting the Indonesian flag singing the Indonesian national anthem in Indonesian while attending Menteng state elementary school. The other scene depicted Obama praying to Mecca and reciting passages from the Koran in Arabic at the Menteng school's *At Taqwa Muslim [musralla]* chapel. Both scenes were cut from the final version of the film for being "too political," according to high-level sources the author spoke to while in Jakarta. Hume reportedly told the film's director and producer that the scenes "were not good for the United States." The rights for the final version of the film were bought by MGM United Artists and the film was due for release in the United States in 2012.

According to well-placed Jakarta sources, the film was partially subsidized by the CIA as a propaganda vehicle. If true, planned distribution across the United States of a CIA-financed film about Obama called into question the role of the CIA in producing propaganda aimed at the U.S. electorate during a major political campaign, a clear violation of the Smith–Mundt Act, which, since 1948, has banned the federal government from directing U.S. agency-funded propaganda to the American public. In 2012, a bipartisan attempt to amend the Smith-Mundt Act, in the form of the Smith-Mundt Modernization Act of 2012, intended to loosen the restrictions on Americans' exposure to government-produced propaganda.

"Young Obama" was produced by Multivision Plus, an Indonesian movie production company with links to India's "Bollywood." The company was owned by Indonesian-Indian Raam Punjabi. When released in Indonesia, "Young Obama" was treated to favorable coverage by *The New York Times*, *The International Herald Tribune*, and CNN.

Some of the characters portrayed in "Young Obama" have not seen their lives improve as a result of their old friend acceding to the highest political office in the United States. When Obama was 9-years old, his "nanny," the Indonesian named Turdi [like many Indonesians, Turdi uses a single name], saw to Obama's every need: cooking his meals, taking him to the Menteng state elementary school, washing his clothes, and for three-and-a-half months sharing a bedroom with him. Although Turdi was 19-years old at the time he shared a bedroom at the Menteng Dalam house with 9-year old Obama and took care of his needs, such an arrangement is not unusual, according to Indonesian standards. However, in the United States, a 9-year old boy sharing a bedroom with a 19-year old male transvestite might raise eyebrows in even the most liberal of households.

Turdi, who turned sixty in 2011, had changed his name to the woman's name of Evi and moved outside of Jakarta to a smaller village in Java. Turdi/Evi, who remained openly gay, was very poor and was reportedly in ill-health.

It is also noteworthy that a classmate of Obama blamed Barry Soetoro for abandoning him after he suffered a serious bicycle accident. The injuries sustained in the accident, which may not have been as serious had the classmate received immediate medical attention, resulted in the man being rejected for military service and a career in the Indonesian armed forces. The man, who is Obama's age, jokingly said that he ought to "sue Obama" for leaving him unaided and injured at the scene of the accident.

And for British actress, Cara Lachelle, who played the role of Ann Soetoro in "Young Obama," the co-starring performance did not prevent her from being arrested by Indonesian authorities for possession of illegal drugs. She was sentenced to a minimum six-month's sentence in an Indonesian prison.

There was something else very apparent with those who were still alive, as well as those recently passed away, who knew the Soetoro family during the late 1960s and early 1970s. There was a definite fear about talking about what they knew about the Soetoros. It was clear that U.S. intelligence agents had swept through Jakarta and other parts of Indonesia looking for those who knew the Soetoros. They feared anyone, especially "bule," who asked too many questions about Barry, Lolo, and Ann Soetoro.

In January 2008, State Department contractors working for The Analysis Corporation, a CIA contractor firm headed by one-time CIA counter-terrorism and rendition and torture architect John O. Brennan, rifled through Obama's passport files at the State Department. Brennan became Obama's Deputy Director of National Security for Counter-terrorism. If Brennan utilized his old CIA torture and rendition colleagues to sweep through Indonesia looking for those who knew the Soetoros, there was little wonder why so many Indonesians who encountered "Family Soetoro" decades ago were afraid to talk about them after Obama became president.

In 1968, one year after moving to Jakarta, Indonesia, Ann Soetoro listed her son's last name as Barack Hussein Obama (Soebarkah) with "Soebarkah" bracketed by parentheses. Obama's mother later used the spelling of "Sutoro" as her own last name.

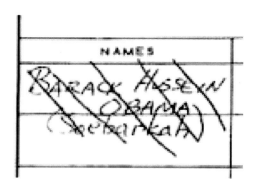

Soebarkah may be Obama's given Indonesian name: a legal requirement in his formal adoption process and his becoming an Indonesian citizen.

The name "Soebarkah" may have been Obama's given Indonesian name upon his formal adoption by Lolo Soetoro. The adoption of an Indonesian name also indicates strongly that Obama became an Indonesian citizen. In Janny Scott's book, *A Singular Woman*, a young Obama is quoted as telling Lolo that he wanted to one day become "Prime Minister of Indonesia," something that only an Indonesian citizen could strive to attain.[85] Indonesian law explicitly states that dual citizenship is not permitted and, according to a 1958 Indonesian law, only Indonesian citizens could be enrolled in the two schools Obama attended in Jakarta: St. Fransiskus Assisi Catholic school and Menteng Elementary. By becoming an Indonesian and possibly by travelling on an Indonesian passport to Pakistan and India in 1981, Obama ceased being a "natural born" citizen and became a "native born" citizen. Although it is an Indonesian custom for family, friends, and even employers of domestic help to informally "adopt" the

---

[85] Janny Scott, *op. cit.*, p. 131.

children of relatives, friends, and employees, Obama's adoption was much more formal and carried out pursuant to Indonesian law.

Obama's mother's listing of her son's name as "Soebarkah" was in all likelihood an attempt by her to avoid breaking U.S. law, which states, "False statements made knowingly and willfully in passport *applications* are punishable by fine and/or imprisonment under U.S. law." Article II, clause 5, is very specific about Obama's ineligibility to serve as President as a "native born" American who held Indonesian citizenship as a child and may have continued holding Indonesian citizenship two years after turning 18: "No Person except a natural born Citizen, or a Citizen of the United States, at the time of the Adoption of this Constitution, shall be eligible to the Office of President."

Obama's eligibility to serve as President has never been about his Hawaiian birth certificate. Obama was born in Hawaii on August 4, 1961, which made him an American citizen until he was adopted by Lolo Soetoro, became a sole Indonesian citizen as a result of Indonesia's prohibition of dual citizens, was possibly given the Indonesian name of Soebarkah, and may have continued to swear allegiance to a foreign power until after he turned 18. There is an ongoing controversy over Obama's attendance at Occidental College in 1979, with reports that he had been awarded a Fulbright Scholarship only available to foreign students and was enrolled in Occidental with financial assistance from the government of Indonesia. Some dubious "conspiracy debunking" web sites, such as Snopes.com, have said the Fulbright scholarship for Obama is a myth. Obama's Occidental records, as well as those from Columbia University, where he transferred, remain largely sealed as a result of restrictions placed on such records by the Family Educational Rights and Privacy Act (FERPA).

Obama has shown no inclination to authorize the release of the records.

With most of Obama's immediate family members dead and those whom he knew in Jakarta who are still alive afraid to talk to the press, Obama has managed to continue to perpetuate a fraudulent presidency on the American people. The "birther" extremists, most of whom are unfamiliar with the history of Indonesia in the 1960s, 70s, and 80s, have managed to muddy the waters by insisting that Obama was born in Mombasa, Kenya, a meme that is intended to paint Obama as an African, thus catering to more racist elements in the Republican Party. There is a significant issue with Obama's eligibility to serve as President but the roads to Mombasa, Kenya and Honolulu are truly dead ends: the only road pointing to the answers about Obama's citizenship status leads to Jakarta.

A knowledgeable source who covered Indonesian politics for twenty years was asked why Indonesia has been so strict on insisting that no dual Indonesian citizenship by nationals of other countries be legal. The Indonesians, like the framers of the U.S. Constitution, particularly Article 2, Clause 5, which states that U.S. presidents must be "natural born" citizens, did not want a foreign usurper from being proclaimed President of Indonesia in the years leading up to Indonesia's declaration of independence in 1945, following World War II.

Indonesian independence leaders feared that the Dutch Queen might have attempted to become a president-regent in a post-war independent Indonesia. an independence that would be in name only. The independence leaders were also aware that the Japanese occupiers during the war suggested that Emperor

Hirohito was offered up as a regent-president of Indonesia in *de facto* colonial relationship with Japan.

Therefore, Indonesian law was crafted to disallow dual citizens to prevent someone with loyalty to a foreign power becoming President of Indonesia. Ironically, it is Barack Obama's own Indonesian citizenship status that has some questioning his constitutional eligibility to serve as President of the United States.

In the years following the fall of the Suharto dictatorship, rather than seeing a disclosure of the U.S. archives from the Suharto "New Order" regime following the CIA-inspired coup in 1965, the archives have been kept under wraps. This situation did not benefit those researchers who wanted more information on the activities of Obama's step-father, mother, and their Indonesian and American colleagues in the years immediately following the coup.

There is one group in Indonesia that has called for more disclosure and transparency of government activities in Indonesia: the Muhammadiya Islamic movement, condemned by some in the West as pro-Islamic state, but in reality, is as reform-minded as the Turkish Justice and Development Party and is just as committed to increasing democratic rule in Indonesia.

Published State Department cables, released by WikiLeaks in 2011, sent shock waves through the administration of Indonesian President Yudhoyono, who was the Minister of Political and Security Affairs in the cabinet of the previous president, Megawati Sukarnaputri, the daughter of President Sukarno. In a fortuitous turn of events, the blow-back over the leaked cables resulted in information being passed to the author by high-level sources in the Indonesian government that contained in Indonesian intelligence files were documents related to the activities of Obama's step-father, Soetoro, and his mother, Ann.

In Lolo's case, the files pointed to his CIA training at the East-West Center at the University of Hawaii in preparation for the September 30, 1965 coup against Sukarno. In the case of Ann, the files showed her involvement in Javanese village- and rural-based Indonesian Communist Party (PKI) and Sukarno cadre eradication efforts in the years following the coup, an operation, Project PROSYMS, which relied on anthropologists like Ann. The program's counterpart in South Vietnam, which targeted Vietcong and Vietcong sympathizers for eradication, was known as Civil Operations and Revolutionary Development Support (CORDS) and the Phoenix Program.

President Obama retained funding for the two programs' modern-day successor, the Human Terrain System, which has targeted villagers and peasants in Afghanistan, Iraq, Pakistan, Somalia, and other countries thought to be sympathizers of "Al Qaeda" and its off-shoots.

Cables sent by Hume to the State Department in November 2009 painted Yudhoyono as leading a corrupt administration and political party, the Democratic Party of Indonesia. The cables from Hume suggested that Yudhoyono and his top officials were involved in corruption with Indonesia's wealthiest business tycoons and bankers. It is noteworthy that Hume made no mention of the close financial relationship between the Lippo Group of Mochtar and James Riady and top U.S. Democrats, including former President Bill Clinton, Secretary of State Hillary Clinton, former Vice President Al Gore, and Obama. Later, the U.S. embassy in Jakarta did not refute the claims made by Hume in the cables.

It was learned from Indonesian government sources that the work that Soetoro and Ann were doing for Indonesian and U.S. intelligence in the years following the coup kept the two away from Jakarta for weeks and months at a time. For that reason, Obama was raised by a Soetoro household staff that was either employed directly by Soetoro or was provided under the aegis of the U.S. embassy and the CIA station in Jakarta.

Ann Soetoro's Russian language training at the University of Hawaii may have been useful to the CIA in Indonesia. An August 2, 1966, formerly Secret memorandum from the National Security Council's Executive Secretary Bromley Smith states that, in addition to Japan, Western Europe, Australia, New Zealand, Malaysia, and the Philippines, the Suharto coup was welcomed by the Soviet Union and its Eastern European allies because it created a non-aligned Indonesia that "represents an Asian counterweight to Communist China." Records indicate that a number of CIA agents posted in Jakarta before and after the 1965 coup were, like Ann Soetoro, conversant in Russian.[86]

By 1970, the Soviets were faced with an Indonesia tied firmly to the West. Indonesia's pro-Western Foreign Minister, Adam Malik, even suggested the creation of a NATO-like defense pact between Ceylon, India, Pakistan, Malaysia, Singapore and Indonesia to "defend" the Indian Ocean from Soviet encroachment.[87] The following year, in 1971, Indonesia grew more important to the West. New oil discoveries were made in Riau by Caltex, south Sulawesi by Iapco

---

[86] National Security Council memo, dated August 2, 1966. Also, the CIA's HA/BRINK project in Indonesia was designed to capture Soviet weaponry transferred to the nation in order to analyze it. David Barnett, the operation's chief CIA agent in Jakarta, later defected to the KGB revealing the entire operation. Ann was posted to Jakarta at the height of HA/BRINK operations in the late 1960s.
[87] Ernest Weatherall, "Magnet for Soviet ships seen in east-of-Suez vacuum," *Christian Science Monitor*, June 11, 1970.

(owned by the San Francisco-based Natomas Oil Company), north of Jakarta in the Java Sea by Atlantic Richfield Company (ARCO), and in the Strait of Makasar by Yapex Union Oil Company.[88]

Ann worked for the elitist Ford Foundation, World Bank, Asian Development Bank, Bank Rakyat (the majority government-owned People's Bank of Indonesia), and the CIA-linked USAID while she lived in Indonesia and later, Pakistan, where she worked in rural development projects in Punjab and where she once traveled to one of the most heavily-garrisoned regions in the world: the mountainous region where the Hindu Kush, Himalayas, and Karakoram Range converge, an area heavily contested by China, India, and Pakistan.[89]

USAID was involved in a number of CIA covert operations in Southeast Asia. The February 9, 1971, *Washington Star* reported that USAID officials in Laos were aware that rice supplied to the Laotian Army by USAID was being re-sold to North Vietnamese army divisions in the country. The report stated that the U.S. tolerated the USAID rice sales to the North Vietnamese since the Laotian Army units that sold the rice found themselves protected from Communist Pathet Lao and North Vietnamese attack. USAID and the CIA also used the supply of rice to force Laotian Meo tribesmen to support the United States in the war against the Communists. USAID funds programmed for civilians injured in the war in Laos and public health care were actually diverted for military purposes.[90]

---

[88] Henry S. Hayward, "Oil Finds Brighten Indonesia's Outlook," *Christian Science Monitor*, July 9, 1971.
[89] Janny Scott, *op. cit.*, p. 268.
[90] "CIA Uses Health Aid Funds For Combat Role in Laos," *St. Louis Post-Dispatch*, March 21, 1972.

In 1971, the USAID-funded Center for Vietnamese Studies at Southern Illinois University in Carbondale was accused of being a CIA front. USAID-funded projects through the Midwest Universities Consortium for International Activities (MUCIA) – comprising the Universities of Illinois, Wisconsin, Minnesota, Indiana and Michigan State – were accused of being CIA front projects, including those for "agricultural education" in Indonesia, as well as other "projects" in Afghanistan, Mali, Nepal, Nigeria, Thailand, and South Vietnam. The charge was made in 1971, the same year that Ann Dunham was working for USAID in the country.[91]

After the 1965 coup, the Western media became cheerleaders for Suharto, with newspaper headlines like "One Cheer for Suharto's democracy" in *The Economist* of June 10, 1971 and "Indonesia: Someone is Doing Something Right," in *The New York Times* of July 19, 1971.

One of Ann's closest East-West Center colleagues in Indonesia, Bill Collier, who arrived in Indonesia in 1968, a year after Dunham, previously saw center-sponsored study tours in three hotbeds of Communist "subversion": Thailand, Malaya, and British North Borneo.[92] Chinese ethnic communities in Malaysia, particularly in Sarawak, were seen as fertile for Communist activities.

One noted dual anthropologist-intelligence agent who served in British North Borneo was Richard Noone, a member of Britain's Secret Intelligence Service (SIS).

---

[91] Dan Cryer, *The University of Minnesota Daily*, November 2, 1971.
[92] Janny Scott, *op. cit.*, p. 79.

Noone had organized Malay tribal networks that fought the Japanese during World War II. After the war, Noone was in charge of Malaya's Aborigines Department where he recruited Malay tribes to fight against the Communists. Noone later led a special operations commando base in Sabah, the former British North Borneo state of Malaysia, to fight Indonesian forces during the military confrontation between Malaysia and Indonesia in the mid-1960s. Noone led a team of ethnic Malay-Polynesian tribesmen from Borneo to help their ethnically-related cousins, the Montagnard tribes of central Vietnam, in the war against the Vietcong and North Vietnam. Ultimately, Noone became a special operations adviser to SEATO.

In a July 10, 1971, *New York Times* report, USAID and the CIA were accused of "losing" $1.7 billion appropriated for the CORDS program in South Vietnam. CORDS was part of the CIA's Operation Phoenix program, which involved CIA assassination and torture of South Vietnamese village elders and Buddhist clerics. USAID money was also directed to the CIA's proprietary airline in Southeast Asia, Air America. In Thailand, USAID funds for the Accelerated Rural Development Program in Thailand were actually masking a CIA anti-Communist counter-insurgency operation. USAID funds programmed for public works projects in East Pakistan in 1971 were used for East Pakistan's military fortifications on its border with India, in the months before the outbreak of war with India, in contravention of U.S. law that prohibited USAID money for military purposes.[93]

---

[93] Tad Szulc, "U.S. report says Pakistan spent aid for defenses," *New York Times*, June 8, 1972.

In 1972, USAID administrator Dr. John Hannah admitted to Metromedia News that USAID was being used as a cover for CIA covert operations in Laos. Hannah only admitted to Laos as a USAID cover for the CIA. However, it was also reported that USAID was being used by the CIA in Indonesia, Philippines, South Vietnam, Thailand, and South Korea. USAID projects in Southeast Asia had to be approved by the Southeast Asian Development Advisory Group (SEADAG), an Asia Society group that was, in fact, answerable to the CIA.[94]

The U.S. Food for Peace program, jointly administered by USAID and the Department of Agriculture, was found in 1972 to be used for military purposes in Cambodia, South Korea, Turkey, South Vietnam, Spain, Taiwan, and Greece. In 1972, USAID funneled aid money only to the southern part of North Yemen, in order to aid North Yemeni forces against the government of South Yemen, then ruled by a socialist government opposed to U.S. hegemony in the region.[95]

One of the entities affiliated with the USAID work in Indonesia was the Asia Foundation, a post-World War II creation formed with the help of the CIA to oppose the expansion of communism in Asia. The East-West Center guest house in Hawaii was funded by the Asia Foundation, which used the East-West Center to recruit foreign agents and CIA case officers. The guest house is also where Barack Obama Sr. first stayed after his airlift from Kenya to Hawaii, arranged by the one of the CIA's major agents of influence in Africa, Mboya.

---

[94] Dan Siegel, *Daily World*, August 10, 1972.
[95] Tom Foley, "South Yemen faces imperialist gang-up," *Daily World*, October 17, 1972.

One of the agents recruited by the CIA through the Asia Foundation was Sir John Kerr. The Asia Foundation sponsored Kerr through the Law Association for Asia and the Western Pacific.[96] Later, Kerr would, as Governor General of Australia, act at the CIA's behest by dismissing from office Labor Prime Minister Gough Whitlam. Whitlam had been a major critic of the CIA's secret activities from the intelligence base at Pine Gap, near Alice Springs.

The San Francisco-based Asia Foundation, founded at the end of World War II as the Committee for a Free Asia, received much of its funding through CIA conduits, including USAID. The foundation's CIA ties resulted in its operations in Indonesia, Burma, and Cambodia being terminated by the governments of those countries.

Ann Dunham would also travel to Ghana, Nepal, Bangladesh, Kenya, Egypt, Malaysia, India, and Thailand working on micro-financing projects. In 1965, Barack Obama Sr. returned to Kenya from Harvard, with another American wife. The senior Obama linked up with his old friend and the CIA's "golden boy" Mboya and other fellow Luo politicians. The CIA station chief in Nairobi from 1964 to 1967 was Philip Cherry. In 1975, Cherry was the CIA station chief in Dacca, Bangladesh. Cherry was linked by the then-U.S. ambassador to Bangladesh, Eugene Booster, to the 1975 assassination of Bangladesh's first president, Sheikh Mujibur Rahman, and members of his family.[97]

The hit on "Sheikh Mujib" and his family was reportedly ordered by then-Secretary of State Henry

---

[96] Toohey and Pinwill, *op. cit.*, p. 76.
[97] Christopher Hitchens, *The Trial of Henry Kissinger,* quoting Lawrence Lifschultz. New York: Verso, 2001. pp. 52-53

Kissinger. Bangladesh was also on the micro- and macro-financing travel itinerary of CIA-linked Ann Dunham.

Chapter Four – East and West of Krakatoa: CIA anthropologist spies

I think its time we held Sukarno's feet to the fire – Frank Wisner, Sr., CIA Deputy Director for Plans.

The CIA influence over President Obama's

anthropologist mother is highlighted in an important report written by University of California-Los Angeles anthropology professor Dr. Ralph Beals for the Officers and Executive Board of the American Anthropological Association (AAA) and delivered to the annual meeting of the AAA on November 17, 1966 in Pittsburgh. This chapter pursues the close relationship between the CIA and the world of anthropology during the Cold War years and today, in the so-called "global war on terrorism."

Beals's significant report remains relatively obscure to those outside the field of applied anthropology but what it detailed is a critical indictment of the CIA and Defense Department in co-opting young and inexperienced field anthropologists like Ann Dunham/Soetoro to conduct "data mining" for CIA and Pentagon covert "counter-insurgency" operations. Ann's receipt of funding from the Ford Foundation is a troubling aspect of President Obama's upbringing. Far from being raised by a leftist "flower child" of the 1960s who for a time reportedly lived on food stamps, young Barack Obama was raised in a family that was never without need or want but benefited from a CIA-funded regime that permitted anthropologists like Ann to collect largely tax-free salaries abroad while conducting dubious research for the CIA via foundation-laundered funding.

In its investigation of U.S. intelligence activities in the 1960s and 70s, the U.S. Senate Select Committee on Intelligence chaired by Senator Frank Church (D-ID) discovered that one-third of all the hard and social sciences grants awarded by the "Big Three" foundations – Ford, Rockefeller, and Carnegie – involved CIA money. In some cases, the CIA-funded "research" was later used for the CIA's torture, counter-insurgency, "termination with extreme prejudice," and surveillance of targets abroad and within the United States.

The CIA's Chief of Plans and Policy Staff, in a 1956 Weekly Activity Report, stated that a meeting was held with the Massachusetts Institute of Technology's Center for International Studies (CENIS) Director Max Millikan to establish a course on "intercultural communications." The report also stated that on January 12, 1952, "Mr. John D. Rockefeller III . . . . offered the Department of State $100,000 to set up a CENIS-type program at Harvard University."[98]

With a Bachelor of Arts in Anthropology from the University of Hawaii under her belt, Ann moved with her seven-year old son to Jakarta to be with her husband, Indonesian Army Lieutenant Colonel Lolo Soetoro – a hit man for the CIA-installed Suharto regime – to ply her intelligence agency apprenticeship in mapping the political and social allegiances of the people of the island of Java, a longtime island of opportunity for CIA machinations.

Ann's work in Indonesia for USAID and the Ford Foundation followed by two years President

---

[98] CIA, Weekly Activity Report No. 5, Secret, dated February 3, 1956.

Lyndon Johnson's dictate to Secretary of State Dean Rusk: "I am determined that no Government sponsorship of foreign area research should be undertaken which in the judgment of the Secretary of State would adversely affect United States foreign relations."[99] According to the seminal Beals Report, this presidential directive placed the government in a commanding role in deciding who and what projects, including foreign anthropology research, would be funded. For good measure, to ensure that such research had a military or intelligence predicate, Rusk assigned oversight for foreign area research to Thomas L. Hughes, the Director of Intelligence and Research for the State Department.

As Dr. David Price, a pre-eminent expert in the use of anthropologists by the CIA and Pentagon in clandestine operations, wrote in a 2009 article in *Critique of Anthropology* titled, "Subtle Means and Enticing Carrots: The Impact of Funding on Cold War Anthropology," the Ford Foundation, State Department, and CIA were "involved in intricate covert political interventions in Indonesia."[100] One of the top witting U.S. assets in Java was Dr. Clifford Geertz, a pioneer in the anthropological surveys of Java for the CIA who would have most certainly known Ann Soetoro in Java or may have even been her de facto "control officer."

In her book, *Surviving Against the Odds*, which largely dealt with village industry in Indonesia, Ann's respect for Geertz as the *eminent grise* of social scientists of her time is on full display. Although she

---

[99] Dr. Ralph Beals, American Anthropological Association, *Anthropology Newsletter*, Vol. 8. No. 2, January 1967.
[100] Dr. David Price, "Subtle Means and Enticing Carrots: The Impact of Funding on Cold War Anthropology," *Critique of Anthropology,* Vol. 23, No. 4, 2003.

96

criticized Geertz for his use of derogatory language to describe Javanese society and culture, Ann's respect for Geertz and CENIS's Project Modjokuto is more than evident. She cites Geertz and her University of Hawaii academic adviser Alice Dewey, the granddaughter of philosopher John Dewey, as inspirations for her book.[101] Dunham is also effusive in her praise of Suharto's "New Order" program, considered fascistic by many of Suharto's opponents.[102]

In a poem written by intelligence and "deep state" expert, the University of California-Berkeley Professor and former Canadian diplomat, Peter Dale Scott about the Indonesian massacre, Geertz is mentioned in a chilling passage:

Clifford Geertz having just
reread your Notes
on the Balinese cockfight

how you were first accepted
by cautious villagers
after you all fled

from the Javanese constabulary
and how slaughter
in the cock ring itself

after red pepper
is stuffed down their beaks
and up their anuses

---

[101] S. Ann Dunham, *Surviving Against the Odds: Village Industry in Indonesia*, edited by Alice G. Dewey and Nancy I. Cooper, Durham, North Carolina: Duke University Press, 2009, pp. 17, 33.
[102] *Ibid.*, p. 336.

joins pride to selfhood
selfhood to cocks
and cocks to destruction

a blood sacrifice
offered to the demons
to pacify their cannibal hunger[103]

Geertz, who was heavily funded by the Ford Foundation, happened to have arrived in Indonesia the day before the coup against Sukarno. Geertz immediately went to Yogyakarta, the PKI hot-bed where Ann Soetoro would conduct her "field research."

Anthropologists like Ann Soetoro were a key factor in the transformation of Indonesia from a non-aligned socialist country to a Western surrogate. The transition plan was spelled out in a CIA "Central Intelligence Bulletin" from December 1965. The CIA saw a gradual political transition from Sukarno to Suharto and agreed with a Suharto plan to initially maintain a semblance of "leftism" without the Communist Party. The CIA and Indonesian junta members concluded that "Indonesian political philosophy existed long before Marx was born or Lenin stole a train ride to St. Petersburg."[104]

The use of cultural anthropologists for CIA work created a furor in the 1960s, especially with their use in South Vietnam and Thailand in support of the war effort. However, one of the most noted anthropologists in the world at the time, Margaret Mead, renowned for her seminal work in 1928, *Coming of Age in Samoa,* and

---

[103] Peter Dale Scott. "Coming to Jakarta."
[104] CIA, Central Intelligence Bulletin, TOP SECRET, December 13, 1965, p. 13.

her controversial views on the sexual morés of the 1960s, defended the CIA's use of anthropologists in field work. In a 1971 report, referred to as the "Mead Report," Mead rebutted the 1966 Beals Report and stated that the use of anthropologists in counter-insurgency "research" met the "traditional canons of acceptable behavior" for anthropologists.

Mead found herself in opposition to senior anthropologists of the AAA who were opposed to the CIA's use of anthropologists in covert operations and counter-insurgency programs. The Beals Report stated: "several anthropologists, especially younger ones who had difficulty in securing research funds, were approached by 'obscure' foundations or were offered support from such organizations only to discover later that they were expected to provide intelligence information to the CIA." The report added, "agents of the CIA have posed as anthropologists, much to the detriment of the anthropological research programs."[105]

Geertz had an unusual interest in the Balinese blood sport of cockfighting. Price cites Professor Nancy Scheper-Hughes, director of the Medical Anthropology program at the University of California-Berkeley, whose later investigation of an Israeli-based ring of human organ traffickers led to a number of arrests by the FBI of a number of perpetrators.[106] [It is interesting to note that in her investigation of the Israeli organ theft operation, which targeted unsuspecting poor people in developing countries, Scheper-Hughes discovered that one of the motivating factors for the Israeli theft of organs from non-Jews was, as she stated in a 2008 lecture, "revenge, restitution, reparation for the Holocaust – the attitude

---

[105] Beals. *op. cit.*
[106] Price, *op. cit.*

being 'we're gong to get every single kidney and liver and heart that we can. The world owes it to us.'"][107]

In the Indonesia context, Scheper-Hughes wrote of Geertz:

"Clifford Geertz's celebrated Balinese 'cockfight" scenario was developed within the larger context of a national political emergency that resulted in the massacre of almost three-quarters of a million Indonesians, though it took Geertz three decades to mention the killings that had engulfed his Javanese field site, now forever associated in our minds with those semiotic fighting roosters."[108]

In the context of current events, where President Obama has, without a thought for the carnage wrought on innocent civilians in Afghanistan, Iraq, Pakistan, and now, Libya, has ordered wanton attacks by drone aircraft, Special Forces units, U.S. Army Stryker units, "precision-guided" munitions (including those tipped with depleted uranium warheads), and, in the case of Libya, stand-off Tomahawk cruise missiles, the involvement of Ann Soetoro with "blood sport" aficionados like Geertz , a member of the Council on Foreign Relations and the CIA-linked Institute for Advanced Study at Princeton, raises troubling questions. If Geertz was a role model for Ann Dunham, and she was a role model for Obama, there is a distinct possibility that the president of the United States was raised within a household where mass murder of civilians was not considered a crime against humanity but a macabre blood sport.

---

[107] Alison Weir, "Israeli Organ Trafficking and Theft: From Moldova to Palestine," *Washington Report on Middle East Affairs*, November 2009. Pp. 15-17.

[108] Price, *op. cit.*

Today, a number of elements of CAMELOT and PROSYMS are integral to the much-discredited "Human Terrain System" (HTS) operations in Afghanistan and Iraq. As with CAMELOT and other covert operations involving anthropologists, HTS was charged with exacerbating tensions between various indigenous groups and tribes to create intelligence opportunities for the U.S. military. The targeting of village leaders, a replay of the CIA's PHOENIX assassination program in South Vietnam, part of CIA Southeast Asia regional chief William Colby's CORDS program, was a charge leveled against those involved with HTS. President Obama did nothing to curtail HTS funding, although there were some moves by some members of Congress to do so.

HTS expert John Stanton, writing in the *Sri Lanka Guardian*, quoted a Sri Lankan soldier who said, "I fear Human Terrain Teams more than the CIA." Stanton revealed that the Human Terrain Teams were active in Operation New Dawn in Iraq and military operations in Afghanistan, and were a major element in the activities of the U.S. Africa Command (AFRICOM).[109] There was once a humorous slogan about the U.S. Army: "Join the Army, meet interesting people, then kill them." However, what was once was considered an example of black humor is now entrenched in U.S. military doctrine.

---

[109] John Stanton, "Congress' Human Terrain Assessment Vanishes: Politically Charged Study Withdrawn from Military Website," *Sri Lankan Guardian*, February 21, 2011.

Obama continued to fund the follow-on to CAMELOT, PHOENIX, CORDS, and MODJOKUTO, the Human Terrain System, which has been responsible for massacres of civilians in Afghanistan, Iraq, Somalia, Yemen and Pakistan.

Geertz was the beneficiary of the largesse of CIA-linked philanthropic foundations, Rand Corporation, USAID, CIA, and Pentagon funding poured into Java and Bali at the same time Ann Soetoro was a young field anthropologist in western Java.

Price writes that Geertz "ignored the Indonesian political setting that gave rise to death squads, military and police terror, institutionalized unemployment, and eventually to the bloodbath that followed the US-backed coup against Sukarno."[110] And it was in this very environment that Ann chose to raise her son, who later wrote that the massacre of between 750,000 and 1 million Indonesians was not known to her before she ventured to join her husband in Indonesia. Obama is either ignorant of history or engaged in a dishonest campaign to divorce his family from genocide in Indonesia for which the record clearly indicates they were involved to varying degrees.

---

[110] Price, *op. cit.*

Geertz's role as a patron for Ann Soetoro is also problematic when one considers that Geertz first entered Indonesia under the aegis of the Ford Foundation (and CIA)-funded Project Modjokuto in 1954. The project was conducted through the auspices of the CIA-funded CENIS at the Massachusetts Institute of Technology (MIT) and at Harvard University.

Geertz worked with CENIS on projects funded by both the CIA and Ford Foundation. In his book, *The Bridge: The Life and Rise of Barack Obama*, David Remnick cites Geertz as one of Ann Soetoro's Indonesian colleagues.[111] Geertz, a specialist in the post-war Javanese economy, believed in modernization of tribal and rural societies and was not sold on Ann Soetoro's quaint ideas of promoting the interests and development of Indonesian village craftsmen and weavers.

CENIS's anthropological work on behalf of the CIA was the brainchild of Millikan, CENIS's first director, and Walt W. Rostow, who, in 1954, convinced CIA director Allen Dulles of the need for CIA involvement in development projects abroad. Rostow later became deputy national security adviser in the Lyndon Johnson White House. Rostow worked for McGeorge Bundy, who, after leaving the White House in 1966, became President of the Ford Foundation, the main source of the laundered CIA funding for Geertz's and Dunham Soetoro's field work in Indonesia.

Many of the pre-1977 CIA files on its interactions with the American Anthropological Association have either been heavily redacted or

---

[111] David Remnick, The Bridge: *The Life and Rise of Barack Obama*. New York: Vintage Books, 2011, p. 84.

destroyed. Many of the MK-ULTRA documents on CIA behavioral science work in the United States and abroad were ordered destroyed in 1973 by CIA director Colby, shortly after he took over at Langley. Some of the CIA's anthropological studies were directed domestically at the Black Panther Party.

CENIS is listed in the official *CIA Historical Staff Chronology 1946-65* as being founded on March 1, 1952 by Millikan.[112] The Chronology states that on June 29, 1964, "MITs Center for International Studies, attacked in a book for CIA connections, acknowledges having been originally subsidized by CIA in '53."[113]

Geertz's Modjokuto was similar to the Pentagon's Project CAMELOT in Chile in the 1960s, which represented the use of anthropologists to conduct counter-insurgency studies among various ethnic groups in countries ripe for U.S. covert intervention.

Geertz was also involved in parapsychology and believed "the Western conception of a person . . . is . . . a rather peculiar idea within the context of the world's cultures."[114] Geertz was also an expert on ghosts, having been cited in David N. Hess's "The Poltergeist and Cultural Values, A Comprehensive Interpretation of a Brazilian and American Case," Colgate University (in CIA archives).

Mysticism in Indonesia is manifested in the Java-based sect known as "Subud," named for its founder Muhammad Subuh Sumohadiwidjojo, also

---

[112] *CIA Historical Staff Chronology 1946-65*, Vol. I, 1946-55, Secret June 1970, p. 47.

[113] *Ibid.*, p. 79.

[114] Hoyt Edge, "The Relentless Dualist: John Baloff's Contribution to Parapsychology," *Journal of Parapsychology*, Vol. 55, June 1991, p. 211.

known as "Bapak" or "Pak Subuh," a charismatic religious figure who believed individuals can be uplifted by spiritual energy from a higher power in an exercise known as the latihan. Subud, which has an international following and became popular in Indonesia and internationally following World War II, attracted as adherents a few Western intelligence operatives assigned to Indonesia. It is not known whether Ann Soetoro, an expert in Javanese culture and peoples, was an actual member of the Java-based sect.

However, Ann maintained close connections with the sect. Ann first encountered Subud members while working for the Institute for Management and Education and Development, while under a grant from the Ford Foundation, in 1971. She hired members of Subud, who lived in the International Subud Center compound in the Jakarta suburb of Cilandak, to teach intensive courses in business English.[115] Given her residence in Semarang, Bapak's hometown and base, from 1978 to 1980, it is inconceivable that Ann was unaware of Bapak and his movement. Bapak and his Subud followers were also well-entrenched at the East-West Center at the University of Hawaii, where Ann met her Kenyan and Indonesian husbands.

Kenya was also not unknown to Subud missionaries. Conversion missions set out from Indonesia in the early 1960s to Kenya, Swaziland, and Northern and Southern Rhodesia.

Before he died in 1987, Bapak toured the world spreading his message of mystical spiritualism. The one goal Bapak wanted to achieve was to create a "Bank for Mankind." Although Bapak died before he could

---

[115] Janny Scott, *op. cit.*, pp. 116-117.

achieve his goal, much of Ann's micro-financing programs achieved part of the goal of banking services for women and the poor. In fact, Subud counted a number of international aid workers and employees of the World Bank and Asian Development Bank – where Obama's mother worked – among its members, or "helpers," as Subud prefers to call its international assistance workers. These Subud assistance workers were found working in Indonesia, Bangladesh, India, Sri Lanka, and Thailand. Subud also attracted a number of Australians and New Zealanders to its ranks and Subud centers sprang up in the major cities of the two countries.

Bapak was not only interested in helping the poor but became a wealthy man in his own right by bringing new adherents into the fold. Bapak owned a construction company that built a hotel and the S. Widjojo office building in Jakarta.

Some of its critics have labeled Subud a cult. The sect attracted a number of 60s-era "hippie generation" adherents, including Jim McGuinn, lead singer and guitarist for The Byrds. It was Bapak who told McGuinn to change his name from Jim to Roger because it would "vibrate" better with the universe.

Subud members often change their names while transitioning into full membership status. New names are assigned by Subud leaders. In Ann Dunham Soetoro's 1968 U.S. passport renewal application, Barack H. Obama, Jr.'s name is listed as Barack Hussein Obama (Soebarkah). There is a possibility that if Ann Soetoro was a Subud member, she changed the name of her son in accordance with Subud teachings. Ann also changed the spelling of her own last name from Soetoro to Sutoro.

Other critics have pointed to the connections between the Subud movement and CIA mind control operations, especially those directed at children and others that administer sodium pentothal to unwitting subjects. Subud maintains a religious compound known as Skymont on the banks of the Shenandoah River near Front Royal, Virginia. In the lead-up to the CIA coup in Indonesia, the PKI accused Subud of being a CIA front. The chairman of Subud Indonesia before the coup was Dr. Achmad Subardjo, the first Foreign Minister of Indonesia. One of those who distrusted Subud was Dr. Subandrio, Sukarno's Foreign Minister, who banned Subud meetings in the weeks leading up to the coup.

Bapak issued orders to his non-Indonesian members to leave the country before the coup and told foreign members abroad not to enter the country. When Suharto ousted Sukarno and declared the PKI illegal, Bapak celebrated the change, proclaiming that Indonesia was free of the Communists.

Subandrio was sentenced to death after the coup but the sentence was reduced to life imprisonment. He was released from prison in 1995 and died in 2004. Bapak's followers believed that their religious icon could bring death upon his enemies. Not only was Subandrio sentenced to death after he quarreled with Bapak but in 1959, the Prime Minister of Ceylon, Solomon Bandaranaike, told Bapak he had to leave the island nation within 48-hours because he was thought to be a threat to the state religion of Buddhism. Shortly afterwards, Bandaranaike was shot to death by a Buddhist monk. Some suspected the CIA of being behind the assassination. Bandaranaike had steered Ceylon away from the West, ejecting Britain from its military bases in the country, and forming a political pact with the Communist Party.

107

There were reports that some child members of the sect were also involved in the horrific sex abuse case at the McMartin pre-school day care center in Manhattan Beach, California in the 1980s. The McMartin pedophile ring was linked to members of the military, Los Angeles Police Department, and the U.S. intelligence community.

Ann Soetoro developed a close friendship with one of the Subud members she hired to teach English at the management institute. He was Mohammad Mansur Medeiros, originally from Fall River, Massachusetts and who attended Harvard University. Medeiros immersed himself so deeply into Javanese culture and religion that he became known as "Mansur Java." Mansur Java died in 2007. [116]

Although there are only some 10,000 Subud members in the world, Hawaii Governor Abercrombie, a friend of Ann Dunham at the University of Hawaii, appointed as the Hawaii Director of Health, sociologist and public health specialist Loretta Fuddy, a former chair of the Bellevue, Washington-based Subud USA from 2006 to 2008. In her position as Health Director, Fuddy had oversight over President Obama's Hawaii birth records, which were the subject of intense controversy.

The Beals Report cites the CIA's use of universities to carry out social science research: "There have also been disclosures of contracts involving the Central Intelligence Agency and certain U.S. universities, undertakings which appear to pose a threat to the integrity both of the universities as sponsors of social research and to the social sciences themselves." [117]

---

[116] *Ibid.*, p. 121.
[117] Beals, *op. cit.*

The Beals Report states that CAMELOT, funded by a contract to the Special Operations Research Office at American University, used American social scientists who attempted to enlist Chilean social scientists, to carry out "a study of the social political factors related to the possibility of internal warfare in that country."[118] The research was conducted some nine years before a bloody CIA-directed coup saw the assassination of democratically-elected President Salvador Allende on September 11, 1973 and the imposition of a fascist regime under General Augusto Pinochet. The history of Obama's mother's involvement with anthropologists who were likely involved in CAMELOT may have been a factor in President Obama's failure to apologize, while visiting Chile, for the CIA's involvement in the assassination of Allende and its suspected involvement in the later murder of Nobel laureate Pablo Neruda and former President Eduardo Frei Montalva. Apologies for past and current CIA crimes do not appear to be in Obama's political lexicon.

Modjokuto was the brainchild of the CIA's former assistant director of research and reports, Millikan, and one of the agency's top economists, Rostow. Supporting Modjokuto, with a view that data gleaned from the project could ultimately be used to oust Sukarno, was Frank Wisner, Sr., a top CIA clandestine services official. Modjokuto's intentions were to transform Indonesia into a modern economic consumer-oriented nation-state, ripe for Western investment but resistant to armed insurgencies. It was a goal championed by Geertz and, later, Ann Soetoro.

---

[118] *Ibid.*

Field data gleaned by Modjokuto would be of some use to the CIA, but the data was from Java and not from the periphery areas, such as Sumatra and the Celebes, that the CIA saw as ripe for a rebellion against Sukarno. Four years after Modjokuto's inception, the CIA gave direct military assistance to rebel groups and mercenaries on Java, Sumatra, and other islands, an operation code named Operation HAIK, also known as the "Archipelago Project," to launch a coup d'etat against Sukarno. The "HA" in HAIK was the CIA's digraph cryptonym indicating a covert operation in Indonesia.[119] On November 30, 1957, there was an attempt to assassinate Sukarno when hand grenades were thrown at him following his attendance at a ceremony marking the fifth anniversary of the school his children attended at Cikini.[120] Sukarno was convinced the CIA was behind the assassination attempt. The head of the Inter-agency Task Force on Indonesia at the time of the Cikini Affair, Hugh S. Cumming, later stated that he was surprised the Senate Select Committee on Intelligence headed by Senator Church did not ask him about the Cikini affair during its 1975 hearings. In its report on the CIA's assassination of foreign leaders, titled "Alleged Assassination Plots against Foreign Leaders," the CIA's Richard Bissell is reported to have testified that the CIA contemplated assassinating Sukarno "but had proceeded no farther than identifying

---

[119] Other CIA cryptonyms include "GT," "AE," and "CK" for Soviet Union, "AM" for Cuba, "LC" for China, "PB" for Guatemala, "SD" for Iran, "WI" for Congo-Kinshasa, and "MK" for CIA's Technical Services Division operations.

[120] Angus McIntyre, *The Indonesian Presidency: The Shift from Personal to Constitutional Rule*, Lanham, MD: Rowman and Littlefield Publishers, Inc., 2005, p. 143.

an 'asset' whom it was believed might be recruited to kill Sukarno."[121]

CIA B-26 aircraft operated by the CIA front company Civil Air Transport, provided air support for the rebel uprising. On May 18, 1958, one of the CIA's B-26s that was based in the Philippines was shot down by Sukarno's army. Indonesia's government captured the pilot, Allen Pope. The plane had bombed a hospital on Ambon. The State Department and U.S. ambassador to Jakarta Howard Jones immediately claimed Pope was a "soldier of fortune" and not connected to the U.S. government. It was a lie. Pope had U.S. Air Force identification on him when he was captured. There were direct links between Operation HAIK and the "Charter of Common Struggle" proclaimed by CIA-supported rebel leaders in Celebes and Sumatra. The Sumatra debacle would be followed three years later by a similar aborted attempt by the CIA to invade Cuba and overthrow Fidel Castro – the Bay of Pigs affair.

Java became the key to the CIA's plans to oust Sukarno. Working closely with the Australian Secret Intelligence Service (ASIS), the CIA began to concentrate its efforts on Java more than the surrounding islands. Australian Foreign Minister Richard Casey (later Lord Casey of Berwick) recounted how Allen Dulles told him at an ANZUS (Australia-New Zealand-U.S.) meeting in Washington in October 1957 that Indonesia was causing the United States "more anxiety than any other country in Southeast Asia."[122]

---

[121] Audrey R. Kahin and George McT. Kahin, *Subversion as Foreign Policy: The Secret Eisenhower and Dulles Debacle in Indonesia,* New York: New Press, 1995, pp. 114-115.
[122] Toohey and Pinwill, *op. cit.*, p. 69.

In his diary entry on his meeting with the Americans on Indonesia, Casey wrote: "I expressed our concern at the growth of Communist influence and the increasingly injurious effects of Sukarno's policies. I said the recent Java elections meant 20 percent increase in Communist vote which might well be reflected in next national elections and that Java represented two-thirds of whole Indonesian electorate." Casey wrote that Allen and John Foster Dulles agreed with his assessment about the importance of Java. However, Allen Dulles also pointed out that provincial leaders remained strongly anti-Communist but cautioned against encouraging separatism since the "breakup of Indonesia should not be regarded as an objective." Dulles said separatism "might have to be accepted as a last resort rather than have the whole of Indonesia under Communism."[123] The importance of the Indonesian provinces and regional separatists would advance the importance of anthropologists in the field in Indonesia to the CIA. Anthropological ethnic mapping data would be important in order to ascertain the political feelings of the various ethnic groups, as well Muslim, Hindu, and Christian leaders, in Padang, Medan, and Aceh, Sumatra; the Moluccas, and Celebes.

The CIA's plans for the provinces went operational in February 1958 when a revolutionary government was established in Sumatra with the CIA's backing. In March, Casey and his ASIS chief, Ralph Harry met with South East Asia Treaty Organization delegates in Manila. After the meeting, it was decided that a secret plan to undermine the Indonesian economy

---

[123] *Ibid.*, p. 70.

be launched. Casey sent a telegram to Canberra with details of the plan:

"It occurs to me as a possible move in the game that the Americans (and others with oil interests in Sumatra) might stop their oil activities in Sumatra on the plea that conditions are too disturbed to enable them to carry on. This might follow some minor *alleged* [emphasis added] sabotage of their installations and/or threats to their employees. Stoppage of oil activity would substantially add to the Djakarta Government's financial difficulties. Danger of such action would be nationalization by the Djakarta Government and substitution of America and other friendly operators by Russians and others.

The above suggestion might equally apply to any other commercial activities conducted by European interests in Sumatra."[124]

It appears that Australia permitted the CIA and U.S. military to use bases in northern Australia, New Guinea, and Christmas Island to carry out covert operations aimed at toppling Sukarno.[125] In 2012, President Obama agreed that U.S. Marines and other military and intelligence personnel would be stationed at new bases in Darwin and Perth and on the Cocos (Keeling) Islands in the Indian Ocean. Indonesia, as well as China, saw the bases as a threat to their own interests in the region.

Another CIA operative who engaged in the use of anthropologists to carry out counter-insurgency campaigns was Colonel Edward Lansdale, who, in the CIA's campaign in the Philippines against Communist

---

[124] *Ibid.*
[125] *Ibid.* p. 73.

Huk guerrillas, broadcast messages in Tagalog from a loudspeaker mounted on a small aircraft flying above heavy cloud layer. The Huk-controlled villages that the curses, based on local myths, being broadcast by the aircraft were messages from the gods. In fact, Lansdale obtained the local cultural information from anthropologists on the CIA's payroll. Lansdale was later implicated in the CIA's and Pentagon's role in the conspiracy to assassinate President Kennedy.

As Professor Price points out in his article, Millikan and Rostow were the brains behind the co-option of anthropologists and U.S. development assistance programs to carry out the war against communism. In a 1954 CIA point paper written by Millikan and "WWR" (Walt Whitman Rostow), titled "Notes on Foreign Economic Policy," it is stressed that . . . "free world success in seeing the underdeveloped countries through their difficult transition to self-sustaining growth would deny to Moscow and Peking the dangerous mystique that only Communism can transform underdeveloped societies."[126]

When Ann Soetoro went to Indonesia in 1967 to help in the CIA's and General Suharto's anti-Communist "mopping up" operations, the use of anthropologists as CIA field agents had the support of McGeorge Bundy, who became the National Security Adviser to Presidents Kennedy and Johnson and who was succeeded by Walt Rostow, one of the masterminds of Modjokuto. After leaving the White House, Bundy became the President of the Ford Foundation, the organization that laundered CIA money for Geertz's Modjokuto work and Ann Soetoro's Communist targeting in post-Sukarno Indonesia.

---

[126] Price, *op. cit.*

An even darker side to the CIA's use of anthropologists in its research was the involvement of the CIA front, the Society for the Investigation of Human Ecology and the Human Ecology Fund, in research projects that involved the study of sex, stress, and refugees. These studies, a personal favorite of CIA director Allen Dulles, involved the study of human pain, methods of persuasion, and enhanced interrogation practices. The CIA "human ecology" projects link the CIA's MK-ULTRA, MK-NAOMI, and MK-DELTA psychological operations to field programs such as those involving both Ann Dunham and her husband, Lolo, a participant in counter-insurgency operations in Indonesia and West Papua on the island of New Guinea. The Beals Report cites "large and unstudied" New Guinea as being "saturated" by an "increasing number of social scientists" who began encountering one another in the field.[127]

The CIA Human Ecology Fund was cited in the Department of State's Bureau of Intelligence and Research List of Current Studies on Political Behavior in 1963 as being involved in studying "Spare Time Education in Communist China," "In the African Mind – Emerging Images of Other Nations (study of city dwellers and villagers in Ghana and Nigeria), and "Anthropological Identification of the Determinants of Chinese Behavior."[128]

Human Ecology Fund researchers were almost never told their funding came from the CIA. By the time the Human Ecology Fund was dismantled in the 1960s, three CIA psychologists, John Gittinger, Robert E.

---

[127] Beals, *op. cit.*
[128] U.S. Department of State, Bureau of Intelligence and Research, External Research Staff, Political Behavior, Spring 1963.

Goodnow, and Samuel B. Lyerly, went to work for the already-established Psychological Assessment Associates (PAA). PAA continued to work for the CIA's Clandestine Services Division.[129]

The Human Ecology Fund was one of many front foundations established by the CIA over a twenty-year period to channel funds to human mind control programs, including LSD testing on humans. The Human Ecology Fund was a part of MK-ULTRA.[130]

On September 25, 1975, Senator Edward Kennedy (D-MA) sent a letter to CIA director Colby asking if MK-ULTRA's Dr. Sidney Gottlieb and Dr. Robert Lashbrook's human experimentation included experiments on drug addicts "in or near Lexington, Kentucky, the University of Kentucky Medical Center, the Kentucky Research Foundation, the University of Kentucky Research Foundation, Columbia University, David Lipscomb College, Georgetown University, Montana State University, New Jersey Mental Health Research and Development Fund, Pennsylvania State University, Vanderbilt University, Vanderbilt School of Medicine, Howard University, University of Miami, Mt. Sinai Hospital of New York City, the Coldspring Harbor Laboratory on Long Island, NY, the Massachusetts Mental Health Clinic in Boston, the Worcester Institute in Worcester, Massachusetts, the New York Psychiatric Institute in New York City, Microbiological Association, Moloscope Project, Communication Contract, Inc., or the Medical Explorations

---

[129] "The CIA Won't Quite Go Public," *Rolling Stone*, June 1974; Lawrence Stern, "Behind Psychological Assessments Door, A CIA Operation, *Washington Post*, June 21, 1974.
[130] Tony Lioce, "CIA chief mum about ties to Brown," *Providence Bulletin*, January 5, 1979.

Communications." A CIA official jokingly wrote "or MASH," a reference to the television show by the same name, on the margin of Kennedy's letter. Kennedy also wanted to know what CIA records on human testing were destroyed in 1973 and to what extent the CIA used the John Macy Foundation, the Geschickler Fund, the Society for the Investigation of Human Ecology, Inc., the Human Ecology Fund or Psychological Assessment Inc. as intermediaries in human experimentation funding.[131]

The CIA's money-laundering process for Obama's mother's anthropology field work in Indonesia and Pakistan

President Obama's upbringing in such an environment may explain his approval for the continued operation of the Guantanamo Bay gulag, the torture of Private First Class Bradley Manning at the Quantico Marine Corps base, and the continued operation of CIA "black sites" that are involved in the worldwide kidnapping and torture of detainees. In other words, the possible exposure of Obama to such practices at a young age may have created a "Manchurian candidate" in reverse, a president who obeys every command emanating from the top secret lairs of Langley.

The University of Hawaii, which hosted the CIA-funded East-West Center, was one of CIA director Richard Helms's five favorite universities for "behavioral sciences" studies. Behavioral science was also of keen interest to the Rockefeller family. The Beals Report states that after President Johnson, on

---

[131] Sen. Edward Kennedy letter to William Colby, dated September 15, 1975.

117

September 15, 1965, presented "a major new program in international education and in the communication of scholarly knowledge and thought on a broadened international basis," the Division of Behavioral Sciences of the National Academy of Sciences-National Research Council formed a committee under Donald Young of Rockefeller University to advise the government on behavioral sciences research, in coordination with the Departments of Defense and State. The Rockefeller Foundation had been involved in funding a number of anthropological studies that were geared to the forced assimilation of the native Indians of northern Central America into nation states, including Guatemala and Mexico. The Rockefeller-funded program, linked to the CIA, was conducted through the "Yucatan Linguistics Surveys."[132]

Senator Fred Harris (D-OK) held hearings before his Subcommittee on Government Research on foreign area research in the area of behavioral studies. Committee files indicate that the "research" involved the State Department, USAID, the Peace Corps, U.S. Public Health Service, National Institutes of Health, and National Science Foundation. The Beals Report cites the National Defense Education Act as an important tool used by the Pentagon and CIA to ensure that universities succumbed to the foreign research dictates of the U.S. military and intelligence or risk losing their funding.[133]

Chairing the Sub-committee on Government Research on February7, 1966, Harris brought up yet another Pentagon-funded anthropological study in Latin America, Project SIMPATICO in Colombia. Harris said

---

[132] Beals, *op. cit.*
[133] *Ibid.*

the project was funded through the Defense Department, USAID, and the State Department but was the brainchild of the Special Operations Research Office (SORO) at American University, a known CIA pass-through operation. SIMPATICO targeted Colombian villagers' attitudes toward joint Colombian Army/U.S. military "assistance" programs. Harris said Peru, Bolivia, Guatemala, and Honduras had originally been considered for SIMPATICO. Harris stressed that such research should be civilianized and he cited the previous controversy surrounding CAMELOT in Chile.

Harris cited a speech titled "Scholars and Foreign Policy: Varieties and Research Experience," delivered by the State Department's Director of Intelligence and Research, Thomas Hughes, at Hamilton College on October 21, 1965, Hughes stressed that the job of field researchers included understanding "which juntas are good and which juntas are bad; where reunification is a hope and where it is hindrance . . . and how a coup d'etat may be preferable to a coup de grace."[134]

The CIA would later refine its counter-insurgency methodology to include a formal program on the "selective use of violence" and "neutralization" of certain regime leaders. In 1984, a CIA psychological warfare expert who used the pseudonym John Kirkpatrick who, along with a team of CIA officers, developed a 90-page manual titled "Psychological Operations in Guerrilla War." The manual called for the hiring of professional criminals to carry out "selective jobs," which included assassinations. The number one target for "selective jobs" was the Sandinista

---

[134] Congressional Record, February 7, 1966, Project Simpatico.

government of Nicaragua.[135] At the time, Barack Obama, Jr. was working for the CIA front company, Business International Corporation, also known as "BIC," "BI," and "Business International," in New York.

As Professor Price points out: "In the 1970s and 1980s, applied anthropologists found a small funding gold mine in the superpowers' competition for clients as USAID, the World Bank, and IMF contested for the debts and loyalties of the Third World." Contrary to the "invented" biography of Ann Soetoro as some female version of Dr. Albert Schweitzer, Price points out the result of the various projects funded by USAID, World Bank, and others: "Arguably, in the end, the debt created by most of these projects turns out to have had a greater societal impact than the social, health, or agricultural benefits they produced."[136]

Price provides a summation of the actual goals of foundations, such as Ford, in their funding of projects such as those of Ann Soetoro in Indonesia and Pakistan:

". . . these foundations serve as intergenerational anti-devolutionary fortresses which protect large portions of amassed capital from inheritance and estate taxes – allowing family members to manage these funds, and direct research in areas of direct interest to the families and their investments."[137]

The chief foundations that use tax-exempt provision to push overt and covert agendas are the "Big Three" – Ford, Carnegie, and Rockefeller – as well as Duke and Kellogg. Price points out of the role of

---

[135] Robert Parry, "Casey Reportedly Ok'd Nicaragua Psy-War Program," Associated Press, December 3, 1984.
[136] Price, *op. cit.*
[137] *Ibid.*

anthropologists in this grand design of the foundation families, "Anthropology was earning its keep as a passive player in America's imperial brain trust."[138]

The Beals Report contains a paragraph that directly applies to the suspicious field work carried out in Suharto's Indonesia by Ann Soetoro beginning in 1967: "There are strong reasons to believe that private research organizations offering 'systems' approaches, but without competent social science staffs or sufficient experience with problems of foreign research, are contracting to do very large CAMELOT-type studies in countries where these are acceptable to U.S. Ambassadors and the host governments. Experienced personnel do not exist for research on this scale. Young, partially trained, and inexperienced people are being recruited and in some cases literally seduced by extravagant salaries. Former Peace Corps personnel are being recruited to provide local country 'expertise,' an action not likely to produce proper advice, and one certain to undermine the integrity of the Peace Corps."

U.S. media reports demonstrated the CIA's use of various charities and scientific funds to conduct subversive activity. The Ford Foundation was one of the "mediatory funds" used by the CIA in 1967 and 1968 to engage in foreign covert activities.[139]

Local suspicions of the activities of anthropologists in nations like Indonesia are described in the Beals Report: "Some problems are particularly acute in the so-called developing countries, especially where there is limited understanding of social science and its purposes and possible utility, or where

---

[138] *Ibid.*

[139] E. Vladimorov, "Imperialist Intelligence Propaganda," *International Affairs*, September 1971.

anthropology formerly was associated with the goals and administration of colonial governments."[140] CAMELOT involved such military and intelligence operations as predicting internal war, psychological operations, socialization within the military, and political activities.[141]

In an extraordinary major criticism of the CIA's use of anthropologists abroad, the Beals Report declared: *It is reported that:* Agents of the intelligence branches of the United States Government, particularly the Central Intelligence Agency, have posed as anthropologists or asserted that they were doing anthropological research. When, in fact they were neither qualified as anthropologists nor competent to do basic anthropological studies. Journalists and others from the United States and elsewhere have also posed as anthropologists, and even though not involved in secret intelligence work for agencies of their governments, they have, through their behavior, created difficulties for legitimate anthropologists and their research." [It should be noted that after graduating from Columbia University in 1983, Barack Obama went to work for Business International Corporation, an entity that admitted to the use by the CIA of its journalists abroad as CIA agents under journalistic "cover."]

Beals launched a second broadside against the CIA for its use of anthropologists abroad (and appears to be a reference to those in Ann Soetoro's category): *It is reported that:* "Some of those qualified by training to call themselves anthropologists, and representing themselves as engaged in anthropological research, have

---

[140] Beals, *op. cit.*

[141] *Congressional Record*, August 25, 1965.

122

actually been affiliated with United States intelligence agencies, especially the Central Intelligence Agency. This has come about through direct employment by these agencies, or *through accepting grants from certain foundations with questionable sources of income* [emphasis added], or through employment by certain private research organizations. In some cases, such persons have falsely represented themselves as still being associated with universities, although their prior academic affiliations no longer existed."[142]

And in a third criticism of the CIA's use of anthropologists (and another possible reference to people like Ann Soetoro), Beals stated: "*It is said that*: Some anthropologists, particularly younger ones, who have encountered difficulties in securing funds for legitimate research, have been approached by obscure foundations or have been offered supplementary support from such sources, only to discover later that they were expected to provide intelligence information, usually to the Central Intelligence Agency. Some anthropologists are reported to have sought such support and to have accepted commissions willingly." Beals stated that some of the foundations and 'alleged foundations' could not be listed by name but could be "identified among those that do not publish balance sheets indicating the sources of their funds." Beals added, "a few anthropologists report that they were approached by U.S. Embassy officials in the countries where they worked, or that they were interviewed by representatives of intelligence agencies after they had returned."[143]

Beals concluded with two additional stark warnings about the use by U.S. intelligence of

---

[142] Beals, *op. cit.*
[143] *Ibid.*

123

anthropologists abroad: "Although some individual anthropologists have been guilty of behavior that threatens to impair the access to foreign areas by their colleagues, the greatest dangers have actually come from contracts, actions, and projects of the United States Government and of some academic and private research organizations, even though these did not primarily involve anthropological activities." In addition, Beals stated, "in several countries of South and Central America, Africa, and Asia financing from certain United States governmental sources is suspect and in some cases completely unacceptable. These sources include such mission-oriented agencies as the Department of Defense, Central Intelligence Agency, U.S. Information Agency, and the Department of State."[144] One of Ann Soetoro's first jobs in Jakarta was one funded by the USIA – one of the suspect agencies cited in the Beals Report.

The CIA's and Pentagon's use of anthropologists like Ann Dunham to stir up insurgencies in countries like Indonesia was not lost on Senator J. William Fulbright (D-AR). In an August 25, 1965 statement on "Department of Defense Research in Foreign Policy Matters," Fulbright said, "I can well imagine how Members of the Senate might react if it were announced that Chilean or British or French 'scientists' were initiating a study of the conditions that might give rise to racial insurgency in Los Angeles or any other American city and what might be done to prevent it." Fulbright revealed that while Project CAMELOT in Chile was canceled, other "similar projects" were planned in Latin America, including Colombia, Peru, and Venezuela.[145]

---

[144] *Ibid.*
[145] *Congressional Record*, August 25, 1965.

125

Chapter Five – Mother and Son: CIA "Flexible Cover" Agents

I never would have agreed to the formulation of the Central Intelligence Agency back in forty-seven, if I had known it would become the American Gestapo – President Harry S Truman.

In this chapter, Hawaii as a center point for the CIA's operations in Asia and the Pacific will be described in detail. Also discussed is how, at the height of the Cold War, the CIA recruited and continued to employ individuals like Ann Dunham, Lolo Soetoro, and President Obama's grandmother Madelyn Dunham. It is a tale of CIA bank slush funds, front operations using NGOs, and constant coups against leaders the United States feared.

Before he was sacked as CIA director in 1976 and replaced by George H. W. Bush, William Colby commissioned a study of the agency's priorities in a five-year plan. The Secret NOFORN plan, titled "Director of Central Intelligence: Perspectives for Intelligence 1976-1981," described the importance of agencies like USAID in the CIA's operations. The report states: "Contributions of such agencies as State, Defense, Treasury, USAID, USIA, Agriculture, and Commerce can be enhanced substantially by more effective approaches to information gathering and in the reporting aspects of their activities. We need particularly, gains in the interrelationships between overt and clandestine and technical and human sources. We must establish more direct lines between our human collectors and our technical collectors."[146]

Classified CIA documents from the late 1970s, while Ann Soetoro was working for USAID, the CIA-linked Development Alternatives, Inc. and the East-West Center of the University of Hawaii, describe in great detail the type of deep agent "flexible cover" under which she worked for the CIA. A Secret paper written by C.D. Edbrook as a basic text for CIA agent training and titled "Principles of Deep Cover," describes the environment in which Obama's mother worked in both Indonesia and later, Pakistan.

Edbrook defines "flexible cover" as "a logical reason for interest in diversified local groups" and "mobility." Ann Soetoro's varied employers in Indonesia suggest that her career met the definition of a "flexible agent," either a non-official cover (NOC) employee of the CIA or a career contract agent. The latter became highly favored in the late 1970s after CIA director Stansfield Turner sacked a number of career clandestine services officers. On career contract agents, Edbrook clearly favored their use in stating: "many of the problems of deep cover are avoided when a service can recruit suitable agents already embarked on legitimate careers."[147]

Between January 1968 and December 1969, Ann Soetoro worked for the Indonesia-America Friendship Institute in Jakarta, a suspected CIA front. Dunham was also co-founder of the Indonesian Heritage Society at the National Museum in Jakarta. She worked at the

---

[146] CIA, "Director of Central Intelligence: Perspectives for Intelligence 1976-1981," SECRET NOFORN.
[147] C. D. Ebrook, SECRET, "Principles of Deep Cover," CIA paper.

Society as a volunteer from 1968 to 1972. In 1969, the CIA Jakarta CIA station chief was Stuart E. Methven whose official cover was embassy political officer. Methven became the CIA station chief in Kinshasa, Zaire in 1974 from where he launched the CIA's covert war against the government of Angola.

From January 1970 to August 1972, Ann Soetoro was an executive at the Institute of Management Education and Development (IMED) in Jakarta, likely a continuation of her CIA flexible cover employment.

From 1972 to 1975, Ann Soetoro double-dipped, returning to the University of Hawaii to obtain her Masters of Arts in anthropology from the University of Hawaii, under a grant from the CIA-funded Asia Foundation, while continuing to serve under contract IMED in Jakarta. The CIA's liaison for various USAID programs in Jakarta was Vincent Michael Shields who operated under official cover as the embassy's economic and commercial attaché.

Between 1972 and 1975, Ann Soetoro taught Indonesian crafts at the Bishop Museum in Honolulu, formerly known as the Bernice Pauahi Bishop Museum (named for Princess Bernice Pauahi Bishop, last legal heir of the Kamehamena royal dynasty), further developing her "flexible cover" credentials. Although the Bishop Museum sounds like a fairly benign place of employment, the CIA's library contains a book on "Survival," titled, "Wartime Activities at the Bishop Museum, Honolulu; Instruction in Survival," by M. Titcomb. The book was published in 1945 and was contained in the CIA's Special Libraries collection.[148] The Bishop Museum provided the Office of Naval

---

[148] CIA, Bibliography: Survival; a Selected List of Books and Articles, For Official Use Only, May 24, 1950.

Intelligence with anthropological and other information on Okinawa during and after World War II.[149]

The Bishop Museum's longtime curator, Edwin H. Bryan, Jr., spent a large part of his career "rapidly accumulating masses of data about Pacific geography, natural history, and the study of man in the Pacific," developing the Pacific Scientific Information Center, which was funded partly by the National Science Foundation.[150] During the Reagan administration, W. Glenn Campbell, a member of the Board of Visitors of the Bishop Museum, served on the President's Intelligence Oversight Board.[151]

In 1975, the year Indonesia invaded East Timor with the support of the CIA, Ann returned to conduct "anthropological field work" on Java. Ann worked in Jakarta in 1975 and moved to work in Yogyakarta in 1976. One of Ann Soetoro's close friends had a valuable connection with the Indonesian dictator. Anton Hillman, an Indonesian of Chinese ethnicity, was the host of an English-language show on Indonesian television and an interpreter for Suharto's wife, Ibu Tien Suharto.[152]

In March 1977, Ann taught a course under Professor Leon Mears at the Faculty of Economics of the University of Indonesia in Jakarta. The course was designed for the staff of the Indonesian National Development Planning Agency (BAPPENAS). From June 1977 to September 1978, Ann returned to Yogyakarta and researched small village industries under a grant from the CIA-linked East-West Center.

---

[149] CIA file: CONFIDENTIAL, "Intelligence in Support of Operational Command."

[150] Congressional Record, January 17, 1966.

[151] President's Intelligence Oversight Board letter, dated August 31, 1982 to William Casey, Director of Central Intelligence.

[152] Janny Scott, *op. cit.*, p. 121.

In May 1978, Ann returned to Jakarta and consulted with the International Labor Organization to develop recommendations on village industries for the Suharto regime's third five-year plan, REPELITA III. On November 24, 1980, Ann divorced Lolo Soetoro. From 1977 to 1980, the CIA station chief in Jakarta was Carl Edward Gebhardt. Case officers at the CIA station during this time frame were economics section officer James D. Anders, Jr.; Ronald M. Cinal, whose previous posting was Nairobi, Kenya; and William H. Wright, who worked in 1977 at the consulate in Surabaya – while Ann Soetoro was working in the Surabaya CIA station city of responsibility Yogyakarta – and who was transferred in 1979 to Jakarta.

The year 1977 was a crucial year in the history of the CIA. President Carter's new director, Turner, was determined to clean house of clandestine services officers who had been committing acts of illegality and running their own off-the-books operations. Turner fired, transferred, forced into early retirement, or eliminated through attrition some 800 clandestine officers.

From October 1978 to December 1980, under contract to USAID and Development Alternatives, Inc. (DAI), a CIA front company, Ann consulted on rural industries development in central Java, living in Yogjakarta and the old port city of Semarang on the north coast of the island. She also traveled extensively to Bogor.

The CIA's station chief in Jakarta in June 1980 was Warren E. Frank and the deputy chief USAID "public administration adviser" in Vientiane, Laos. Also at the CIA station in Jakarta in 1980 was Robert H. Mills, operating under official cover of embassy First Secretary and who, form 1972 to 1974, was operating at the U.S. Consulate in Surabaya, eastern Java, as a USAID "public safety program" officer.

The identities of the CIA agents assigned to Indonesia in the late 1960s, 70s, and 80s were compiled in various writings by the whistle blowing former CIA agent Philip Agee.

From January 1981 to November 1984, Ann worked under the cover of the Ford Foundation's Southeast Regional Office in Jakarta. Ann's immediate supervisor was Thomas Kessenger, Ford Foundation's country representative in Indonesia, and a veteran of the Peace Corps and Ford Foundation in India.[153]

Ann's financial work in Indonesia was at the outset of Suharto's five-year economic plan from 1979 to 1984. The plan saw the devaluation of the Indonesian rupiah by 33 percent, the severance of the rupiah's link to the U.S. dollar, and a rapid growth of non-oil exports. Ann Soetoro's work in Indonesia also coincided with "increased internal security problems in East Timor, Irian Jaya, Aceh, and Kalimantan, as well as potential threats to Southeast Asia regional security from Vietnam and China."[154] Ann traveled throughout Indonesia, from Bali and Sumatra to Sulawesi and Java to Nusa Tenggara Timur.

Edbrook's paper on "deep cover" describes Ann Soetoro's checkerboard employment record to a tee: "The cover with the best chance of enduring in any area is one that does not feed off the area but contributes needed skills or knowledge or a commodity that is lacking . . . non-commercial cover may be more desirable in some places: in newly independent

---

[153] Janny Scott, *op. cit.,* p. 222.
[154] CIA National Foreign Assessment Center, Economic Intelligence Weekly Review, SECRET, December 22, 1978. pp. 12, 16.

countries, for instance, teachers or technicians may be more needed and welcome than business representatives and the desire of the new governments to get them elsewhere than from the former colonial power may provide another nation with cover opportunities for its own nationals or for third-national agents."[155]

In post-coup Indonesia, neither the Dutch -- the former colonial rulers -- nor the Chinese, who were linked to the previous Sukarno government, were held in high esteem. Thus, "teachers" like Ann Soetoro were able to make instant inroads in urban and rural areas alike while keeping her CIA cover intact. Similarly, Obama's 1981 trip from Indonesia to Pakistan and India, reportedly using an Indonesian passport issued to "Barry Soetoro," describes Edbrook's "cover opportunities" for "third-national agents."

The pressure the Obama administration applied to newspapers like *The New York Times* to hold off on publishing details on Raymond Davis, the sometimes CIA contract employee and later, its acting station chief in Pakistan, who was jailed by Pakistan for murder in February 2011, but later released, exemplifies Obama's strong support, even empathy, for CIA covert operations. Similarly, the Obama administration applied strong pressure on Cuba to release jailed accused CIA spy Alan Gross, who operated in Cuba under Development Alternatives, Inc., the same CIA-USAID front company that employed Obama's mother in Indonesia.

In fact, Obama's own work in New York for CIA front company BIC, after graduating from Columbia University, came after President Reagan signed the classified National Security Council Decision

---

[155] Edbrook, *op. cit.*

Directive 77. NSCDD-77 authorized the CIA and other intelligence agencies to produce mountains of disinformation, biased news, propaganda, and planted news stories in the name of "Project Democracy" and the renewed ideological war against Communism. The plan was the reincarnation of CIA Plans Director Frank Wisner, Sr.'s "Mighty Wurlitzer," the CIA's worldwide propaganda and deception operation that relied on, in part, firms like BIC. Wisner was also the originator of the CIA's program to recruit foreign students attending U.S. universities – students like Barack Obama, Sr. and Lolo Soetoro – to serve as CIA agents after they returned to their home nations. Funding for the students tuition was either made directly by the CIA or through foundations like the East-West Center at the University of Hawaii. Perhaps not coincidentally, Wisner's son, Frank Wisner, Jr., was dispatched as President Obama's special envoy to Egypt during President Hosni Mubarak's waning days in office.

In 1965, Wisner, Sr. placed a 20-gauge shotgun to his temple and pulled the trigger. It was just a few weeks after the CIA's coup in Indonesia. Wisner, Sr. retired from the CIA in 1962, reportedly suffering from mental depression.

CIA files contain a 1967 letter to the editor of the *Daily Emerald* from three anthropology professors at the University of Oregon supporting a decision of the American Anthropological Association condemning the "intelligence meddling" of the CIA and Defense Department in anthropological field work. In the same year, 1967, Ann Soetoro was performing such anthropological "field work" for USAID, a front for the CIA, in Java, Indonesia. The AAA's Professor Beals [from UCLA] report stated that the Pentagon and CIA "repeatedly interfered with anthropological work abroad, and have clearly jeopardized our chances, as anthropologists, to do meaningful foreign research."[156]

And in what is the clearest evidence yet that Ann was working for the CIA in Indonesia and elsewhere, the Beals Report stated: "several anthropologists, *especially younger ones* who had difficulty in securing research funds, were approached by 'obscure' foundations or were offered support from such organizations only to discover later that they were expected to provide intelligence information to the CIA." The report added, "agents of the CIA have posed as anthropologists, much to the detriment of the anthropological research programs."[157]

Harvard anthropologist Dr. Irven DeVore told a Utica high school audience in 1969 that "CIA men" were using the "cover of anthropologists for spying missions, as well as the cover of teachers, engineers, and economic aid personnel in a 'hotbed of American espionage'" He added, "when one of these government men blows his cover, it sets back the work of hundreds of anthropologists, or whatever, in a dozen countries – they're no longer welcome." Emphasizing that the American Anthropological Association was working to stop this, DeVore, said it was "not an easy task."[158]

The AAA had its own internal feud over the CIA's use of anthropologists as spies. In 1971, documents from UCLA anthropologist Dr. Michael Moerman, leaked by the Student Mobilization Committee to End the War in Vietnam to AAA ethics committee member Dr. Eric Wolf, proved the CIA, USAID, and the Pentagon were using anthropologists to

---

[156] *Ibid.*

[157] *Ibid.*

[158] William Welt, "Outdated Bodies, the CIA, All part of being 'modern,'" Utica Press, January 21, 1969.

spy on hill tribes in northern Thailand. Wolf and Dr. Joseph Jorgensen quit the ethics committee in protest.[159]

In 1965, Senator Wayne Morse (D-OR) revealed Pentagon and U.S. intelligence plans to conduct counter-revolutionary warfare using "research projects in the field of social sciences." Morse named the targeted nations as Indonesia, Ghana, Sudan, Nigeria, Ethiopia, Brazil, Venezuela, Panama, Cuba, Korea, Liberia, Egypt, Guinea, Cyprus, and Japan.[160]

In the previously-cited December 19, 1971, article in the *Boston Globe* by Dan Pinck, titled "Is everyone in the CIA?" it is alleged that identifying U.S. Agency for International Development (USAID) officers as CIA agents was a "reasonably accurate accounting of certain leading operatives and associates of the CIA."[161]

The American Political Science Association (APSA) also weighed in against the CIA's abuse of social scientists abroad. Gabriel Almond, the president of APSA, said the Pentagon and U.S. intelligence agencies were injuring foreign research by U.S. scientists. Charging that Pentagon contracts were used to mask CIA activities, Almond said the intelligence programs were highlighted by "too much clumsy and short-sighted use of scientific research abroad."[162]

The Boston Globe article states the CIA had a massive presence in Third World nations, including 32 agents in Nigeria, 24 in Ethiopia, 71 in Hong Kong, 8 in Uganda, 132 in South Vietnam, 14 in Ghana, 42 in

---

[159] Stephen Isaac's, "Asia Anthropology: Science or Spying?" *The Washington Post*, November 22, 1971.

[160] *San Francisco People's World*, September 11, 1965.

[161] Dan Pinck, "Is everyone in the CIA?" *The Boston Globe*, Dec. 19, 1971.

[162] UPI, June 28, 1966.

Chile, and 90 in Mexico. Ann Soetoro, who worked for USAID at the time "Who's Who in the CIA" was published, was employed by the CIA-infiltrated Ford Foundation and Asian Development Bank. This fits with what *The Boston Globe* article reported was the common use of non-official cover (NOC) officers abroad. One of the tactics of USAID operatives in Indonesia was the smuggling of aid staples to Indonesian generals so they could buy the loyalties of local village elders against Sukarno and the Communist Party of Indonesia.

President Obama has never explained his mother's role in the CIA's smuggling operation carried out through USAID. However, Obama has snubbed his nose at the memory of the Indonesians killed by Suharto's CIA-supported troops by restoring U.S. training contacts with the Indonesian KOPASSUS, the Red Beret special forces of the Indonesian army. As President, Obama has done nothing to alleviate the blocks placed by the previous Bush administration on Freedom of Information Act requests for CIA and other agency files on CIA and USAID human rights violations.

One of the closest CIA contacts for Suharto was former CIA Jakarta embassy officer Kent B. Crane. Crane was so close to Suharto after "retiring" from the CIA, he was reportedly one of the only "private" businessmen given an Indonesian diplomatic passport by Suharto's government. Crane's company, the Crane Group, was involved in supplying small arms to the military forces of the United States, Indonesia, and other nations. A foreign policy adviser to Vice President Spiro Agnew, Crane was later nominated as U.S. ambassador to Indonesia by President Ronald Reagan but the nomination was dead-on-arrival because of Crane's dubious links to Suharto. The ambassadorship would instead go to John Holdridge, a close colleague of Kissinger. Holdridge was succeeded in Jakarta by Paul Wolfowitz.

Suharto's cronies, who included Mochtar and James Riady of the Lippo Group, would later stand accused of funneling over $1 million of illegal foreign contributions to Bill Clinton's 1992 presidential campaign.

In the 1970s and 80s, Dunham was active in micro-loan projects for the Ford Foundation, the CIA-linked East-West Center, and USAID in Indonesia. One of the individuals assigned to the U.S. embassy and helped barricade the compound during a violent anti-U.S. student demonstration during the 1965 Suharto coup against Sukarno was Dr. Gordon Donald, Jr. Assigned to the embassy's Economic Section, Donald was responsible for USAID micro-financing for Indonesian farmers, the same project that Ann Soetoro would work on for USAID in the 1970s. In "Who's Who in the CIA," Donald is identified as a CIA officer who was also assigned to Lahore, Pakistan, where Dunham would eventually live for five years in the Hilton International Hotel while working on micro-financing for the Asian Development Bank.

Another "Who's Who in the CIA" Jakarta alumnus is Robert F. Grealy, who later became the director for international relations for the Asia-Pacific for J P Morgan Chase and a director for the American-Indonesian Chamber of Commerce.

In addition, *The Boston Globe* article stated that among NOCs used by the CIA were agents working abroad for *Time, Life, Forbes, Newsweek*, the *New York Times*, CBS News, AFL-CIO, the Massachusetts Institute of Technology (MIT), Bankers Trust, *Fortune, Sports Illustrated, US News and World Report*, First

National City Bank, Westinghouse, NBC News, RCA, Gulf Oil, Standard Oil Company, Bank of America, Litton Industries, and Kimberly-Clark Corporation of Canada. The article also reported "the directors of Asian and Russian research centers at leading American universities" worked for the CIA abroad.[163] The revelation calls into question what circumstances prompted Obama's mother and father to meet in the Russian language class at the University of Hawaii, Manoa campus, in 1960. A CIA document, titled "Training Selection Board Courses," dated December 18, 1963, lists the East-West Center at the University of Hawaii as a favored campus for full-time, intensive courses. Others listed include the University of California at Berkeley, Cornell, and the University of Washington.[164] In addition to the University of Hawaii, Ann also attended courses at the University of Washington.

Pinck, who served as an Office of Strategic Services (OSS) officer in China and later wrote a book about his experiences, wrote in *The Boston Globe* that USAID officers operating as CIA agents abroad included Dan Mitrione, who served in Brazil and Uruguay from 1960 to 1970 under USAID cover. [165]

Mitrione's actual job was providing counter-insurgency training to Brazilian and Uruguayan security forces, which reportedly included training police in the use of torture. Mitrione was kidnapped and executed by Uruguayan Tupamaro guerrillas in 1970. Mitrione reportedly used homeless people as torture training

---

[163] Pinck, *op. cit.*
[164] CIA, "Training Selection Board Courses," SECRET/CIA INTERNAL USE ONLY, December 18, 1963.
[165] Pinck, *op. cit.*

subjects. The homeless were disposed of after they served their purpose.

In 1970, Ann Soetoro's mother, Madelyn Dunham, became one of the first female vice presidents of the Bank of Hawaii in Honolulu. Madelyn handled a number of escrow accounts through which the CIA paid off leaders and politicians in various Asian countries where the "BankoH" maintained branches, including Indonesia. 1970 was the same year that Australian banker Frank Nugan and U.S. Green Beret officer and CIA agent Michael Hand formed Australasian and Pacific Holdings, Ltd., a CIA proprietary firm that shared investors with executives of the CIA's Air America and USAID.

In 1973, using the profits from Australasian and Pacific Holdings, Nugan and Hand established the Nugan Hand Bank, with branches or offices in Chiang Mai, Thailand; Manila; Taipei; the Cayman Islands; Honolulu; Singapore; Kuala Lumpur; Hong Kong; Washington, DC; Cape Town; and Sydney. The Chiang Mai branch laundered profits from drug smuggling while the other branches paid off Pacific region politicians and handled accounts used for weapons smuggling. In January 1980, when Nugan's body was discovered in his Mercedes on a quiet road in Sydney, the business card of William Colby was found in his pocket. Nugan Hand Bank was established while Colby was CIA director.

Nugan Hand Bank also financed the supply of bombs and other explosive materials, as well as weapons like machine guns, helicopter gunships, and rocket launchers, to terrorists. The terrorist arming operation was carried out largely by a CIA military carve-out known as U.S. Navy Task Force 157, which likely used the CIA's paramilitary training base at Harvey Point, North Carolina as one of its operational centers. The

Nugan Hand-Task Force 157 operations involved secret arms deals with Thailand, Brazil, Taiwan, Malaysia, Singapore, Philippines, Saudi Arabia, Lebanon, Iran, Angola, and Libya. The operation was linked to CIA arms smugglers Edwin P. Wilson, Frank Terpil, Nugan Hand's Saudi branch chief Bernie Houghton, CIA oil specialist Walter McDonald, CIA Canberra station chief John D. Walker, and former CIA White House liaison officer John Paisley. Paisley's body was found in 1978 in the Chesapeake Bay, weighed down with anchor chain and with a single gunshot wound to the head. Paisley's death was later ruled a suicide. In 1996, Colby's body was also found underwater in the Chesapeake Bay. Colby's death was ruled a drowning after suffering a heart seizure. Most of Nugan Hand's business records were destroyed in a high-priority and global CIA black bag operation.

Grandmother Madelyn's bank also had dealings with Nugan Hand Bank of Australia, through which the CIA funded the constitutional coup d'etat against Australian Labor Prime Minister Gough Whitlam in 1975. After Nugan Hand collapsed in the late 1970s, co-founder Frank Hand was found slumped over the steering wheel of his parked car near Sydney. Hand was shot through the head although a rifle on the seat beside him had been wiped clean of fingerprints. The world of Pacific finance in which Obama's banker grandmother was immersed in the 1970s and 1980s dealt with much more than loaning money for beachfront properties in idyllic South Pacific settings.

As Nugan Hand Bank was collapsing, in 1979, the CIA quickly moved to establish a replacement firm in Honolulu, Bishop, Baldwin, Rewald, Dillingham, and Wong (BBRDW). The name of the firm borrowed the names of prominent Hawaii families, including Bishop, whose name graces the Bishop Museum of Honolulu, where Ann Soetoro worked from 1972 to 1975 while studying under a grant from the CIA-linked Asia Foundation. Operating as an international investment firm, BBRDW quickly filled the vacuum left by Nugan Hand and it opened offices in all the countries where Nugan Hand maintained branches, including Hong Kong, Taipei, Jakarta, Singapore, Cayman Islands, and Sydney, with additional locations in Auckland, Stockholm, London, Paris, Sao Paulo, and Santiago. BBRDW also did business with BankoH when Madelyn was still handling the secretive escrow accounts.

After the CIA allowed the firm to collapse in 1983 amid charges that BBRDW was merely a Ponzi scheme, Senator Daniel Inouye of the U.S. Senate Intelligence Committee said the CIA's role in the firm "wasn't significant."[166] It would later be revealed that Inouye, who was one of the late Alaska Senator Ted Stevens's best friends in the Senate, was lying. In fact, BBRDW was involved heavily in funding covert CIA programs throughout Asia, including economic espionage against Japan, providing arms for Afghan mujaheddin guerrillas in their war against the Soviets and covertly supplying weapons to Taiwan. One of BBRDW's principals was John C. "Jack" Kindschi, who, before he retired in 1981, was the CIA station chief in Honolulu. BBRDW's chairman Ron Rewald had a counterfeit college degree certificate provided for the wall of his office by the CIA's forgery experts and his name was inserted in university records as an alumnus.

Buried in CIA files is a letter, dated April 13, 1984, sent from the U.S. Attorney for the District of Hawaii to the Justice Department's Internal Security

---

[166] Charles Memminger, "Inouye: No Significant Rewald-CIA Link Is Found," *Honolulu Star-Bulletin*, April 2, 1984.

Criminal Division and the CIA's Legislative Office forwarding a Honolulu article on the firm. [167] The article reveals that the CIA stepped in to halt an Internal Revenue Service (IRS) investigation of BBRDW in January 1983. IRS Honolulu agent Joseph A. Campione confirmed that his IRS bosses in Washington, DC had ordered him to halt his investigation of BBRDW. The CIA's station chief in Honolulu, Jack Kindschi, retired from the CIA and joined BBRDW after it was established. [168]

In its TOP SECRET Weekly Report of September 10, 1984, it is reported that the counsel to the President's Intelligence Oversight Board, Bretton Sciaroni, requested to be briefed on September 26 at the CIA headquarters on the Rewald case. In a letter to Senator James Exon (D-NE), dated November 26, 1984, Charles Briggs, the Director of the CIA's Office of Legislation Liaison, castigates ABC News for its coverage of the BBRDW case:

"We regret that ABC has chosen to air a series of reports wrongly accusing the CIA of engaging in an attempted assassination and other improper practices. These accusations were made by certain persons interviewed in connection with ABC's series on Ronald Rewald, a Honolulu businessman now awaiting trial under a 100-count federal criminal indictment . . . The Agency obviously is constrained from responding to the series because the case is in litigation. CIA believes, however, that it is important the public know that the

---

[167] Letter, Daniel A. Bent, U.S. Attorney, District of Hawaii, to Edward J. Walsh, Internal Security, Criminal Division, US Department of Justice, dated April 13, 1984.
[168] "The CIA played a devious but leading role in the rise and fall of Bishop, Baldwin: Ron Rewald's defunct consulting firm was a front in the most embarrassing tradition," *Hawaii Investor*, March 1984.

report issued by ABC is an example of irresponsible journalism . . . The ABC report does a great disservice to the many dedicated men and women who work selflessly without seeking the recognition that is duly theirs in protecting this nation's security."[169]

However, the British Broadcasting Corporation (BBC) also reported that BBRDW was a CIA front and that Rewald was a "CIA kingpin." The BBC reported that U.S. Air Force Captain Ned Avary, Rewald's assistant, arranged for the delivery of tanks to Taiwan on behalf of the CIA. The BBC also identified as BBRDW as key component in an espionage program carried out on behalf of Philippines dictator Ferdinand Marcos that spied on anti-Marcos Filipino students at the University of Hawaii.[170]

Rewald was recruited in 1976 by the CIA's chief officer in Chicago. In addition to BBRDW, Rewald created a number of other CIA front firms in Honolulu, including H&H Enterprises and Canadian Far East Trade Corporation. Other firms that were joint CIA ventures with foreign millionaires, included Hawaiian-Arabian Investment Company and U.S. and United Arab Emirates Investment Company, registered in Hawaii and involving Rewald, millionaire Indonesian Indri Gautama, and UAE prince Saud Mohammed of the emirate of Sharjah.[171]

Rewald told the *Hawaii Investor* that millions of dollars in CIA funds were "freely co-mingled" with the funds of innocent investors in accounts such as those maintained in the Bank of Hawaii, as well as in overseas

---

[169] Letter from CIA Director, OLL, to Senator James Exon, dated November 26, 1984.

[170] Charles Memminger, "BBC Calls Rewald CIA Kingpin," *Honolulu Star-Bulletin*, April 7, 1984.

[171] *Hawaii Investor, op. cit.*

accounts. BBRDW accounts in Hawaiian and overseas banks were used to launder money for the Sultan of Brunei, Philippine banker Enrique Zobel and his close friend President Ferdinand Marcos, Indian Prime Minister Indira Gandhi, Gandhi's son and future Prime Minister Rajiv Gandhi, and President Suharto of Indonesia.[172]

A false history for BBRDW was concocted by the CIA claiming the firm had operated in Hawaii since it was a territory.

BBRDW conducted its business in the heart of Honolulu's business district, where the Bank of Hawaii was located and where Obama grandmother oversaw the escrow accounts. The bank would handle much of BBRDW's covert financial transactions.

BBRDW collapsed in 1983 but there was another CIA replacement already ramped up: the Bank of Credit and Commerce International (BCCI), which had taken over First American Bank of Washington, DC. First American handled the secret financial operations for some 200 CIA proprietary companies established after William Casey became director of the CIA in 1981.

Casey appointed CIA veteran Douglas Mulholland to act as the CIA's point man at the Treasury Department, with a side liaison function to the Federal Reserve Bank, to ensure that the CIA's secret financial deals remained that way – secret. Eminent Democratic Party politicians like former Defense Secretary Clark Clifford and Robert Altman were brought in to run First American to provide the First American's CIA drug money and weapons smuggling

---

[172] *Ibid.*

laundering operations with cover and legitimacy. When BCCI's unsavory operations became known in 1988, Senator John Kerry (D-MA), a member of the Senate Foreign Relations Committee, suddenly began to waffle on conducting a thorough investigation of BCCI after it was discovered that two top Democrats – Clifford and Altman – as well as the CIA, were using the bank for covert and illegal activities.

House Banking Committee chairman Henry Gonzalez (D-TX) suspected that Kerry and House Intelligence Committee chairman Lee Hamilton (D-IN) were covering up for Langley. Before BCCI collapsed in 1990, the CIA ensured that key bank documents held by Treasury and the Fed were destroyed in another major bank shredding operation.

BCCI's international branches were more ubiquitous than those of Nugan Hand and BBRDW combined. BCCI, with its headquarters in Luxembourg, maintained branches in Washington, DC; Grand Cayman; London, Chicago, New York, Abu Dhabi, Karachi, Jeddah, Kuwait, Shenzhen, Geneva, Hong Kong, Los Angeles, Miami, Willemstad, Amsterdam, Toronto, Paris, Muscat, Gibraltar, Singapore, Istanbul, Manila, Atlanta, Monte Carlo, Houston, Nassau, Tampa, Boca Raton, Encino, Islamabad, and Dubai.

Nugan Hand was used to finance the 1975 dismissal of the Australian Labor Party government of Prime Minister Gough Whitlam in an operation conducted jointly with Britain's MI-6, which received the backing of Queen Elizabeth II who gave the necessary instructions to her Governor General of Australia, Sir John Kerr, known to be a CIA asset, to sack Whitlam. The CIA overthrow of Whitlam may not have been the last time the agency interfered in Australian politics. The June 2010 "midnight overthrow" of Australian Prime Minister Kevin Rudd by his deputy, Julia Gillard, was reportedly engineered by the CIA. Gillard, more than Rudd, was seen as a reliable ally to help the American case against WikiLeaks' founder and Australian national Julian Assange, who had overseen the leak of over 250,000 sensitive and classified U.S. State Department cables to the media.

It is significant that the Governor General who appointed Gillard to the post of Prime Minister, Quentin Bryce, was launched into political prominence by Prime Minister Malcolm Fraser, who was installed as prime minister after the overthrow of Whitlam in the 1975 CIA-engineered coup. Bryce has been described by her associates as a "control freak."

According to Indonesian government and media sources in Jakarta, at the same time he was attending Occidental College in Los Angeles from 1979 to 1981, Obama, using the name Barry Soetoro and an Indonesian passport issued under the same name, possibly with the added Indonesian name of "Soebarkah," given to him at the time of his acquisition of Indonesian citizenship as a youth, traveled to Pakistan during the U.S. buildup to assist the Afghan mujaheddin.[173] Informed sources in Kabul revealed that, as president, Obama has been extremely friendly, through personal correspondence on White House letterhead, with a private military company that counts among its senior personnel a number of Afghan mujaheddin-Soviet war veterans who fought alongside the late Northern Alliance commander Ahmad Shah Masood.[174]

---

[173] Background interviews in Jakarta, August 19 and 29, 2011.
[174] Background e-mail correspondence from private military contractor assigned to Kabul in 2009.

In 1981, Obama spent time in Jacobabad and Karachi, Pakistan, and appeared to have an older American 'handler,' possibly a CIA officer. Obama also crossed the border from Pakistan and spent some time in India.[175] At the time of Obama's stay in Pakistan, the country was being built up as a base for the anti-Soviet Afghan insurgency by President Carter's National Security Adviser Zbigniew Brzezinski and later by President Reagan's CIA director William Casey. Obama has suspiciously refused to release his transcripts from Occidental or Columbia University and he has remained cagey about his post-Columbia employment with BIC.

A U.S. intelligence source revealed that Obama's tuition debt at Columbia was paid off by BIC. The source also revealed that when Obama lived in Indonesia with his mother and his adoptive father Lolo Soetoro, the 20-year-old Obama, who was known as "Barry Soetoro," traveled to Pakistan in 1981. He was hosted by the family of Muhammadmian Soomro, a Pakistani Sindhi who became acting President of Pakistan after the resignation of General Pervez Musharraf on August 18, 2008. According to U.S. intelligence sources in Pakistan, the Obama/Soetoro trip to Pakistan, ostensibly to go 'partridge hunting' with the Soomros, was related to unknown CIA business. The covert CIA program to assist the Afghan mujaheddin was already well underway at the time and Pakistan was the major base of operations for the CIA's support.

The U.S. intelligence source also stated that Ann Soetoro was in Indonesia when the Soviets invaded Afghanistan in 1979. In 1981, Barack Obama visited

---

[175] *Ibid.*

Lahore, Pakistan, where his mother worked as a "consultant."

USAID was a major component of the U.S.-funded mujaheddin war against the Soviets in Afghanistan. The major covert assistance program run by USAID from Pakistan was the Cross Border Humanitarian Aid Program, established by Deputy Undersecretary of State for Political Affairs Gerald Helman. Helman would later help coin the term "failed state," something he helped create in Afghanistan with covert support for the mujaheddin.[176]

The USAID covert assistance program for the mujaheddin operated behind a cipher-lock on the second floor of the U.S. embassy in Islamabad, one floor below the CIA station.[177]

According to a declassified Top Secret CIA document titled "Worldwide Reaction to the Soviet Invasion of Afghanistan," dated February 1980, Indonesia became a hotbed of anti-Soviet student demonstrations after Moscow's invasion of Afghanistan. The report states, "Indonesian students have staged several peaceful demonstrations in Jakarta and three other major cities. They have also demanded the recall of the Soviet Ambassador because of remarks he made to a student delegation on 4 January and have called for a severance of Soviet-Indonesian relations."[178]

Obama's mother was in Lahore as a consultant for the Asian Development Bank, a perfect NOC (non-

---

[176] George Crile, *Charlie Wilson's War*, New York: Grove Press, 2003. p. 362.
[177] *Ibid.* p. 371.
[178] CIA, "Worldwide Reaction to the Soviet Invasion of Afghanistan," February 1980.

official cover) job at the time the CIA, under William Casey, was beefing up its covert presence in Pakistan to battle the Soviets in Afghanistan.

Madelyn retired from the Bank of Hawaii in 1986. It is suspected that the Bank of Hawaii acted as a financial vehicle for CIA operations in Asia and the South Pacific well into the 1980s.

The Bank of Hawaii, according to financial sources familiar with the bank's operations, had been linked to a number of CIA-connected operations in the Asia-Pacific region, including links to the Indonesian Lippo Group and Mochtar Riady's contributions to the presidential re-election campaign of Bill Clinton. The bank was also linked to American International Group (AIG) – bailed out by Obama; the CIA's Nugan Hand Bank in Australia; another CIA-influenced bank, the Bank of Credit and Commerce International (BCCI) and an affiliate bank in the Cook Islands, Commercial Bank of Commerce Cook Islands, Ltd. (CBCCI) headquartered in Rarotonga – which in the 1980s were funneling money to South Pacific islands to counter Soviet influence in the region.

There were additional links between Grandma "Toot's" bank and the USAID officer in Suva, Fiji, William Raupe, who was actually a CIA official cover agent; global bullion trader Deak International; European Pacific investments; and the CIA front company in Honolulu BBRDW, Ltd. BBRDW also maintained close links with the chiefs of the New Zealand Security Intelligence Service – which acted on behalf of the CIA in South Pacific small island states.

Hawaiian banks also reportedly maintained slush fund accounts in the Cayman Islands, the Cook Islands, Spain, and South America. The CIA cut-out BBRDW, which took over the assets of the collapsed Nugan Hand

Bank in Australia, also used actor Jack Lord, from *Hawaii 5-0* fame, on its promotional material as a way to "open doors" and maintained close links with the US Pacific Command based in Hawaii.

In the 1960s, the Bank of Hawaii began opening up branches all over the Pacific: Palau, Guam, Yap, Ponape, and Kosrae. It also bought the Bank of American Samoa and the First National Bank of Arizona and had gained significant, if not fully controlling, financial stakes in the Bank of New Caledonia, Bank Indosuez in Vanuatu, National Bank of the Solomon Islands, Bank of Queensland, Bank of Tonga, and Bank Indosuez Niugini in Papua New Guinea, and Bank Paribas Polynesia. The Bank of Hawaii also opened up branches in Suva, Saipan, and Tokyo.

The Bank of Hawaii was also a key bank in a global CIA financial network used to finance the Nicaraguan contras; Southern Air Transport; Air Asia and its North Hollywood, California CIA cut-out and pass-through front, Air-Sea Forwarders, Inc.; and various Iran operations, including the 1980 "no hostages-for-arms" October Surprise that sealed President Jimmy Carter's political fate, and the Reagan administration's "arms-for-hostages" caper. Also included in this CIA web were BCCI, Manufacturer's Hanover (the major bank for CIA's Air America),[179] Citibank, Credit Suisse, Chase Manhattan Bank, First Hawaiian Bank, Mellon Bank, and Wells Fargo Bank.

By the time Madelyn Dunham retired in 1986, the bank was also deeply connected to John Waihee, the first Native Hawaiian governor of Hawaii. The CIA's

---

[179] Todd E. Fandell, "CIA is apparent seller of a charter airline, but nobody's talking," *Wall Street Journal*, August 29, 1973.

BBRDW and an affiliate, Canadian Far East Trading Corporation, also maintained close links with Waihee and Governor George Ariyoshi.

When Barack Obama graduated from the exclusive private Punahou High School in Hawaii in 1979 and transferred to Occidental College in Los Angeles, Eugene Welch was the CIA's station chief in Hawaii. Punahou High School was also the alma mater of U.S. Senator Hiram Bingham III of Connecticut, who was said to be the inspiration for Indiana Jones, the daredevil anthropologist movie character popularized by George Lucas and Steven Spielberg. The CIA was engaged in a major recruiting campaign, including on college campuses, after Admiral Turner, the CIA director, was ordered by President Jimmy Carter to clean up the agency after previous scandals that were exposed during and after the Watergate affair that brought down the administration of President Richard Nixon.

The CIA's Hawaii-based Asia-Pacific financial operation appears to have been the brain child of retired CIA deputy director for intelligence Ray S. Cline, a proponent of the CIA's paying pro-American strongmen around the world large sums of cash to ensure their loyalty, including Mobutu Seso Seko of Zaire, King Hussein of Jordan, Chiang Kai-shek in Taiwan, General Lon Nol of Cambodia, the Shah of Iran, Suharto, and Marcos. Helping to assist these operations was Madelyn in her capacity as controller of the Bank of Hawaii's secretive escrow accounts. During her grandson's presidential campaign in 2008, Madelyn refused all media interview requests. She died in Hawaii, two days before her grandson was elected president. With the death of Toot, the early chapters of the life of Barack Obama, Jr., as well as those of his father, mother, and step-father, also went to the grave.

At the time Obama's mother and father met in Russian language class in Hawaii, the CIA was embarked on an aggressive covert campaign in Asia, one that involved starting a Soviet-Chinese war and aiming to assassinate Sukarno of Indonesia. The CIA was similarly involved in an aggressive covert war with the Soviets in Africa, vying for control of the continent's newly-independent states. In the world of the CIA there are no coincidences, such as the Obama Sr.-Ann Dunham meeting in the Russian language class.

According to published biographical material, Ann Dunham/Soetoro worked in Indonesia and Pakistan for USAID in Java, the Regional Southeast Asia Office of the Ford Foundation in Jakarta, the Asian Development Bank for Pakistan Agricultural Development Bank's Gujranwalla Agricultural Development Program in Lahore and Gujranwalla, all reportedly CIA fronts involved, respectively, in the post-Sukarno agency activities in Indonesia and CIA mujaheddin support activities in Pakistan. She also spoke, to varying degrees of fluency, Bahasa Indonesian, Javanese, Dutch, Urdu, Russian, and more interestingly, French. Dunham's presence in Indonesia and Pakistan would explain her knowledge of Bahasa Indonesian, Javanese, Dutch (which many Indonesians spoke from the colonial days), and Urdu, and her taking Russian at the University of Hawaii, along with Obama's Kenyan father, explains her knowledge of that language. However, it is Dunham's knowledge of French and the only other reported country she visited in Africa, other than Kenya and Egypt – Ghana – that raises suspicions as to her true mission when she was in West Africa.

Ann visited Kenya at least once after the birth of her son. She expressed a desire to move there with her son to be with her husband.

While working for the various CIA front entities, including the Ford Foundation, World Bank, and International Labor Organization, Ann also spent time in Bangladesh, India, Nepal, Philippines, and Thailand, all of which are of no surprise considering her Asian ties. Ann re-applied for her U.S. passport in Honolulu on April 27, 1986. She supposedly left Hawaii for Indonesia in 1988 to complete her PhD in anthropology from the University of Hawaii. However, she also reportedly lived in Pakistan from 1987 to 1992 working for the Asian Development Bank.

In a May 1978 letter from CIA director Turner to Harvard University President Derek Bok, the CIA director admitted the CIA used academic researchers and professors to gather information in countries where regular visitors found access restricted or barred altogether. MIT professor Peter Molnar said his seismological survey in Afghanistan after the April 1978 leftist coup by Nur Muhammad Taraki was not in any way linked to the CIA but he said such research served as "a hypothetical example of how scientists might be useful to the CIA," such as "recording Russian underground nuclear tests."[180]

Ann was officially registered as a student at the University of Hawaii from the fall semester of 1984 to the summer semester of 1992, when she finally earned her PhD. Ann's two-year employment contract for the Ford Foundation ended in December 1982, before which

---

[180] Elaine Douglass, American professionals abroad aid CIA," *The Tech* (MIT), September 22, 1978.

she may have been involved as a Javanese speaker with the Suriname exile community to help plan the CIA's overthrow of the country's left-wing dictator Desi Bouterse. Ann reportedly returned to Jakarta to work for Ford until 1984. There is no indication as to when Ann went to Ghana but in the mid-1980s, the country and one of its northern neighbors, Burkina Faso, were hotbeds of CIA activity.

It is also not known whether Barack Obama, Jr.'s first visit to Kenya, in 1987, before he attended Harvard Law School, coincided with his mother's visit to Ghana and whether the two had met in Africa as they reportedly did when Obama visited his mother in Indonesia in 1981. Obama visited his mother in Indonesia before he went to stay with "friends" in Pakistan and India. Obama also reportedly visited Pakistan later, when his mother was living there.

The inconsistencies in Ann's employment, academic, and travel records coincide with suspicions concerning Obama's college transcripts, all sealed, from Occidental College, a favorite CIA recruiting campus, and Columbia University, a favorite CIA think tank contractor. Little is known about Obama's post-Columbia employment in New York City for BIC, the well-known CIA front company responsible mainly for reaching out to Communist and Marxist governments and political parties around the world.

In 1987, two leaders in West Africa had the full attention of the CIA's Africa division: Flight Lieutenant Jerry Rawlings of Ghana, who overthrew Ghana's civilian leadership in a 1981 coup, and Captain Thomas Sankara of Burkina Faso, formerly Upper Volta. Although Rawlings was considered a leftist, his commitment to sustainable development projects earned

154

him the support of the World Bank and possibly, "Mrs. Rural Development Micro-loan" Stanley Ann Dunham.

However, Rawlings commitment to sustainable development and anti-corruption did not save him from an attempted CIA-backed coup in 1983, oddly during one of those periods when Ann's whereabouts, following her departure from the Ford Foundation in New York, remain uncertain. It should be recalled that one of the reasons for the CIA's Airlift Africa project that brought Dunham's first husband from Kenya to Hawaii in 1960 was to influence future leaders of newly-independent African states. Obama. Sr.'s Kenyan mentor, Tom Mboya, became the arch-nemesis of Africa's most popular socialist leader, Kwame Nkrumah. Nkrumah was ousted in a CIA coup in 1966, one year after Ann's second husband, Lolo Soetoro, assisted General Suharto in the CIA-planned coup against President Sukarno of Indonesia.

In 1983, a Ghanaian named Godfrey Osei tried to launch a coup against Rawlings, who was considered to be a Marxist by the CIA. Osei managed to escape from a Ghanaian prison with the help of the CIA in June 1983 and he ended up in the United States where he made plans for another coup against Rawlings. Osei was based in Queens, New York a few months after the termination of Ann's employment contract in New York for the Ford Foundation. Although Congress banned any further CIA attempts to overthrow Bouterse in Suriname, the ban did not extend to Ghana or Burkina Faso.

Osei was supported by the CIA and Israel's Mossad during his exile in New York. Apparently, Israeli crime syndicates were promised lucrative gambling casino, diamond, gold, cocoa, and coffee concessions in Ghana after Rawlings was overthrown and Osei was installed as president. Osei arranged with the CIA to purchase post-Falklands War surplus Argentinean weapons from a Texas arms broker who was also linked to the Mossad.

In 1986, a tug called the *Norbistor* departed Argentina with weapons bound for Ghana. Osei had also contracted with CIA mercenaries who were veterans of wars in Rhodesia, Laos and El Salvador. The mercenaries were also linked to a Solomon Schwartz of New York, someone who had suspected Mossad links. Upon setting sail for Ghana, the *Norbistor's* captain and mercenaries mutinied and docked near Rio de Janeiro, Brazil, where they were arrested and jailed by Brazilian police for illegally transporting weapons into Brazilian waters. There are reports that since Osei, who was witnessed wearing Nazi SS regalia and believed to be mentally unstable, was ordered not to join the ship on its voyage to Ghana.

CIA mercenaries subsequently aborted the mission. The entire CIA operation to land mercenaries and weapons in Accra after rendezvousing with Ghanaian soldiers off the Ivory Coast to start a coup against Rawlings had been compromised by the CIA on purpose. Two Americans jailed in Brazil later "escaped" from prison and returned to the United States. Rawlings, who may have also been tipped off to the coup plot, began to moderate his leftist position and announced plans for a return to civilian rule.

However, the CIA was not as sanguine about Rawlings's colleague to the north, Sankara, the leftist leader of Burkina Faso who praised Fidel Castro and Ché Guevara. Sankara, like Daniel Ortega in Nicaragua, became a public enemy as far as the CIA was concerned. If Ann Soetoro was anywhere near West Africa in 1987, with her command of French, the language of Burkina Faso, she would, with her experiences with Indonesia's

156

coup and, possibly, attempted coups in Ghana and Suriname, have been a perfect fit for the CIA to act as a liaison with French intelligence and Burkina Faso government coup plotters in Ouagadougou, the Burkinabe capital; Abidjan, the French-speaking Ivorian capital; and Accra, a CIA support station for a planned move against Sankara.

The CIA's operations against Sankara also reportedly involved a number of CIA-backed English-speaking guerrilla assets in West Africa, including Charles Taylor of Liberia, Foday Sankoh of Sierra Leone, and Yahya Jammeh of Gambia. All three enjoyed close relations with Libya's Qaddafi. Taylor and Jammeh would later overthrow the civilian leaders of Liberia and Gambia, respectively, with CIA help. Sankoh would head the Sierra Leone Revolutionary United Front (RUF) that would help plunge the country into a bloody civil war that was marked by the RUF's penchant for chopping off of the limbs of children. In October 1987, Sankara praised Guevara at a commemoration ceremony honoring the 20th anniversary of the execution of the Cuban revolutionary leader at the hands of a CIA hit squad in Bolivia. Sankara said, in praise of Guevara's revolutionary ideals, "revolutionaries can be killed but you cannot kill ideas." Sankara also rejected aid from the International Monetary Fund (IMF) and World Bank because he did not want to subject Burkina Faso to debt and taking orders from foreign powers. Sankara pressed for public health care, roads, railways, rural development, and pushing back desertification of the one-time French colonial backwater known as Upper Volta. Upon making his decision to reject IMF and World Bank loans and grants, Sankara stated at a news conference, "We must speak in one voice, saying this debt cannot be paid.

And since I am the lone voice, I will be assassinated. We must say together, we cannot pay, because we have to work to build a future for our people. If only Burkina Faso refuses to pay, I will not be here at the next conference."[181]

Two weeks after making those remarks, on October 15, 1987, Sankara's second-in-command, Captain Blaise Campaore, walked into a room where Sankara was sitting and fired two shots at Sankara who slumped in his chair and died. Campaore had coordinated his coup with the CIA station at the US embassy in Ouagadougou and the French General Directorate for External Security (DGSE) station at the French embassy. There was also strong suspicion of Mossad involvement in the coup. Apparently, Qaddafi had also soured on Sankara, possibly because of his pan-Africanist revolutionary ideas, something Qaddafi reserved for himself, and quietly supported the French- and American-backed coup.

The voice of the man who said, "As an army at the service of the revolution, the National Popular Army will have no place for any soldier who looks down on, scorns, or brutalizes his people . . . this will be a struggle against those who starve the people, the agricultural speculators and capitalists of all types . . . health care available to everyone . . . trade with all countries on an equal footing and on the basis of mutual benefit . . . it fills me with indignation to think of the Palestinians, who an inhuman humanity has decided to replace with another people – a people martyred only yesterday . . . I wish to also feel close to my comrades of Nicaragua,

---

[181] Thomas Sankara, *We Are Heirs of the World's Revolutions*. New York: Pathfinder Press, 2002.

whose harbors are mined, whose villages are bombed, and who, despite everything, face their destiny with courage and clear-headedness . . . the most pitiful and appalling – yes, the most appalling – record in terms of arrogance, insolence, and incredible stubbornness, is held by a small country in the Middle East, Israel. With the complicity of its powerful protector, the United States – which words cannot describe – Israel has continued to defy the international community for more than twenty years . . . Ideas do not die," that voice was gone.[182]

Left to right: Chantal Campaore, Michelle Obama, Blaise Campaore (assassin of Sankara), and President Obama.

It is not certain what role Barack Obama's mother may have played in the coup against Sankara in 1987. But in 2009, Obama and the First Lady feted Sankara's assassin, Campaore, and his wife at a reception in New York at the time of the UN General Assembly summit. Sankara's ideas about non-

---

[182] *Ibid.*

interference in the affairs of other countries, health care for all, rejection of international banking schemes, and self-sufficiency obviously fell on deaf ears for the first African-American president of the United States, who appears more interested in backing CIA machinations against his own cousins on the African continent. However by meeting Campaore and, later, snubbing Surinamese President Bouterse, Obama may have been paying homage to the CIA activities of his dear old mom.

Campaore returned Obama's friendship by bringing Burkina Faso firmly into the web of U.S. military and surveillance activities in Africa. U.S. AFRICOM was permitted to open a surveillance base at Ouagadougou International Airport in a classified program known as Operation Creek Sand and a classified regional intelligence fusion center known as Aztec Archer was also established in Burkina Faso.[183] Sankara's revolutionary ideals were dead and buried with Burkina Faso's entry into the American global intelligence web.

---

[183] Craig Whitlock, "U.S. expands secret intelligence operations in Africa," *The Washington Post*, June 13, 2012.

161

Chapter Six – The Spy Who Loved Him: Obama's Mother's Classified Mission in Indonesia

What do you think spies are: priests, saints, and martyrs? They're a squalid procession of vain fools, traitors, too, yes; pansies, sadists, and drunkards, people who play cowboys and Indians to brighten their rotten lives. – John LeCarré, *The Spy Who Came in from the Cold.*

Ann Soetoro worked in Indonesia for USAID embassy cover operation that helped identify some 5000 key members of the Indonesian Communist Party – *Partai Komunis Indonesia* (PKI) -- that were targeted for assassination by Indonesian armed forces units, of which her husband and her son's step-father, Lolo Soetoro, was a participant. The 5000 targets' names appeared in what was referred to by the CIA as "the shooting list." President Obama has glossed over the Indonesia chapter of his life for a major reason. To understand Indonesia in post-coup Indonesia is to also understand Obama's love affair with covert operations, special warfare, psychological operations, and all the new war gadgets and methods he has used to the maximum extent, including remotely-piloted aircraft, invasive mass and personal surveillance technology, and "smart" weaponry.

Furthermore, the contacts of the key 5000 PKI members were also used by the CIA, in part using USAID official cover agents like Ann Soetoro, to identify Indonesian sympathizers with the government of President Sukarno and the PKI, with the net total of Indonesians killed ranging from 250,000 to 1 million.

Ann Soetoro began working for CIA/USAID front, *Lembaga Persahabatan Indonesia Amerika (LIA)*– the Indonesia-America Friendship Institute. In 1972, Ann returned to Hawaii to continue her CIA work in Indonesia under the non-official cover of two agency fronts, the Asia Foundation and the East-West Center at the University of Hawaii. Ann Soetoro returned to Indonesia in 1975 to conduct "anthropological field work." The year 1975 is key. It was the year East Timor gained independence from Portugal and when the CIA, working with Suharto, planned the Indonesian invasion and bloody occupation of East Timor, a move that had been given the green light by then-Secretary of State Henry Kissinger. Kissinger later served as a foreign policy adviser on Russian matters for President Obama.

The Ford Foundation, on behalf of the CIA, began currying favor with top Indonesian military officers as early as 1954. Ford's chief liaison to the officers, as well as to members of the Indonesian Socialist Party, was Ford researcher Guy Parker. The CIA's involvement with village politics in Indonesia, began when the Ford Foundation started the Modern Indonesia Project, a CIA cover program during the Sukarno regime that was run out of Cornell University, the University of California at Berkeley, and MIT, an academic cover operation into which Ann Soetoro was later placed.

Ford Foundation-funded scholarships were used to provide education to a number of Indonesian military officers and economists who would become leaders in Suharto's government.

After Suharto's "New Order" government came to power, key Indonesian assets of the CIA were placed into top positions in Indonesia's mining, oil, and timber industries. One was Lolo Soetoro who later went to work for Exxon.

Ann Soetoro's USAID/CIA cover in Java continued from 1975 to the end of 1980 through the auspices of various employers, including BAPPENAS (*Badan Perencanaan Pembangunan Nasional*) – the Indonesian National Development Planning Agency, the UN's International Labor Organization, the Ministry of Industry Provincial Development Program (PDP I), and most significantly, the notorious USAID/CIA cover company, Development Alternatives, Inc. (DAI) of Bethesda, Maryland.

USAID had, since 1968, been secretly financing CIA overseas programs, including business and student groups. The programs became known as the "CIA orphans" after their CIA financing was disclosed.[184]

The Obama administration demanded that Cuba release Alan P. Gross, a DAI employee charged with espionage under the cover of providing telecommunication support for the Cuban Jewish community. Leaders of Cuba's Jewish community stated they were not familiar with Gross. DAI was also involved in funneling National Endowment for Democracy (NED) funds on behalf of the CIA to the Venezuelan opposition to President Hugo Chavez and covert funding for Iraqi groups during the U.S. Coalition Provisional Authority regime of U.S. viceroy for Iraq Paul "Jerry" Bremer, a Henry Kissinger understudy.

Like BIC, DAI, which employed Obama's mother from 1978 to 1980, has been a long-time CIA front. Ann Soetoro worked for DAI during the time period that Barack Obama was attending Occidental College. In the book, *A Singular Woman: The Untold*

---

[184] Richard Dudman, "Confidential Report Urges More Secrecy in CIA Spying," *St. Louis Post-Dispatch*, September 26, 1974.

Story of Barack Obama's Mother, Janny Scott describes DAI's close ties to the Suharto regime. Ann Soetoro's work for DAI was funded by an Asian Development Bank grant to the Indonesian State Ministry for the Role of Women. The contract for the state ministry's work was awarded to a joint venture of DAI and a firm linked to the Suharto family.[185]

The 1970s saw the CIA resort to the use of more "deep cover" agents. In a report by the Council on Foreign Relations, issued on January 8, 1968 and classified "Confidential: Not for Publication, Restricted to Group Members Only, Not to be Quoted or Cited" and titled "Intelligence and Foreign Policy," a panel composed of former CIA deputy director Richard Bissell, Allen Dulles, former CIA deputy director Robert Amory, Jr., former assistant secretary of defense for electronic intelligence Eugene Fubini, Douglas Dillon, former director of the State Department Bureau of Intelligence and Research Thomas J. Hughes, and President Kennedy's special assistant Theodore Sorensen called for the CIA to expand its use of private institutions for "deep cover" and "cut out" purposes and employing non-U.S. nationals for projects "which cannot be traced back to the CIA."[186] Bissell, before he became Allen Dulles's chief deputy at the CIA, was the president of the Ford Foundation, the sponsor of a number of deep cover and cut-out activities.

While Barack Obama was at Columbia and BIC, his mother was under non-official CIA cover from 1981 to 1984 in Jakarta as the program officer for women and employment for the Ford Foundation's Southeast Asia

---

[185] Janny Scott, *op. cit.*, p. 324.
[186] "CIA Fears a Mass Exposure," *Chicago Sun-Times*, September 28, 1971.

regional office, a job that took Ann to other nations in the region, including the Philippines, Thailand, and Malaysia. Ann's cover was as a Ford Foundation micro-financing project leader.

Fluent Russian speaker Robert J. Martens was a member of the political section [CIA station] of the U.S. embassy in Jakarta from 1963 and in the years leading up to the Suharto coup. Edward Masters was number three in the embassy's chain-of-command. In the years during which the Indonesian communists and their sympathizer were tracked down and murdered, Martens, as a key Indonesia expert, would have been a key player in Ann Soetoro's USAID CIA cover chain-of-command during the CIA's mopping up operations in the Indonesian rural villages. Martens, who previously served in Naples, Vienna, Salzburg, Oberammergau, and Moscow, before being posted to Jakarta, was considered one of the CIA's top operatives in Jakarta where he helped craft the CIA's "shooting list." Others in Ann's CIA chain in Jakarta were CIA station chief Bernardo Hugh Tovar, CIA deputy station chief Joseph Lazarsky, and Jakarta embassy political section chief Masters. Tovar, a native of Colombia, had been assigned previously to the CIA stations in Kuala Lumpur and Manila.

Masters, who was fluent in Hindi, had been posted in Frankfurt, Karachi, and Madras before being assigned to Jakarta to help plan the CIA coup against Sukarno. Ann Soetoro was assigned to Java villages to conduct "anthropological" research since the CIA had identified Indonesian village cadres, including members of the *Gerwani* women's organization and SOBSI labor federation, as primary supporters of the PKI and Sukarno.

In a November 1974 CIA "Interagency Memorandum on Asian Regionalism," Martens,

166

representing the State Department, along with Jack Froese of the National Security Council and Morton Abramowitz of the International Security Agency (and later the ambassador to Thailand and Turkey), were invited to a November 21, 1974, meeting at CIA headquarters by the National Intelligence Officer for Japan and the Pacific.[187] Martens's seniority in the Intelligence Community would have given Ann Soetoro's operations a high priority in the Johnson and Nixon administrations.

With his CIA connections, Lolo Soetoro's dual chain-of-command, in addition to his reporting to Suharto and his top men, would have also included the U.S. embassy's defense attaché, U.S. Army Colonel Willis G. Ethel. Colonel Ethel worked closely with Indonesian intelligence chief Ali Murtopo.

The CIA officials in Indonesia reported to William Colby, the director of the CIA's Far East Division. Colby was the brains behind the Phoenix Program in South Vietnam.

From 1989 to 1990, States News Service reporter Kathy Kadane conducted a series of interviews with former CIA personnel who were involved in the 1965 coup and the subsequent mass killings of communists. Martens revealed the role of the CIA "shooting list" for Suharto's army, in which Lolo Soetoro served, in the systematic assassination of PKI members: "It was really a big help to the army . . . they probably killed a lot of people. And I probably have a lot of blood on my hands, but that's not all bad. There's a time when you have to strike hard at a decisive moment." Asked whether the CIA sent Martens to Indonesia in 1963 to compile kill

---

[187] National Intelligence Officers office of the Director of Central Intelligence memorandum dated November 19, 1974.

lists, Colby responded, "Maybe. I don't know. Maybe we did. I've forgotten."[188]

In order to communicate the names of suspected communists from outlying villages like those where Ann Soetoro worked, the CIA provided Indonesian military officers and CIA agents with Collins KWM-2 radios, requisitioned from U.S. Air Force stocks at Clark Air Force Base in the Philippines and flown to Jakarta on U.S. Air Force C-130 transport planes. National Security Agency intercept stations in Southeast Asia also picked up the radio transmissions from the Indonesian army field officers and CIA overseers like Ann Soetoro to ensure that all suspected PKI members were identified for elimination by matching the "field" human intelligence with other NSA information compiled from intercepts of Indonesian commercial and government communications, i.e., signals intelligence or "SIGINT."

Others at the Jakarta embassy who directed CIA operations against the PKI included U.S. ambassador Marshall Green and deputy chief of mission Jack Lydman. Green dropped dead from a heart attack on a Washington, DC golf course in 1998. He worked for Nixon national security adviser Kissinger after leaving Indonesia in 1969. Lydman later was involved in the State Department's review of Indonesian military operations in West New Guinea in 1969, after the Indonesian annexation of the former Dutch territory. Lieutenant Colonel Lolo Soetoro was involved in the bloody Indonesian army crackdown on West Papuan secessionists in the territory.

On March 11, 1966, while Lolo Soetoro continued to assist Suharto in the identification and

---

[188] Kathy Kadane, U.S. Officials' Lists Aided Indonesian Bloodbath in the 60s." *The Washington Post*, May 21, 1990.

rounding up of PKI members for execution, the U.S. embassy in Jakarta sent airgram A-654 to Washington. The airgram was drafted by Martens and signed by Masters. The airgram stated it was necessary to compile a new list of PKI members because information on PKI officials "remains extremely fragmentary but sufficient additional information has been received to make a new compilation advisable." The airgram contained a list of 80 PKI leaders and their status.[189]

The Indonesian army's and CIA's kill list would not end with the elimination of PKI members and their sympathizers. Kill lists would play out in West Papua, East Timor, and Aceh province during the time of Obama's "Mommy Dearest's" bloody work in Indonesia on behalf of her bosses at the CIA, USAID, and the Ford Foundation.

The problem for Barack Obama is not shouldering blame for sins of his mother and step-father but the fact that he has lied completely about their histories. In his book, *The Audacity of Hope*," Obama writes about his mother's first trip to Indonesia in 1967: "In later years my mother would insist that had she known what had transpired in the preceding months, we never would have made the trip. But she didn't know – the full story of the coup and the purge was slow to appear in American newspapers. Indonesians didn't talk about it either."[190] If they were truly Ann Dunham Soetoro's words, we can be certain of one thing: she trained her son to lie just as well as she did.

---

[189] *Ibid.*
[190] Obama, *The Audacity of Hope*, pp. 322-323.

Chapter Seven–MK-ULTRA Hawaiian Style

Why is my CIA daily brief the same as what I just read in the morning paper? – President Jimmy Carter.

There are volumes of written material on the CIA backgrounds of George H. W. Bush and CIA-related activities by his father and children, including former President George W. Bush. Barack Obama, on the other hand, cleverly masked his own CIA connections as well as those of his mother, father, step-father, and grandmother (there is very little known about Obama's grandfather, Stanley Armour Dunham, who was supposedly in the furniture business in Hawaii after serving in Europe during World War II). What was the purpose of all of this family secrecy? This chapter will delve into one of the darkest secrets of the CIA, that of mind control and mass manipulation.

Presidents and vice presidents do not require security background checks, unlike other members of the federal government, to hold office. That job is left up to the press. In 2008, the press failed miserably in its duty to vet the man who would win the White House. With the ties of Obama's parents to the University of Hawaii and its links to MKULTRA and ARTICHOKE, a nagging question remains: Is Barack Obama a real-life "Manchurian Candidate?"

Although CIA geo-political covert operations at the University of Hawaii are well-documented, the agency's darker side of research and MK-ULTRA type operations has not generally been associated with the University of Hawaii.

170

Curiously, buried deep in the CIA files is an obscure invitation to then-CIA director Stansfield Turner to attend a "30th Anniversary of Teaching" for "Gil's" award from the American Chemical Society at the East-West Center [Appendix 6] at the University of Hawaii on April 3, 1979.

Oddly, the name of the group celebrating the anniversary is redacted in the unclassified invitation, which also reveals "Gil's" 30 year teaching stint at the University of Hawaii and University of Illinois. The ceremony for "Gil" follows a "Division of Chemical Education Dinner." The return address on the invitation's envelope is also redacted [Appendix 7] and two pages of the file on the anniversary and award ceremony are withheld [Appendix 8] from disclosure. The University of Hawaii served as one of five universities favored by CIA director Richard Helms for the CIA's behavioral modification projects, part of the CIA's Office of Science and Technology's MK-ULTRA and Project Artichoke programs, which employed the use of, among other drugs, LSD for the CIA's human subjects.

Many of the CIA's files on MK-ULTRA and its behavioral science operations have been destroyed or heavily redacted.

A series of formerly Confidential CIA memoranda, dated May 15, 1972, points to the involvement of both the Defense Department's Advanced Research Projects Agency (ARPA), the CIA, and the University of Hawaii in the CIA's behavioral science program. The memos are signed by then-Deputy Director of the CIA Bronson Tweedy, the chief of the Intelligence Community's Program Review Group (PRG) [name redacted], [Appendix 14] and CIA Director Richard Helms. The subject of the memos is

171

"ARPA Supported Research Relating to Intelligence Product," [Appendix 15] The memo from the PRG chief discusses a conference held on May 11, 1972, attended by Lt. Col. Austin Kibler, ARPA's Director of Behavioral Research. Kibler was the chief for ARPA research into behavior modification and remote viewing. Others mentioned in the PRG chief's memo include CIA Deputy Director for Intelligence Edward Proctor, the CIA Deputy Director for Science and Technology Carl Duckett, and Director of the Office of National Estimates John Huizenga.

In 1973, after CIA Director James Schlesinger ordered a review of all CIA programs, the CIA developed a set of documents on various CIA programs collectively called the "Family Jewels." Most of these documents were released in 2007 but it was also revealed that Dr. Sidney Gottlieb, the CIA's director of MKULTRA, the agency's behavior modification, brainwashing, and drug testing component, had been ordered by Helms, before he resigned as CIA director, to be destroyed. Duckett, in one memo from Ben Evans of the CIA to CIA Director William Colby, dated May 8, 1973, conveys that he "thinks the Director would be ill-advised to say he is acquainted with this program," meaning Gottlieb's drug testing program under MKULTRA.

Senior Gerald Ford administration officials, including Chief of Staff Dick Cheney and Defense Secretary Donald Rumsfeld, ensured that after the production of the "Family Jewels" documents, no CIA revelations were made about CIA psychological behavior-altering programs, including MKULTRA and Project ARTICHOKE.

The May 15, 1972, set of memos appears to be related to the CIA's initial research, code named

SCANATE, in 1972 into psychic warfare, including the use of psychics for purposes of remote viewing espionage and mind control. The memo discussed Kibler from ARPA and "his contractor," which was later discovered to be Stanford Research Institute (SRI) in Menlo Park, California.

In a memo from CIA Director Helms to, among others, Duckett, Huizenga, Proctor, and the Director of the Defense Intelligence Agency, which later inherited remote viewing from the CIA under the code name GRILL FLAME, Helms insists that ARPA had been supporting research into behavioral science and its potential for intelligence production "for a number of years" at "M.I.T., Yale, the University of Michigan, U.C.L.A., and University of Hawaii [Appendix 16] and other institutions as well as in corporate research facilities."[191]

Dr. Robert Doktor, a University of Hawaii business professor, actually wired the brains of several corporate chief executive officers to electro-encephalograms (EEGs) to demonstrate the Gestalt psychology tenet that a dominant right hemisphere of the brain is the most desired for leadership qualities. The article is contained in archived CIA files.[192]

In addition to the five universities mentioned as favored centers for the CIA's behavioral science activities, Princeton professors were revealed in 1977 to

---

[191] DCI Memorandum for Director, Bureau of Intelligence and Research, Department of State; Director of DIA; Deputy Director of CIA for Intelligence; Deputy Director of CIA for Science and Technology; CIA Director of National Estimates, Subject: ARPA Sponsored Research Relating to Intelligence Production, May 15, 1972.

[192] "Those Business Hunches Are More Than Blind Faith," *Fortune*, April 23, 1979, p. 112.

have been involved in MK-ULTRA research. The research included the use of hallucinogenic drugs for mind control experiments.[193]

A 1966 memorandum for the record written by the CIA's Deputy Director for Research and Development states that while he was committed to expanding the CIA's role in life sciences, "particularly behavioral and social," he was alarmed at the CIA's lack of capability in this area. The memo stated that the CIA's Office of Research and Development was involved in life sciences as they pertained to "behavior, human factors, animal studies, use of drugs, the man-machine interface, and . . . the BW/CW [biological warfare/chemical warfare] effort." The CIA deputy director for research and development also indicates that he has an information sharing relationship with Agriculture Secretary Orville Freeman, later the president of Business International Corporation (BIC). The CIA's top research and development official also states that Helms "reaffirmed a statement made at an earlier meeting that he expected us to follow up on all cases of ESP-like activity and that he was 'telling people' we do this." The R&D deputy director replied to Helms that "we were following most of the ones we heard about," but Helms again injected the word "all." Helms also stated he was reading Austrian ethologist Konrad Lorenz's book *On Aggression*, which concerned intra- and inter-species violence and planned to read *King Solomon's Ring*, on the ability of humans to communicate with animals. Lorenz was a member of the Austrian Nazi Party who later helped start the Austrian Green Party. The memo also states that Admiral Rufus

---

[193] John Cavanagh, Sally Frank, and Laurie Kirby, *The Daily Princetonian*, November 12, 1979.

King, the director of the Office of Naval Intelligence, shared Helms's views on life and behavioral science research.[194]

The role of the University of Hawaii in CIA psych-war operations continues to this day. The chief of research for DIA's Defense Counterintelligence and Human Intelligence Center (DCHC) Behavioral Sciences Program, Dr. Susan Brandon, who was reportedly involved in a covert program run by the American Psychological Association (APA), Rand Corporation, and the CIA to employ "enhanced interrogation" techniques, including sleep and sensory deprivation, intense pain, and extreme isolation on prisoners held at Bagram airbase in Afghanistan and other "black prisons," received her PhD in Psychology from the University of Hawaii. Brandon also served as assistant director of Social, Behavioral, and Educational Sciences for the Office of Science and Technology Policy in the George W. Bush White House.

The CIA's close connections to the University of Hawaii continued to the late 1970s, when the former President of the University of Hawaii from 1969 to 1974, Harlan Cleveland, was a special invited speaker at CIA headquarters on May 10, 1977. [Appendix 17] [195] Cleveland served as Assistant Secretary of State for International Organization Affairs from 1961 to 1965 and Lyndon Johnson's ambassador to NATO from 1965 to 1969 before taking up his position at the University of Hawaii.

A CIA Director of Training memo dated May 21, 1971, reports on the active recruitment of a U.S.

---

[194] CIA Deputy Director for Research and Development Memorandum for the Record, dated October 31, 1966.
[195] Memorandum for DCI from John F. Blake, Deputy Director for Administration, dated April 27, 1977.

Marine officer who was entering graduate school at the University of Hawaii.[196]

The CIA's program of behavior modification, creative leadership, and phenomenological research programs were at full throttle while Obama was an employee of CIA front, BIC.

In 1984, while Obama was working as an editor at BIC in Manhattan, CIA deputy director for intelligence Robert Gates, who Obama retained as his Secretary of Defense from the Bush administration, renamed the CIA's Political Psychology Division the Political Psychology Center (PPC) [Appendix 18] and transferred the group from the Office of Global Issues (OGI) to the Office of Scientific and Weapons Research (OSWR).[197]

The CIA's political psychology program is directly linked to its overall psychological and behavioral science programs. In fact, the CIA continues to send CIA officers for training to the Stanford Institute for Political Psychology program at Stanford University. Stanford and Stanford Research Institute (SRI) figure prominently in the CIA behavioral science and modification programs that enabled Barack Obama to hurdle into political office.

A CIA memorandum from the chief of OSWR/PPC to the Associate Deputy Director for Intelligence, dated 1984, requested that a consultant member of the PPC's Senior Behavioral Science Panel

---

[196] Memorandum, Chief, Career Training Program, to Director of Training, Confidential, dated May 21, 1971.
[197] CIA, Organizational Change. Political Psychology Division, Office of Global Issues, Administrative-Internal Use Only, April 18, 1984.

be permitted to publish an unclassified paper prepared by the PPC at the University of Chicago. At the time of Gates's push for political psychology programs at the CIA, Obama was working on the very same psychological-propaganda "journalism" projects at BIC, a CIA front. The paper in question sought to depict Iranian Ayatollah Khomeini as intent on bringing down "'Western' supported regimes and to establish in their place one 'united Islamic Nation' guided by the Islamic Republic of Iran and Ayatollah Khomeini." The paper suggests Khomeini would accomplish his goals by stirring up the Shi'a populations of "Saudi Arabia, Kuwait, the United Arab Emirates, Syria, Lebanon, Oman, Qatar, Bahrain, and Iraq" and maintain "the Gulf and the Arab world in a state of crisis."

The CIA's push for political action on the international and domestic media is seen in a formerly SECRET/SENSITIVE agenda for a meeting on "Political Action," dated August 5, 1982 [Appendix 19] and attended by Secretary of State George Schultz, Secretary of Defense Caspar Weinberger, Deputy Defense Secretary Frank Carlucci, CIA Director William Casey, U.S. Information Agency director Charles Wick, and National Security Adviser William Clark.

The CIA's Project MOCKINGBIRD, developed under the aegis of Cord Meyer, was a Cold War-era program designed to influence the foreign and domestic media and its successor programs governed the CIA's use of BIC journalists, of which Obama was one, to push propaganda and disinformation at home and abroad. With the approval of the new Political Action doctrine by the Reagan administration, there was a major push to use companies like BIC and other private sector operations to push U.S. propaganda abroad. The cover for the Reagan administration had to be in the private sector for, as the memo states, "Obviously as a government we cannot and should not simply emulate Soviet methods. Nor will our political parties be able in the foreseeable future to play the international role of European parties. But there is much that we can do."

The memo states that there should be a private sector campaign to challenge the Soviets abroad and states that "even the *New York Times*" supported such an effort. The private sector propaganda effort was called PROJECT TRUTH and its details are outlined in a formerly Confidential memorandum from Wick to Clark dated April 23, 1982.

A major propaganda effort against the Soviets, using U.S. and foreign private – unions, parties, youth, church, business, etc. – and public persons and elements, is described. Particular targets for the initiative included the May 13-16 Bilderberg meeting in Norway, the Fall UN General Assembly meeting, the April 28 Washington meeting of the Conference of Non-Governmental Organizations, and a contrivance known as "International Afghanistan Day."

The Reagan national security team was clearly intent, using cut-outs like BIC and others, to increase the U.S. "ability to generate political initiatives and conduct political campaigns, using overt and covert resources and combining government and private efforts here and abroad."

CIA files indicate the PPC was partially involved with a project called LOOKING GLASS, which involved a group of CIA and top business officials whose mission included "cultivating talent" from an early age.

Key to the CIA's interest in early "talent spotting" is the agenda from the "Conference on Cultivating Talent," held in Greensboro, North Carolina from January 17-18, 1984, and co-sponsored by the Center for Creative Leadership (CCL). CCL was founded in 1970 by H. Smith Richardson, founder of the Vick Chemical Company.

Among the participants were the CIA's director of training and education, former National Security Agency (NSA) director Admiral Noel Gayler, and William Verity, Jr., the former chairman of the U.S. Chamber of Commerce and a director at BIC in Manhattan. Gayler also served as Commander of the U.S. Pacific Command in Hawaii from 1972 to 1976, succeeding Admiral John S. McCain, Jr., the father of Obama's 2008 challenger, Senator John S. McCain III of Arizona.[198]

Verity, who was also chairman of Armco steel corporation, later succeeded Malcolm Baldrige, Jr. as Secretary of Commerce in the Reagan administration. Verity became Commerce Secretary after Baldrige died in a freak rodeo accident in California. During his directorship at BIC, Verity also served on the boards of Eli Lilly and Chase Manhattan Bank, as well as serving as chairman of the board of trustees of Ford's Theater in Washington, DC.

Most of the CCL participants at the two-day conference were behavioral scientists. CIA director Richard Helms considered the University of Hawaii, the alma mater of Obama's mother and father, as one of five top centers for the CIA's behavioral science research

---

[198] Research Sponsor Conference on Cultivating Talent, January 17-18, 1984, Participant List, from CIA archival files.

work. The others were MIT, Yale, University of Michigan, and UCLA.

Speaking at the CCL conference, in addition to Verity, were Billie L. Alban, President of Alban & Williams, Ltd., an international consultancy. Alban was a core faculty member at UCLA and previously served on the staff of the Tavistock Institute in London. Currently, she teaches at Columbia University. Part of Alban's biography held in CIA archival files, which states her clients included the CIA-linked Bankers Trust, is redacted. Today, CCL's board of governors includes faculty members from Columbia and Harvard universities.[199]

Verity was joined at the conference by two executives of Armco. One cartoon from the conference found in the CIA archives [Appendix 20] depicts two men with one pointing to a group of people representing the bottom rungs of society and exclaiming, "There is the raw material for a new, dynamic world!"[200] The presence of Verity of BIC at the conference attended by the CIA's chief of education and training raises the specter of BIC's role in supplying "raw material" from its ranks, individuals like Obama, for the CIA's "new, dynamic world."

---

[199] Report on Conference at the Center for Creative Leadership. January 17-18, 1984, Director, CIA Office of Training and Education, January 25, 1984.
[200] Research Sponsor Conference on Cultivating Talent, January 17-18, 1984, from CIA archival files.

The CIA and Tavistock

Also known as the "Freud Hilton," Tavistock has long been involved in brainwashing techniques and CIA work since its foundation. The institute also has links to the Harvard Psychology Clinic, the CIA, and Stanford Research Institute (SRI), a major contractor for CIA psychic warfare activities in the 1970s and 80s. Alban told the 1984 CCL seminar, "talent should be nurtured and developed for tomorrow not today. If one focuses on today's requirements, by the time talents are nurtured one will find they are the talents required of yesterday. The focus must be visionary and look to the needs of the future."

The Tavistock Institute has long been linked with the CIA's MK-ULTRA and Projects BLUEBIRD and ARTICHOKE mind control and brain-washing operations, conducted by the CIA's top scientist for such matters, Dr. Sidney Gottlieb. Much of the records about MK-ULTRA and other CIA programs were destroyed on the order of Helms in 1972. BLUEBIRD documents describe what the CIA was trying to accomplish with behavioral modification in the early 1950s: "Can we 'alter' a person's personality? Can we devise a system for making unwilling subjects into willing agents and then transfer that control to untrained agency agents in the field by use of codes or identifying signs?" In other words, the movie "The Manchurian Candidate," was not purely a fictional account within the CIA's research and scientific community.

The CIA appeared to have been interested in media reports linking Tavistock to anthropologists. CIA archives contain an article from the *Executive Intelligence Review* publication of perennial presidential candidate Lyndon LaRouche that describes a network involving "Columbia University East European studies head Zbigniew Brzezinski" and "radical sociology, anthropology, and history department operations deployed through Eugene Genovese's Marxist Perspective group." The report stated that anthropologists had been recruited by the U.S. government in supporting radical terrorist groups and funding came through various groups, including the Wenner-Gren Foundation, a Manhattan-based fund that supports global anthropological research.[201]

Considering the sex scandals that have plagued the upper echelons of political circles in Washington, the questions about a continuation of Gottlieb's OPERATION MIDNIGHT CLIMAX are still germane. A sub-program of MK-ULTRA, MIDNIGHT CLIMAX employed prostitutes in the San Francisco Bay Area and New York City to lure targeted individuals into CIA safe houses where they would then be plied with drugs like LSD. They would then be tested for their susceptibility to sexual blackmail. The program was "officially" halted in 1966, but the continuing use of prostitutes by the CIA for blackmail purposes has been verified to the author by workers in the sex escort industry.

Twelve pages in the CIA's director for training and education's January 25, 1984, report to the deputy director for administration remain classified to this day, [Appendix 21] but in a hand written note on the CIA transmittal sheet, he states "I think you will find Tab B to be very interesting." [Appendix 22] The deputy director for administration replies, also in a handwritten

---

[201] "How Britain runs the 'radical left,'" *Executive Intelligence Review*, January 16, 1979.

note, "I did – though I don't [subscribe]? To call the community on Tab C."

Tab B is the training and education director's comments to the CCL. The talking points include:

"- Pleased to be invited to participate and to exchange ideas on the cultivating and nurturing of talent.

- Our recent visibility has been both an asset and a liability in this regard. More people know of the CIA and its activities than when I joined (tell the labor union story), and this attracts some good people. By the same token, it brings out the weird ones.

- We have an exceptional screening process involving security investigation, testing, (assessment – OSS-CCL) psychological screening, medical review, interviewing, polygraph, etc. (and a long processing time!) [Note: a likely reference to the CIA's Office of Special Security. CCL appears to indicate a past and on-going relationship between the CIA and the Center for Creative Leadership.]

- So, the people who come to us are, for the most part, exceptionally talented, thoroughly screened, and represent a real challenge for us to stretch, nurture and retain.

- Eventually reach the point where at least some people are identified early on as having high potential for senior agency-wide positions and are consciously developed toward that end."

CIA university recruitment the year Obama graduated from Columbia

A September 11, 1984 memo to Dan Carlin, the assistant director of the President's Foreign Intelligence Advisory Board (PFIAB) from the CIA's executive assistant/executive director to director William Casey points out the academia sources for the past year's CIA undergraduate recruits. Two recruits came from Columbia University. Obama graduated from Columbia in 1983 after reportedly studying under Zbigniew Brzezinski, the former National Security Adviser to President Carter. The chairman of the PFIAB at the time of the stepped-up CIA college recruiting campaign was Anne Armstrong, the Ford administration's ambassador to London from 1976 to 1977 and a major backer of George H.W. and George W. Bush. A one-time board member of Halliburton, Armstrong was a mentor for Karl Rove when she served as co-chairman of the Republican National Committee from 1971 to 1973.

By way of comparison, one undergraduate was recruited from Harvard, one from Occidental College (where Obama attended before transferring to Columbia), one from Claremont Men's College, one from Pepperdine. Topping the list are five each from Georgetown and Dartmouth. Graduate recruits include one from Harvard Law, where Obama attended law school after his "community service" work in Chicago; three from the University of Michigan (one of Helms's favored behavioral science research campuses), and, trumpeting other graduate schools, American University in Washington, with five new recruits.

CIA archival records also indicate an on-going relationship between Obama's former college, Occidental, and the CIA in 1983. A MacNeil-Lehrer Newshour transcript shows a guest, Lawrence Caldwell of Occidental, as having been a scholar in residence at the CIA's Office of Soviet Analysis for two years.[202]

---

[202] MacNeil-Lehrer Newshour, November 11, 1983.

Behavioral science, the CIA, and SRI

A formerly Secret NOFORN [not releasable to foreign nationals] proposal for the CIA, dated December 31, 1992, [Appendix 23] and prepared for the CIA by Science Applications International Corporation (SAIC) describes in great detail the agency's behavioral science programs, which included anomalous cognition (AC) and anomalous perturbation (AP). AC is defined as "the awareness of information that is considered otherwise shielded from all known sensory channels" and AP is "the perturbation of physical matter under conditions of complete physical and sensorial isolation."[203]

The document states that research into both field began in 1973 with the CIA engaged in such research and was followed by U.S. military service and Defense Intelligence Agency (DIA) research with SRI through fiscal year 1990. The document also states "beginning in 1986, the U.S. Army Medical Research and Development Command (USAMRDC) [Fort Detrick, Maryland] initiated the first coordinated long-term examination of AC and AP phenomenon."[204]

SAIC proposed to conduct various research projects for the CIA are similar to some of the "enhanced interrogation" techniques used on detainees in Guantanamo Bay, Bagram airbase in Afghanistan, and other CIA "black sites" in the wake of the 9/11 attacks. The experiments, conducted by SRI since 1974, included exposing individuals to flashing light or no light to discover how their central nervous systems reacted to the visual stimuli. Experiment subjects were fitted with EEGs (electroencephalogram) monitors to

---

[203] SAIC, Technical Proposal, December 31, 1992, p. 2.
[204] *Ibid.*

measure their reaction to the flashing light stimuli. Part of the SAIC proposal remains redacted.

A sub-contractor to SAIC was the Lucidity Institute of Napa, California, founded in 1987 by Dr. Stephen LaBerge for the conduct of "research on lucid dreams and to help people learn to use them to enhance their lives.[205] Lucid dreaming means dreaming while knowing that one is dreaming and allows people to consciously guide the direction of their dreams." Ironically, one of 2010's blockbuster movies, "Inception," dealt with the subject of invading people's dreams to steal secrets. Leonardo DeCaprio plays a secretive agent named Dorn Cobb who is an "extractor" agent operating in the para-psychological dream invasion program. What may be fiction in Hollywood was far from it in the CIA research with SAIC, SRI, and the Lucidity Institute.

One of the methods used by the SRI and SAIC program to determine "the differences between effective and ineffective liars" was called the Q-Sort technique. The technique was used to separate "highly talented" individuals in test "clusters."

The paragraph on the intelligence applications of anomalous cognition is 90 percent redacted from the SAIC proposal as are at least three reference works cited in the document. Academic institutions involved in the project included, in addition to SRI, Stanford University, Brookhaven National Laboratory, the Institute of Buddhist Studies in Berkeley, and UCLA (one of Helms's favorite CIA behavioral science research centers).

---

[205] *Ibid.* p. 7.

The CIA-SAIC-SRI project principals had either worked at or attended the Biofeedfack Institute of San Francisco; SAIC; Yale (another of Helms's favored research centers); Columbia University; Harvard; Bellevue Hospital in New York; the U.S. Army Medical Research Unit in Kuala Lumpur, Malaysia; the Stanford Hypnosis Research Laboratory; Carnegie-Mellon University; MIT (another one of Helms's favored behavioral science centers); the World Bank; the Air Force Institute of Technology at Wright-Patterson Air Force Base, Ohio; University of Minnesota; the Brain Research Institute; the Behavioral Research Foundation of St. Kitts, West Indies; the Tavistock Institute in London; the A.K. Rice Institute of Rainier, Washington, an off-shoot of the Tavistock Institute; Sleep Disorders Clinic, Provo, Utah; Neurology Study Section of the National Institutes of Health, Bethesda, Maryland; Tibetan government-in-exile, Dharamsala, India; U.S. Veterans Administration; University of Wisconsin-Madison; US Naval Research Laboratory, Washington, DC; and perhaps, most interestingly, the University of Hawaii (also designated by Helms as one of the CIA's favored behavioral science research centers and where two of the principals involved in the SAIC-CIA project had an affiliation).

The research director for the CIA-SAIC program was Dr. Edwin C. May, an internationally-recognized parapsychology expert who is the executive director for the Cognitive Sciences Laboratory of the Laboratories for Fundamental Research in Palo Alto, California. May was a lead researcher for the DIA's and CIA's STAR GATE remote viewing and ESP project until it was closed down in 1995. The program moved from the CIA to the National Security Agency and involved research carried out with Johns Hopkins University in Baltimore and the Monroe Institute of Applied Science in Faber, Virginia, south of Charlottesville The Monroe Institute was also heavily involved in the STAR GATE program. The current research is also linked to the Parapsychology Foundation of New York City. The Monroe Institute's Robert A. Monroe developed the "advanced training program using the hemispheric synchronization process" used by remote viewers.[206]

Other members of the team included a retired Army Major General who now specializes in human bionics a radio astrophysicist; an expert who maintains that sexual orientation may be influenced by experiences in childhood; a counselor for survivors of the People's Temple cult of Reverend Jim Jones (itself linked to a CIA MK-ULTRA behavioral modification and mind control operation); a current specialist with the Farsight Institute of Atlanta, a remote viewing research center; a neuro-linguistic programming expert; a toxicology specialist; a principal of the Pentagon's PANDORA project on the use of electro-magnetic weapons to roboticize human beings; an expert in the imaging and computer mapping of the human brain; an inventor of the cochlear implant; an expert on the mass popular opposition of Okinawans to the U.S. military presence on the island; a future warfare expert for the Pentagon and member of the National Security Agency Scientific Advisory Board and Defense Intelligence Agency Scientific Advisory Committee; a former Army Undersecretary for acquisition; a Defense Intelligence Agency psi-tech officer who worked on electro-magnetic weaponry for battlefield psychological

---

[206] First draft of briefing for Secretary of the Army, presented to Major General Albert Stubblebine by Lt. Col, Buzby, dated September 23, 1983.

purposes – PROJECT SLEEPING BEAUTY – and who worked with another Army Intelligence psi-tech officer who was partially the inspiration for the movie "Men Who Stare At Goats;" a specialist on the brainwashing techniques, including sleep deprivation, by the North Koreans on American prisoners of war and by the Church of Scientology on its members, who was also an expert witness on the brainwashing techniques of the Symbionese Liberation Army on heiress Patty Hearst; and, lastly, a University of Hawaii-linked specialist on the psychological effects of prison and prison brutality on prisoners who later defended, as an expert witness, one of the prison guards at Abu Ghraib in Baghdad.

OSS and CIA clandestine services veteran Miles Copeland, Jr., who had once been a trumpet player in the Glenn Miller band, believed that much of MK-ULTRA's secrets were kept from congressional investigators and that an MK-ULTRA off-shoot program was used to psychologically destroy 1972 Democratic presidential candidate Edmund Muskie. Copeland also believed that the CIA played a part in founding the Church of Scientology.

The presence of a Jonestown de-programmer on the CIA-SAIC team is noteworthy. During the time of the Jonestown massacre, the People's Temple's ship, the 'Cudjoe,' was en route to Trinidad with members of the Temple on board. Temple members soon set up operations in Trinidad and Grenada, where Prime Minister Eric Gairy, a CIA client, who, in a 1977 speech before the UN General Assembly, called for the UN to establish an Agency for Psychic Research into Unidentified Flying Objects and the Bermuda Triangle, was in charge. According to *The Oakland Tribune*, the St. George's University Medical School in Grenada had on its staff one Dr. Peter Bourne, the son of the university's vice chancellor Sir Geoffrey Bourne. Peter Bourne is a graduate of the Walter Reed Army Institute of Research (WRAIR), where he studied the psychological effects of stress on those in combat. He also served one year in Vietnam as the head of the Army's psychiatric research team. Bourne later became an Assistant UN Secretary General and an adviser to then-Congressman Bill Richardson. It was under the guise of rescuing American medical students at the university, that the Reagan administration launched a 1983 invasion to overthrow Bernard Coard, who had ousted and executed Bishop in a coup. Both Bournes said the medical students were never in any danger. [Some believe that author Robert Ludlum got the idea for CIA mind-controlled assassins in his novel "The Bourne Identity" and its sequels from Geoffrey Bourne's work.]

The Jonestown connection to the U.S. war in Southeast Asia does not end with the Bourne/Grenada connection. The U.S. ambassador to Guyana at the time of the Jonestown massacre was John Burke, who served with his Deputy Chief of Mission Richard Dwyer, were allegedly working for the CIA in Bangkok during the Vietnam war. Dwyer was wounded in the Port Kaituma shootings where Representative Leo Ryan and the others were killed.

Ironically, Ryan appeared before a House International Relations subcommittee hearing chaired by Representative Donald Fraser (D-MN) on December 18, 1976. The hearing dealt with President Ford's desired increase for aid to Indonesia. Mrs. Carmel Budjiardjo, a former British Communist whose husband, a PKI official in the Sukarno government, was still in an Indonesian jail after the 1965 coup, testified against resuming aid to the Suharto regime. Ryan blasted

Budjiardjo's appearance before the committee: "I do believe that adherents of a government and a former Communist Party that terrorized their own people and vilified the United States have the guts to appear before this body as defenders of human rights and as accusers of anyone." Ryan was drinking the CIA's Kool Aid two years before the Jonestown massacre. Representative Wayne Hays (D-OH) asked Budjiardjo why she had not complained about human rights violations when she worked for PKI leader Aidit and Foreign Minister Subandrio in the Sukarno government. [207]

On September 27, 1980, Jack Anderson reported that Dwyer was a CIA agent and a friend of Jones. Anderson reported that on one of the tapes made during the mass suicide Jones was heard saying, "Get Dwyer out of here before something happens to him." Dwyer reportedly left Guyana for Grenada after the massacre. The U.S. Consular Officer at the embassy in Georgetown, Guyana was Richard McCoy, who allegedly liaised with Jim Jones and was a U.S. Air Force intelligence official. Another alleged CIA employee, operating under State Department cover, was Dan Webber, who also visited the Jonestown the day after the massacre. Joe Holsinger, Ryan's assistant and friend, later said that he believed that Jonestown was a massive mind control experiment and that the CIA and military intelligence was involved in the program.

An August 14, 1974, Memorandum for the CIA's chairman of the Scientific Intelligence Committee (STIC) from the chief of the Life Sciences Division for Scientific Intelligence, called for increased funding for

---

[207] Rowland Evans and Robert Novak, "Aid vs. Human Rights," *Washington Post*, January 15, 1976.

STIC. The memo also opposed the demise of the CIA's scientific research efforts. The Life Sciences chief called for an increased CIA effort in the areas of "potential biological threats (non-military), and mass behavior control." In addition, the key areas of "human factors" and "human engineering" in behavioral sciences are stressed as important to America's intelligence goals."[208]

The nexus of Obama's almae mater: Occidental, Columbia, and Harvard, as well as that of his parents, the University of Hawaii, in the CIA's mind control, behavioral modification, and mass hypnosis projects is deeply troubling. The fact that Obama has failed to provide a full accounting of his past academic and professional employment history, coupled with the presence of a major CIA presence within his and his parents', grandparents', and step-father's backgrounds opens up the real possibility that Obama was, to use the CIA's own term, "nurtured," for a higher calling. Obama told the nation that his would be the most open and transparent in recent history. However, Obama's biography and those of his parents and guardians are full of more holes than a slice of Swiss cheese. It is well past time for the President to make good on that promise and fully release his past academic, passport, employment, and overseas travel records.

CIA archives contain two relatively obscure articles with notes appended to the margins that reveal a classified CIA program to conduct personality assessments on college campuses to identify potential recruits. Considering the fact that one of the articles is dated January 15, 1979, the year Barack Obama enrolled, courtesy of a scholarship, at Occidental

---

[208] Memorandum for Chairman, STIC, SECRET, dated August 14, 1974.

College in Los Angeles, a school cited by the CIA as a favored campuses for agency recruitment efforts, there may be a logical explanation for the sealing of Obama's transcripts from Occidental and Columbia, where he transferred in 1981. Obama's financial records from Occidental have also been sealed.

Occidental was, for many years, a top target for CIA recruiting efforts. A CIA memorandum, formerly Secret and dated February 8, 1967, that details the CIA's "100 Universities Program," which, as stated by the author, "originally conceived [redacted] as a recruitment technique. Its purpose was to make better known on the campuses of America the very existence of the CIA and its mission and role in Government, to illustrate the vast range of vocational opportunities in the Agency."[209]

A formerly SECRET CIA memorandum for the Deputy Director for Administration from the acting Director of Personnel, [Appendix 24] dated February 8, 1979, discusses an active CIA recruitment effort at Occidental College on February 1, 1979. Obama reportedly attended Occidental later in 1979. The memo states, '[redacted] our [redacted] recruiter, reports that he briefed approximately seventy students at Occidental College in Los Angeles on 1 February and was very well received. He added that while they did not interrupt his presentation, about fifteen to twenty members of the Socialist Democratic Alliance demonstrated outside as he spoke and that their chanting of 'CIA, go Away' could be heard. Larry also reported that the seventy attending his briefing was the largest number ever to attend a briefing at the school by an employer.' A burning question is whether "Larry" ever tried to recruit a young Barack Obama, Jr. at Occidental and whether he

---

[209] CIA Memorandum, February 8, 1967.

was successful at the enthusiastically pro-CIA campus in 1979."[210]

In a January 15, 1979, *Village Voice* article by Ed Kiersh, discovered in the CIA archives, it is revealed that the Educational Testing Service (ETS) held a "highly-secret" conference, titled the "Future of the World" conference, in a building in Princeton, New Jersey secluded by 400-acres of woods and streams. Attending the Spring 1978 conference were David Rockefeller, Henry Kissinger, Alexander Haig, IBM Chairman Frank Cary, various prime ministers from around the world, and Zbigniew Brzezinski, then-national security adviser for President Jimmy Carter and two years later, one of Obama's reputed professors at Columbia University. Since Obama's Columbia records are sealed, there has been no independent confirmation of Brzezinski's role as one of Obama's professors.

Kiersh's article reported that the Princeton site was chosen for the meeting to securely discuss "world destruction scenarios, defense pacts, and trade alignments." Kiersh describes ETS as a fitting host for such a meeting and he dubs the testing service as the "gatekeepers to the world."

ETS was created in 1948 by the College Entrance Examination Board, American Council on Education, and Carnegie Foundation as a non-profit test developer. However, Kiersh points out that ETS's links soon extended to the White House and CIA. The administrator of the Scholastic Aptitude Test (SAT) and Graduate Record Examination (GRE), Kiersh refers to ETS as an "Orwellian empire," which, in 1979, administered over 300 testing programs, from bar examinations and law and business school admission

---

[210] CIA Memorandum, February 8, 1979.

tests to tests for barbers, professional golfers, and police officers.

Kiersh also reveals that upon its founding in 1948, ETS hired psychometricians from the Office of Strategic Services (OSS), the forerunner of the CIA. ETS also happens to develop CIA entrance examinations. Kiersh also revealed that foreign students also file personal and financial reports with the ETS and there were suspicions that the CIA had access to the records for purposes of recruitment.[211] With Obama's status at Occidental as either a U.S. enrollee or a foreign national enrollee from Indonesia still an open question, there may be an additional reason why Obama's records at Occidental remain sealed. Present at Occidental when the school was a top CIA recruiting campus and with the possibility that he enrolled as a foreign student from Indonesia, Obama and his handlers may realize that to open up Obama's transcripts would begin to unlock other doors into his murky past.

Another article held in the CIA archives, a *New York Times* piece by Joseph Treaster, dated August 7, 1977, has a handwritten note in the top right-hand corner that reads "MK-ULTRA," even though the CIA's top secret behavioral modification program is mentioned nowhere in the article. [Appendix 25] The article, titled "CIA Mind Probes Now More Benign," discusses a CIA program to create its own "Manchurian candidate." The article describes the CIA's then-ongoing "personality assessment" program. The program was designed to probe an individual's "weaknesses and strengths," as well as predict actions and reactions, and devise ways of how to influence an individual's behavior. Personality

---

[211] Ed Kiersh, "Testing is the Name, Power is the Game," *The Village Voice*, January 15, 1979.

assessment factors given weight by the CIA included where an individual was from, whether he was a chain smoker, and who his father was.

Treaster described the CIA's personality assessment program as largely the brainchild of CIA director Dulles, who authorized CIA funding for the Society for the Investigation of Human Ecology at the Cornell Medical Center in New York in the early 1950s. [212] Other CIA-funded personality assessment programs existed at Rutgers University, where Hungarian refugees were guinea pigs; McGill University of Montreal, where there was a program to study the "effects of repeated verbal signals upon human behavior ['Yes we can,' 'Hope and change,' for example]; the Massachusetts Mental health Center in Boston , where LSD experiments on humans were carried out; and ETS in Princeton, where studies were conducted on "two broad theories of personality."

The Society for the Investigation of Human Ecology was shut down in 1965 and was largely replaced by "Psychological Assessments, Inc.," a CIA front led by psychologist and senior CIA intelligence officer, Colonel James L. Monroe. In the mid-1970s, Psychological Assessments was terminated and Monroe moved the operations to Texas.

The CIA's use of the American Anthropological Association and its new Society for the Anthropology of Consciousness (SAC), established to "support interdisciplinary, cross-cultural, experimental, and theoretical approaches to the study of consciousness," was seen as an important contribution to the Defense Intelligence Agency's para-psychology program, Project

---

[212] Joseph Treaster, "CIA Mind Probes Now More Benign," The *New York Times*, August 7, 1977.

STAR GATE. Specifically, SAC's assistance "in the development of foreign data" was discussed.[213]

STAR GATE was an off-shoot of the Army's special collection program code named CENTER LANE.[214] The DIA's code name for the program before it became STAR GATE was SUN STREAK.[215] The security briefing for the project stated: "Since 1972, the U.S. government, including the Department of Defense, has been involved in examining potential uses of psychoenergetics. Three specific aspects of psychic phenomena were of interest: Remote viewing (clairvoyance), psychokinesis, and remote communications – or telepathy."[216]

Another Army code name for the program was GONDOLA WISH. The Army and DIA later used the code name GRILL FLAME.[217]

It is also more than a minor historical footnote that Dr. Max Millikan, before he started CENIS at MIT, where he began funding CIA anthropology personnel in Indonesia, was involved in the CIA's "Psychological Intelligence" program. Millikan argued that the responsibility for Psychological Intelligence should be centralized within the CIA.[218] Millikan was also heavily involved in the establishment of the CIA's

---

[213] Defense Intelligence Agency, Project STAR GATE Research and Peer Review Plan, SECRET, NOFORN, LIMDIS, May 1994, p. 13.

[214] First draft of briefing for Secretary of the Army, *op. cit.*

[215] Letter, from Assistant Deputy Director for Scientific and Technical Intelligence, DIA to Terry Ryan, Staff member, Senate Select Committee on Intelligence, SECRET NOFORN, dated June 12, 1991.

[216] First draft of briefing for Secretary of the Army, *op. cit.*

[217] *Ibid.*

[218] CIA, Memorandum of Conversation, Subject: Psychological Intelligence, January 22, 1951.

Psychological Strategy Board and the issuance of the "Troy Report" on propaganda operations.[219]

After eight brutal years of George W. Bush and Dick Cheney, the nation was ready for any change and any change agent, no matter how insincere. Unfortunately, the CIA, through LOOKING GLASS, MK-ULTRA, STAR GATE, ARTICHOKE, PANDORA, and other behavioral science programs were ready to answer the call. The CIA answered the call with Obama and most of us bought him and his "Hope and Change" propaganda fecundity "nurtured" by CIA programs going back some sixty years.

Buried deep in the CIA archives is an undated memorandum for a "Colonel Sands" from the Chief of the CIA's Operations Coordination Branch, Psychological Staff Division. Likely from the 1960s when Ann Dunham was ready to fly off to Jakarta, the memo states that CIA psychological operations unit required the following: a psychiatrist or clinical psychologist, a psychological warfare operator, and, more interestingly, a "cultural anthropologist." The memo states the primary mission of such psy-ops units is "undermining collective emotional stability" of targeted peoples and nations.[220]

---

[219] CIA, Memorandum, Troy Report, Propaganda, Defectors, March 5, 1952.
[220] Undated memo for Col. Sands. Underwent a NSA review prior to declassification on June 23, 2010.

Chapter Eight -- New York, New York and the CIA

I will splinter the CIA into a thousand pieces and scatter it into the winds – President John F. Kennedy.

President Obama and many of his biographers have glossed over the importance of Obama's post-Columbia employer, BIC. Far from being a publisher of newsletters for corporations, BIC was one of hundreds, if not thousands, of CIA fronts that operated in both the sunshine and the dark shadows of the Cold War with cleverly-concocted cover stories. BIC was linked to economic intelligence gathering for the CIA. This chapter explains in detail the role and importance of BIC in shaping U.S. foreign policy and in the political development of a young 22-year old college graduate named Barack H. Obama, Jr.

In his book, *The Audacity of Hope*, it is interesting to read how Obama treats his one-year employment at BIC, "I personally came of age during the Reagan presidency – I was studying international affairs at Columbia, and later working as a community organizer in Chicago . . ."[221] Obama's failure to mention BIC was just another gaping hole in a biography that resembled a large slab of Swiss cheese.

For one year, Obama worked as a researcher in BIC's financial services division where he wrote for two BIC publications, *Financing Foreign Operations* and *Business International Money Report*, a weekly

---

[221] Obama, *The Audacity of Hope, op. cit.* p. 288-9.

199

newsletter. In *Dreams From My Father*, Obama wrote that after graduating from Columbia, he eventually worked for "a consulting house to multinational corporations" where he was a "research assistant." Obama claimed that he had his own secretary and interviewed "Japanese financiers or German bond traders."[222] It should be noted that the CIA employed then and still employs a number of economists who do nothing but monitor international financial transactions and produce financial intelligence reports. The CIA also outsources such functions to a myriad of front companies embedded in Wall Street and other major financial centers.

Biographer David Maraniss, in his biography of Obama, *Barack Obama: The Story*, cites Obama as a rather withdrawn low-level employee of "BI.". Obama's early demeanor was highlighted in letters between him and a female friend from his days at Occidental, Alex McNear, and diary entries by another female acquaintance, Genevieve Cook, who he dated in New York while working for BIC. Cook was an Australian from an upper-crust family. In fact, Cook's father, Michael J. Cook, was an Australian diplomat in 1967, during part of the same time frame when Obama lived there with Ann and Lolo Soetoro. Cook's mother, Helen Ibbitson, who divorced Genevieve's father, hailed from a banking family in Melbourne. Both McNeary and Cook described Obama as complicated, with Cook describing Obama as acting much older than his age. In her diary entry for January 26, 1984, Cook writes of Obama: "How is he so old already, at the age of 22? I have to recognize . . . that I find his 'thereness' very threatening . . . Distance, distance, distance, and

---

[222] Obama, *Dreams From My Father*, op. cit., p. 135.

wariness."[223] Normally, such a description would be creepy, unless Obama had been trained for something else, a mission that did not require any romantic closeness with anyone who might be attracted to him. Genevieve Cook eventually married an Egyptian accountant, Mohamed Moustafa, from Alexandria, Egypt. Helen Ibbitson had something in common with Ann Dunham: both were experts in Indonesian art and crafts. [224]

Genevieve Cook had her own link with intelligence. Cook's father, Michael J. Cook, not only served in Indonesia and as Australian ambassador to Vietnam and the United States, but was the director general of the Office of National Assessments (ONA) in Canberra. ONA is the main coordination agency for providing intelligence from the Australian Security Intelligence Organization (ASIO), Defense Intelligence Organization, Australian Secret Intelligence Service (ASIS), and Defense Signals Directorate (DSD) (the Australian counterpart to the U.S. National Security Agency (NSA)) to the Prime Minister and the Cabinet.[225] Had Obama married Cook, no doubt their respective families would have been able to share many intelligence-related stories from their past postings in Jakarta and other parts of the world.

The covert CIA program to assist the Afghan mujaheddin was already well underway at the time and Pakistan was the major base of operations for the CIA's support. Obama also reportedly traveled to India, again,

---

[223] David Maraniss, "Becoming Barack," adapted from *Barack Obama: The Story, Vanity Fair*, June 2012.
[224] "Genevieve Cook weds accountant, *The New York Times*, October 23, 1988.
[225] *Ibid.*

201

on unknown business for U.S. intelligence. According to knowledgeable intelligence sources in Indonesia and the United States, Obama has, in the past, traveled on at least two passports: U.S. and Indonesian, information that may have been contained in Obama's passport files, which were of keen interest to Brennan and The Analysis Corporation contractors.

BIC had long been associated with CIA activities since being founded in 1954 by Eldridge Haynes, a self-professed liberal Democrat. The BIC headquarters was located at the prestigious address of 1 Dag Hammarskjold Plaza in Manhattan. BIC held a series of off-the-record, no press, meetings between top U.S. business executives and top government officials, including the President, and the Secretaries of State, Defense, Treasury, Commerce, and Labor; the Attorney General, Senate leadership, and the heads of the Export-Import Bank and the Inter-American Development Bank.

BIC also maintained a European subsidiary, Business International S.A., in Geneva. BIC held international meetings in locations like Brussels and Mexico City. In 1961, a BIC meeting in New Delhi was attended by Indian Prime Minister Jawaharlal Nehru and Foreign Minister Morarji Desai, who would later become Prime Minister.

One month after Leonid Brezhnev, other Soviet Communist Party officials, and KGB chief Vladimir Seminchastny conspired to overthrow Soviet Communist Party General Secretary and Premier Nikita Khrushchev, Haynes was in Moscow in November 1964 sponsoring a business conference between Khrushchev's successor as Premier, Aleksei Kosygin, and top U.S. businessmen. In the years following the conference, Haynes often crafted together other U.S.-Soviet business meetings and became close to Kosygin. In November 1971, Haynes put together another U.S. businessmen's conference with Kosygin at which Commerce Secretary Maurice Stans was in attendance as President Richard Nixon's personal envoy. The president of BIC at the time was Orville Freeman, a former secretary of agriculture during the Kennedy and Johnson administrations. Joining Freeman in Moscow were officials of DuPont, IBM, General Electric, Union Carbide, and Westinghouse. The Moscow meeting also dealt with the opening up of Soviet natural gas supplies to the United States.

CIA and OSS veteran agent Miles Copeland, Jr. may have tipped his hand on the real purpose of BIC in a 1973 letter to *The Times* of London. Copeland wrote that the "CIA rarely, if ever, employs American citizens as agents. The CIA's agents are citizens of the USSR, East Germany, the other block countries, Communist China, and Cuba – all, incidentally, Communist Party members in good standing."[226] Copeland was differentiating CIA case officers from the agents it used in the field. BIC certainly fit the mold for such activities behind the Iron Curtain.

Freeman's business connections with the Soviet Union had long incurred the ire of some congressional Republicans. In 1973, while Freeman, the then-Agriculture Secretary, was touring the Soviet Union and four eastern European countries, Representative Paul Findlay (R-IL) said, "if Secretary of Agriculture Orville Freeman wants a break from his legislative and administrative chores, he could take a listening trip through America's farmlands rather than visiting the

---

[226] Letter to the editor, "CIA staff cuts," *The Times*, May 5, 1973.

Soviet Union."[227] Haynes resigned as chairman of BIC in 1970 and retired to St. Croix. He remained as chairman until his death of 1976. In St. Croix, Haynes started the Virgin Islands Economic Development Bank.

During the time Obama worked for BIC in 1984, the firm had a full-time analyst tracking events in Nicaragua. The Reagan administration's Iran-contra covert operations would begin in a matter of months from the time Obama went to work for BIC. The firm also appeared to have had established business connections with Nicaragua's Sandinista government in order to protect U.S. banking and other business investments in the country.

A business card for a BIC researcher for Europe and the Middle East [Appendix 9] was obtained from declassified CIA files.

In 1985, BIC named John Haley as chairman and chief executive officer succeeding Hugh Parker, who was Obama's ultimate boss in 1984. Haley had previously served as deputy chairman of Kissinger Associates, Inc. founded by former Secretary of State Henry Kissinger. Although Kissinger endorsed Obama's GOP opponent John McCain in the 2008 election, Obama sought advice from Kissinger during the campaign and later named Kissinger as his special envoy to talk to Russian Prime Minister Vladimir Putin.

BIC's connections to the CIA were revealed by Haynes's son, Elliott Haynes, who co-founded BIC with his father. Elliott Haynes was quoted in a December 27, 1977, *New York Times* article, as saying that BIC "provided cover for four CIA employees in various countries between 1955 and 1960." The same article

---

[227] *Congressional Record,* July 9, 1963.

revealed that the CIA had one agent devoted to liaison with the press who worked out of the CIA's Manhattan office.

A BIC Business Executives Report from 1975 and maintained in CIA files describes the 1975 "constitutional coup" [Appendix 10] against Australian Labor Prime Minister Gough Whitlam but makes only single reference to CIA culpability in the affair.

From CIA files there is a copy of a BIC corporate brochure from 1975 that lists the officers of the corporation: Eldridge Haynes, President; Orville L. Freeman, President; Elliott Haynes, Executive Vice President; William Persen, Senior Vice President; Richard P. Conlon, Vice President; Jose A. Mestre, Vice President; Norman M. Wellen, Vice President and Treasurer; and Robert S. Wright, Vice President. Directors named in the brochure are: Robertson F. Alford, Norfolk, Connecticut; R. Stanton Avery, Chairman, Avery Products Corp., San Marino, CA.; Atherton Bean, Chairman, International Multifoods, Minneapolis; Ambassador Sol M. Linowitz, Senior Partner, Coudert Brothers, Attorneys, Washington; Lord Pilkington, Chairman, Pilkington Bros., St. Helens, UK; and C. William Verity, President, Armco Steel Corp., Middletown, OH.

Linowitz, who was once chairman of Xerox, was the U.S. diplomat who negotiated the return of the Panama Canal to Panama during the Carter administration. Verity was Secretary of Commerce in the Reagan administration between 1987 and 1989. From 1987 to 1984, Verity chaired the U.S.-U.S.S.R. Trade Economic Council made up of U.S. and Soviet business leaders.

Freeman was, in addition to being secretary of agriculture, a former Governor of Minnesota. Although

205

he is not confirmed as the same Richard P. Conlon who served as a BIC Vice President, Richard P. Conlon was a former journalist for the *Duluth Herald & News* and the *Minneapolis Tribune*. Conlon arrived in Washington in 1963 on a congressional fellowship while Freeman was secretary of agriculture. Conlon went on to work as a press assistant to Senator Walter Mondale and he was also close to Vice President Hubert Humphrey.

Conlon also became the head of the powerful Democratic Study Group in the House of Representatives. Conlon opposed U.S. military assistance to the Nicaraguan contras and the naval presence in the Persian Gulf ordered by President Reagan as violations of the War Powers Act. On June 19, 1988, Conlon died in a boating accident in the Chesapeake Bay. He was knocked overboard and his body was not discovered until four days later. Chesapeake boating accidents had already claimed the life of CIA clandestine officer John Paisley in 1978 and would later claim the lives of former CIA director William Colby and Dick Cheney friend and Export-Import Bank chief and Assistant NATO Secretary General Philip Merrill.

Conlon testified before the Commission on the Organization of the Government for the Conduct of Foreign Policy. In the commission's June 1975 report, there was a recommendation to rename the Central Intelligence Agency the Foreign Intelligence Agency, with clear jurisdiction over foreign intelligence activities and with Intelligence Community-wide responsibilities. The commission also recommended that the President's Foreign Intelligence Advisory Board be strengthened and enlarged with participation from outside the Intelligence Community. The chairman of the commission was Robert D. Murphy, honorary chairman of Corning Glass International. Also on the commission were Vice President Nelson Rockefeller and chairman of the Export-Import Bank William J. Casey. Also testifying before the commission were "representatives of the United States Labor Party," the party of anti-Rockefeller activist Lyndon LaRouche.[228] Later, under Casey's directorship, LaRouche provided regular intelligence briefings to the CIA.

The BIC brochure describes the firm's Global Program, which included five elements: the Corporate Headquarters Program operating from New York in conjunction with centers in Washington, DC, Chicago, San Francisco, Geneva, and Tokyo; the European Regional Program operated by Business International, S.A. in Geneva; the Latin American Regional Program operated out of Geneva; the Asia-Pacific Regional Program operated out of Tokyo and Hong Kong; and the East European Service operated out of Geneva and Vienna.

BIC offices were located, in addition to New York, in Chicago (1 IBM Plaza), Geneva (12-14 chemin Rieu), Hong Kong (201 Asian House), Montevideo, Uruguay (Gallerias Diri), San Francisco (600 California Street), Tokyo (Pola Aoyama Building), Vienna (Prinz-Eugenstrasse 4), Washington (1625 Eye Street, NW), Buenos Aires (Cia. De Asesores Latinoamericanos S.A.), Bombay, London, Mexico City, Paris, Rio de Janeiro, and Sydney. There were also BIC "correspondents" in 50 other cities around the world.

BIC also became involved in tracking terrorist and security threats to air passengers, especially after the

---

[228] *Commission on the Organization of the Government for Conduct of Foreign Policy,* June 1975.

1985 hijacking of TWA flight 847 to Beirut while the plane was en route from Athens to Rome. BIC described Athens and Beirut as the world's most dangerous airports, followed by Karachi, New Delhi, Manila, Tehran, Tripoli (Libya), Conakry (Guinea), Lagos, and Yaounde (Cameroon).

Obama's work for a company having ties to the CIA barely registered a blip on the 2008 presidential campaign radar screen. At the very least, Obama helped in providing economic intelligence to the CIA as a contract employee. At most, Obama was, like previous BIC employees who operated abroad for the CIA, a full-fledged non-official cover (NOC) agent. Since President Obama has backpedaled on CIA renditions and torture, as well as warrantless electronic surveillance by U.S. intelligence, he owed the American people a full explanation of the circumstances behind his being hired by BIC, what his job actually entailed, and whether he continued to have a relationship with BIC or any other CIA operation while attending Harvard Law School and thereafter. Obama entered Harvard during another surge in CIA college recruiting efforts, although Georgetown University provided more CIA recruits than any other university in the nation.[229] The CIA was particularly focused on Ivy League universities like Harvard for its recruitment efforts.

When a reporter for the *Washington Star-News* was outed as a covert CIA agent in 1973 after a report was commissioned by then-CIA director William Colby on the CIA's use of journalists abroad as agents, Colby revealed that the CIA would continue to use journalists for "small, limited-circulation specialty publications,

---

[229] Cary Brazeman, "The Company's Campuses," *City Paper* [Washington, DC], April 10, 1987.

such as certain types of trade journals or commercial newsletters." [230] Colby's statement, which appeared in the *New York Times* on December 1, 1973, appears to describe the CIA's later relationship with BIC.

Colby's revelations in 1973 that the CIA would continue to employ journalists working for "small, limited-circulation specialty publications, such as certain types of trade journals or commercial newsletters" coincides with what the son of BIC founder Eldridge Haynes, Elliott Haynes, revealed in an interview reported in the December 27, 1977, *New York Times* the nature of the CIA's longtime relationship with BIC. The younger Haynes stated that BIC "provided cover for four CIA employees in various countries between 1955 and 1960." The same article revealed that the CIA had one agent devoted to liaison with the press who worked out of the CIA's Manhattan office at 1 Dag Hammarskjold Plaza, a stone's throw from the United Nations headquarters.[231]

CIA-archival documents point to a link between Barack Obama's post-Columbia University CIA front employer, BIC, and his mother's two employers, the U.S. Agency for International Development (USAID) and the Asian Development Bank. CIA files also point to the use of field anthropologists abroad, working under foundation cover, by the CIA. Obama's mother, Stanley Ann Dunham/Obama/Soetoro/Sutoro worked as a field anthropologist in Indonesia under the cover of the Ford Foundation.

---

[230] "40 Newsmen Reported Serving As Secret CIA Informants," *New York Times*, December 1, 1973.
[231] John M. Crewdson and Joseph B. Treaster, "CIA Established Many Links to Journalists in US and Abroad, "*New York Times*, December 27, 1977, pp.1, 40-41.

BIC and the Ford Foundation maintained a close relationship through the BIC's running of the Business International Roundtable. Papers maintained at the John F. Kennedy Library provide a linkage between David E. Bell, the Director of the Bureau of the Budget from 1961 to 1962 and administrator of the USAID from 1963 to 1966, and the Ford Foundation, where Bell served as executive vice president from 1966 to 1981, and Business International, where Bell participated in one of their Business International Roundtables on December 17, 1965, at the National Academy of Sciences in Washington. The Joseph P. Kennedy Foundation helped fund the CIA's Airlift Africa project that saw it used to bring Barack H. Obama, Sr. to the University of Hawaii in 1960, as well as over two hundred other African students to other American universities, as part of the CIA's program to counter the Soviet Union's efforts to provide scholarships to African college students in newly-independent African nations at the People's Friendship University in Moscow (later Patrice Lumumba University).

BIC also attempted to infiltrate members of Students for Democratic Society (SDS) at Columbia University in the 1960s by offering them money from Rockefeller family coffers. BIC, which ran Business International Roundtables, was cited in its attempts to infiltrate SDS and other leftist groups.

BIC, which helped propel Obama into international affairs and, later, a profession in politics, was a key to the co-option of leftist groups by Rockefeller and other corporate interests.

In a book titled *The Strawberry Statement: Notes of a College Revolutionary*, James Kunen described Business International, as related by an unnamed 1968 SDS conference attendee, as leading an effort to finance

SDS demonstrations in Chicago in the late 1960s. BIC is described in the book as "the left wing of the ruling class."[232] In fact, journalist Tom Braden, who had once worked for the CIA, admitted on CNN's *Crossfire* and to his co-host Pat Buchanan that for a few years the CIA bankrolled the Communist Party USA newspaper, the *Daily Worker.*[233]

From 1983 to 1984, Obama edited a BIC newsletter titled "Financing Foreign Operations," a topic that his grandmother, who he called "Toot," was more than familiar considering her role in back channeling CIA pay-offs through the BankoH. In addition to writing for "Business International Money Report," Barack Obama specialized in writing about the financial situations in Mexico and Brazil. BIC was allegedly involved in politics in Australia and Fiji in the 1980s, supporting the CIA's initiatives to discredit politicians seen as anti-American, including Australian Labor Party lobbyist David Combe, former Australian Attorney General and High Court judge Lionel Murphy, and Fijian Prime Minister Timoci Bavadra. It has been reported that eleven CIA agents were present in Suva on May 14, 1987, when Fijian Lieutenant Colonel Sitiveni Rabuka ousted Bavadra's government in a coup said to have been the mastermind of retired General Vernon Waters, the old CIA hand who served as Reagan's ambassador to the UN. BIC's headquarters were located at 1 Dag Hammarskjold Plaza, across the street from the UN headquarters. Bavadra accused Walters of helping to engineer the coup in Fiji. "Toot" Dunham had retired from BankoH in 1986, the year before the coup.

---

[232] James Kunen, *The Strawberry Statement: Notes of a College Revolutionary*, Hoboken, New Jersey: Wiley-Blackwell, 1969.
[233] CNN, *Crossfire*, September 15, 1983.

In 1984, Obama left his high-paying job at BIC to literally "parachute" into south Chicago to become a "community organizer." Obama's mission had little to do with organizing a blighted community – after the CIA's OPERATION CHAOS, a domestic spying operation against radical groups was shut down after the Watergate scandal, President Reagan and William Casey restored it under a different name and greatly expanded its operations. In Chicago, the surveillance targets for Obama included the feared El Rukn gang, thought to have links to Muammar Qaddafi's Libyan government, the Black Panthers, and the Nation of Islam.

Obama's membership in a leftist organization at Occidental College in Los Angeles appears to have been a continuation of the infiltration efforts by BIC and its major funder, the CIA. Obama was a key asset to the penetration of radical black organizations in south Chicago in the mid-1980s. Of particular interest to the CIA after Obama's graduation from Columbia were the connections of the El Rukns and Nation of Islam to the Muammar Qaddafi government in Libya, in addition to foreign connections of the Hispanic gang, the Latin Kings, which was also active in Chicago.

After Obama moved to Chicago, BIC was sold in 1986 to The Economist Group in London and merged with the Economist Intelligence Unit. [BIC had maintained "Business International UK Ltd.," which, according to an internal CIA memorandum, subscribed to all the CIA's unclassified publications]. There have been a number of reports that the EIU works as closely with Britain's MI-6 intelligence service as BIC once worked with or for the CIA. One of BIC's directors was the late Lord Pilkington, who was also a director of the Bank of England.

The BIC International Roundtables appear to continue under various academic and foundation auspices, including at Obama's former guest law lecturing employer, the University of Chicago. In addition, the BIC International Roundtables appear to be a continuation of the Roundtables first organized by Africa's greatest colonialist plunderers, Cecil Rhodes. Rhodes's business roundtables of the wealthiest elites eventually morphed into the Council on Foreign Relations (CFR. In fact, Obama, the first African-American president of the United States, is a direct product of BIC and its Roundtables, originally founded by Africa's most infamous looter and pillager of diamonds, gold, and other natural resources and promoter of white minority rule and colonialism, Rhodes.

On June 14, 1976, Senator John Durkin (D-NH) said there was little the Senate could do to reduce the ability of "the Business Roundtable or the Chamber of Commerce . . . to attempt to influence votes, either through sheer force of logic or sheer force." On June 19, 1975, Representative Wright Patman (D-TX) railed on the House floor that "in 1973 and 1974 – when the previous audit bill was up – the Federal Reserve and its Chairman entered into some highly questionable lobbying tactics, ending up with the involvement of the big banks and the big business combines including the fat cat Business Roundtable." Obama's current subservience to Wall Street and the Federal Reserve can be seen through the lens of his employment with BIC, a virtual mouthpiece for what Patman described as the "fat cats."

BIC was also used by the State Department as a diversion for a delegation of General Accounting Office (GAO) representatives who visited Hong Kong in

213

August 1974 looking for information on possibilities for U.S.-Chinese trade after Richard Nixon had opened China up to the United States. A formerly Confidential cable from the U.S. Consulate General in Hong Kong to the State Department, with copies to the U.S. Liaison Office in Peking and U.S. embassy in Tokyo, dated August 21, 1974, bragged about the consulate's success in diverting the GAO's interest from consulate files on "PRC economic affairs (general), foreign trade and trade promotion, (which includes our files on the Canton Trade Fair)" even though the GAO team told the consulate it was "not supposed to do that."[234] The consulate's problem appeared to be that some of the files were classified. In order to stymie the GAO group, the consulate directed them to conversations with "companies, third country representatives (identified as UK, Canadian, Australian, and West German trade officials in Hong Kong), *Far Eastern Economic Review*, and Business International staffs." The GAO delegation was particularly interested in potential oil and mining deals with China.[235]

It is apparent that the consulate and BIC wanted to keep what they knew about Chinese trade under wraps, even from Congress. [Appendix 11]. A few weeks after the GAO team was in Hong Kong, a new head of the U.S. Liaison Office in Peking replaced Ambassador David Bruce. His name was George H. W. Bush.

BIC was commissioned by the State Department and CIA to keep tabs on U.S. firms on the Arab boycott blacklist for investing in or trading with Israel. A

---

[234] Cable from the U.S. Consulate General in Hong Kong, August 21, 1974.
[235] *Ibid.*

214

Congressional Record insertion in 1965 stated, "Business International reported in January 1964 that there were 164 U.S. firms on the Arab blacklist, adding that, "many American businessmen who have wanted to trade or invest in Israel have been deterred by Arab threats."

BIC enjoyed a cozy relationship with USAID in 1982, the year before Barack Obama graduated from Columbia and joined BIC's staff in New York. Obama's mother had been a long time employee of USAID, itself linked closely to the CIA.

On June 8, 1962, in a hearing on "U.S. Policies and Programs in Southeast Asia" held by the Senate Subcommittee on East Asian and Pacific Affairs and chaired by Senator S. I. Hayakawa (R-CA), Elise R. W. DuPont, the Assistant Administrator for Private Enterprise for USAID, testified that her agency was "working with Business International to develop country specific information on laws, regulations, and policies in developing countries that affect investment." DuPont specifically stated that USAID was using the information from BIC to conduct "bureau reconnaissance missions" in Indonesia and Thailand and this included support for "a venture capital firm and a leasing firm in Indonesia." BIC, along with a CIA-connected firm called InterMatrix, also conducted country risk analyses for the CIA.

Obama's first employer acted as a bridge between the U.S. intelligence world, with USAID and other government fronts as cover, and the print media. On May 4, 1967, Acting Secretary of Commerce Alexander B. Trowbridge told the East-West Trade Conference as Bowling Green State University that U.S. trade missions to the Soviet Union and Eastern Europe were facilitated by "TIME, Inc. and Business

215

International." Trowbridge said the use of "trade publications," such as those for whom Obama worked after graduating from Columbia, "stimulated" the exchange of information between East and West.

BIC's relationship with the U.S. government's sensitive trade channels with the East Bloc continued through 1979. A "Cuban Chronology," dated April 1979, and issued by the CIA's National Foreign Assessment Center, states that from November 20 to 25, 1977, BIC sponsored "meetings in Havana of representatives of 50 U.S. firms and their contact points in the Cuban government."[236] A reliable source revealed that Obama's grandfather, Stanley Dunham, had traveled to Cuba in 1960 on CIA business with Obama's mother, Ann Dunham. It has also been strongly rumored by informed sources with connections to the Cuban government that Barack H. Obama, Sr. was not the father of Barack Obama, Jr. but that his actual father was an Afro-Cuban who Ann Dunham met during the 1960 trip with her father.

Allen Dulles ordered destroyed all records and evidence of the CIA's provision of small arms to Castro in his insurrection against Cuban dictator Fulgencio Batista, itself a violation of the Neutrality Act. As a member of the Warren Commission, Dulles also resisted a probe of the activities of one of the arms smugglers involved in arming Castro, an individual who was in Dallas on the day that President John F. Kennedy was assassinated.[237]

A formerly classified CIA "East Europe Branch Notes," report, dated February 4, 1974, [Appendix 12]

---

[236] CIA's National Foreign Assessment Center, "Cuban Chronology," April 1979.
[237] Observations, *Washington Observer*, May 1, 1971 (article maintained in CIA archives).

states "A three-day roundtable conference between Business International and East German officials concerned with the promotion of trade opened in East Berlin on February 4. Orville Freeman, President of Business International, heads the foreign participants, comprising presidents, vice presidents, and board members of important US and West European enterprises. GDR Premier Sindermann told the group further steps toward detente have a favorable effect on the expansion of foreign economic activities. He also said that East Germany plans to expand substantially its economic relations with non-socialist countries." The remainder of the report from East Germany's roundtable with BIC is redacted.[238]

BIC, along with the CIA, participated in private conclaves sponsored by an entity called the "Center for the Study of Democratic Institutions," operating from Post Office Box 4068 in Santa Barbara, California and funded by a non-profit corporation called "The Fund for the Republic," which were held periodically on top of Eucalyptus Hill, overlooking the Pacific Ocean, in Santa Barbara. A fellow of the Center was Edward Engberg, the Managing Editor for Business International who was also a former assistant editor for *Fortune* magazine.[239] Other center fellows and consultants included Associate Justice of the U.S. Supreme Court William O. Douglas; former President of the University of California Clark Kerr; former President of the University of Chicago Robert M. Hutchins (also the President of the center); and Isidor Rabi, Professor of Physics at Columbia University; Stanley Sheinbaum, former consultant to the

---

[238] CIA, "East Europe Branch Notes," February 4, 1974.
[239] Brochure, Center for the Study of Democratic Institutions, CIA archival files.

government of South Vietnam; John R. Seeley, Chairman of the Sociology Department at Brandeis University; and Harvey Wheeler, co-author of the book "Fail Safe."

There is little doubt that BIC was a major covert CIA influence-peddling operation targeting the Third World. The nexus between BIC, Ford Foundation, and USAID is unmistakable. In Indonesia, USAID, for whom Obama's mother worked, was primarily involved in infiltrating the labor unions and student movements to ferret out Communists. Indonesian army officers like Obama's step-father would target Communist leaders for execution. It was in central Java, where Obama's mother worked for USAID in the late 1960s, where Suharto began his anti-Communist massacres in 1965, two years before Obama and his mother arrived in Indonesia. Soon, knife-wielding paramilitaries working for Suharto murdered entire families in east Java, Bali, Aceh, the Celebes, and Borneo. The CIA's chief of clandestine activities in Southeast Asia, including the CIA's support for Suharto's massacre of Communists, was William Colby, who would later insist on keeping intact the agency's relationship with niche journalists working for companies like BIC. In 1983, one of those journalists fitting Colby's bill was Barack Obama, Jr.

In October and November 1981, while Obama was supposedly studying at Columbia University after his unexplained activities in 1980 and 1981 in Indonesia and Pakistan, the CIA held a major seminar titled "Third World Intelligence," according to a formerly Secret CIA document. The seminar attendees included CIA director William Casey, Assistant Marine Corps Commandant General Paul X. Kelley, the Director of the CIA's Office of Near East South Asia [name redacted], a representative of the CIA's Office of Soviet Analysis

218

[name redacted], the chief of operations of the National Security Agency's G Group [name redacted], the Deputy Director of the CIA's Office of Near Eastern and South Asian Analysis [name redacted], the NSA's Signals Intelligence National Intelligence Officer (SINIO) for the Middle East [name redacted], and the CIA National Intelligence Officer [name redacted].

In 1981, as the CIA was making a major push into South Asia, Obama stayed in Karachi, Jacobobad, Lahore (where his mother was working), and Hyderabad.

During the late 1970s, the CIA was actively recruiting on campuses across the United States, including University of California at Berkeley, University of California at Los Angeles, University of California at San Diego, and New York University. Obama entered Occidental College in Los Angeles in 1979, but his activity there is sketchy.

In a September 14, 1978, memorandum from CIA deputy director for administration John F. Blake to senior CIA staff on Freedom of Information and Privacy Act requests, it is stated the second-most prevalent requests to the CIA for information was the "CIA's past and present relationships with academia." Blake wrote "the American Civil Liberties Union and the Center for National Security Studies have encouraged such requests." Interestingly, the fourth most prevalent requests, according to the Blake memo were those dealing with "past programs of the Agency in the field of drug and behavioral control experimentation."

In his book, *Dreams from My Father,* Obama does not even mention BIC as the company he went to work for after graduating from Columbia in 1983. However, BIC, for years, had been a conduit to leaders, fascist, communist, and democratic, around the world.

The main business of BIC appears to be opening up nations, regardless of political leanings, to U.S. business investments. CIA files contain a translated article from the Paris periodical, "Marches Tropicaux et Mediterranean," dated September 26, 1980. The article states that Mozambique's Marxist President, Samora Machel, offered the assurance to the representatives of Business International Corporation, an American company, that 'Mozambique, as a socialist country, is well-organized enough to work with private enterprise, multinational or not, by preserving the principle of mutual advantage.'"[240]

A BIC brochure issued in the mid-1970s is testament to the influence the CIA front company had around the world. It is the same world of extraordinary global access to which Barack Obama was introduced in 1983.

The brochure states: "BIC held more than 50 government roundtables over the past 19 years, including:

Africa H.I.M. Haile Selassie and 87 ministers and officials of 33 countries and multinational organizations (Addis Ababa 1969)

Andean Bloc (2) President Lleras of Colombia; authorities, business and labor leaders of six Andean Bloc countries (1968, 1972)

Argentina (2) President Frondisi and Ongania and their cabinets (1958, 1966)

Australia (2) Prime Ministers Holt and Whitlam and their cabinets (1967, 1973)

---

[240] *Marches Tropicaux et Mediterranean,* September 26, 1980.

Brazil (3) Presidents Kubitschek, Castello Branco, Medici and their cabinets (1956, 1965, 1970)

Canada Prime Minister Pearson and his cabinet (1963)

Colombia President Valencia and his cabinet (1964)

EEC & EFTA (4) Presidents Hallstein, Rey and Mansholt and other members of the EEC Commission; Secretary General Figures and other EFTA officials (1960, 1963, 1968, 1972)

France (2) Prime Minister Pompidou and his cabinet; Prime Minister Chaban-Delmas and his cabinet (1963-70)

Germany (2) Vice Chancellor Erhard and Federal Chancellor Brandt and their cabinets (1963, 1973)

Hungary Prime Minister Jeno Fock and his cabinet (1969)

India Prime Minister Nehru and his cabinet (1961)

Indonesia (2) President Suharto and his cabinet (1968, 1972)

Italy (2) Prime Ministers Zoli and Colombo and their cabinets (1958, 1970)

Japan (3) Prime Ministers Kishi and Sato and their cabinets (1959, 1965, 1971)

LAFTA & CACM (2) Executive Secretary Sola and other members of the LAFTA Secretariat; Secretary General Delgado and other CACM officials (1963, 1969)

Mexico President Lopez Mateos and his cabinet (1962)

Poland Prime Minister Jaroszvicz and members of the Council of Ministers

Romania President Ceausescu and members of the Council of Ministers

Spain (2) Generalissimo Franco and his cabinet (1962, 1967)

Sweden Prime Minister Palme and his cabinet (1971)

USSR (2) Premier Kosygin and his cabinet and more than 250 government officials and Soviet industrial managers (1964, 1971)

United Kingdom (3) Prime Ministers Macmillan, Wilson and Heath and their cabinets (1961, 1966, 1972)

United Nations Secretary-General U Thant; heads of 22 principal UN organizations (1967)

United States (15) Presidents Kennedy, Johnson and Nixon and/or their cabinets year by year

Venezuela President Leoni and his cabinet (1967)

Yugoslavia President Tito and members of the Federal Executive Council (1968)

BIC promoted the future leadership of Spain of then-Prince Juan Carlos. It is noteworthy that First Lady Michelle Obama and the Obamas' daughter were feted at the royal resort in Mallorca of King Juan Carlos. Obama remained in the United States. The following is what Business International's Executive Briefing of October 31, 1975, had to say about Juan Carlos:

"The consensus in Spain is that Prince Juan Carlos is inheriting a good administrative organization and that his appointment as Chief of State will put an end to the political uncertainty which has plagued Spain in recent years. Franco's departure from the political scene will speed up the introduction of democratic reforms and reopen the doors for negotiations with the European Economic Community.

The new king will have 'supreme power of administration,' but he will have less power than Franco had. So to ensure his position, Juan Carlos may hold a referendum to get majority approval of the reforms he intends to introduce. For the present, he may also keep Carlos Arias Navarro as prime minister and name a 'Cabinet of National Union,' incorporating some representatives of opposition groups (excluding the communists), members of the current establishment, and a sprinkling of technocrats. Thus far, everything points in Juan Carlos' favor. Since his designation as successor to Franco a year ago, he has gained in popularity and has the support of the Catholic church and the army, especially the new generation of officers."[241]

As a political risk firm,[242] BIC apparently had good insight into the future plans for Juan Carlos, especially since Franco did not die until a few weeks after the Madrid report was written by the firm's Madrid correspondent. Franco died on November 20, 1975. Juan Carlos acceded to the Spanish throne on November 22, 1975. Juan Carlos had been named the next ruler of Spain in 1969, two years after BIC held a meeting with Franco. The BIC report ignored the fact that the original Spanish Republic, overthrown by Franco with the help of Adolf Hitler and Benito Mussolini, still had support

---

[241] Business International, Executive Briefing, October 31, 1975.
Peter H. Stone, "CIA Agents Never Die . . . High Times In the Political Risk [242] Business," *The Nation*, December 25, 1982.

among many Spaniards, especially in Catalonia and the Basque region. Until 1977, a Spanish Republican government-in-exile existed in Paris and it was recognized by Yugoslavia, the USSR, and Mexico.

Obama's former employer maintained close relations with a number of foreign leaders, including Suharto of Indonesia and Franco and Juan Carlos of Spain. Suharto was closely linked, through Obama's step-father Lolo Soetoro, to young Obama in Jakarta while Juan Carlos continued to be close to the Obama family. None of these relationships are found in Obama's book, *Dreams from My Father*.

Chapter Nine – A Star Is Born

The Rockefeller Foundation and the Ford Foundation and the Mellons and the Carnegies get the laws passed they want so they don't pay taxes. – Alabama Governor George C. Wallace.

Barack Obama, Jr. and his mother entered college during the height of the CIA's campus recruiting efforts. Ann Dunham's recruitment was at the height of the U.S.-Soviet Cold War in the early 1960s. After a brief détente with the USSR in the early to mid-1970s, Obama, Jr. was ripe for recruitment as an agent just as the Cold War heated up again with the Soviet invasion of Afghanistan and other show downs between Washington and Moscow around the Third World. This chapter delves into the aggressive recruiting tactics of the CIA and how the agency became a lucrative option for mother and son.

Barack Obama's employment as an editor for BIC after his graduation from Columbia University in 1983, came at a time when such small business and political risk consulting firms were mushrooming and their ranks growing with retired senior CIA personnel. The expansion of BIC and similar firms in the early 1980s also came at a time when major corporations were phasing out their internal risk departments and relying more on companies like BIC.

However, Obama's contacts with the CIA came earlier than his work for BIC. Obama's attendance at Occidental College in Los Angeles from 1979 to 1981 is significant considering the college's close ties with the CIA. Occidental's President, Richard C. Gilman, who retired in 1988, was a habitué of Los Angeles's version of New York's Council on Foreign Relations, the Los Angeles World Affairs Council (WAC). As a director of the WAC, Gilman rubbed shoulders with fellow WAC directors John McCone, a former CIA director; Simon Ramo, chairman of top CIA contractor TRW, Inc.; and the wealthy oil magnate Armand Hammer, chairman of Occidental Petroleum, himself no stranger to intelligence-oriented intrigue.

Occidental was, for many years, a top target for CIA recruiting efforts. A CIA memorandum, formerly Secret and dated February 8, 1967, details the CIA's "100 Universities Program," which, as stated by the author, "originally conceived [redacted] as a recruitment technique. Its purpose was to make better known on the campuses of America the very existence of the CIA and its mission and role in Government, to illustrate the vast range of vocational opportunities in the Agency."

A formerly SECRET CIA memorandum for the Deputy Director for Administration from the acting Director of Personnel, [Appendix 26] dated February 8, 1979, discusses an active CIA recruitment effort at Occidental College on February 1, 1979. Obama reportedly attended Occidental later in 1979. The memo states, "[redacted] our [redacted] recruiter, reports that he briefed approximately seventy students at Occidental College in Los Angeles on 1 February and was very well received. He added that while they did not interrupt his presentation, about fifteen to twenty members of the Socialist Democratic Alliance demonstrated outside as he spoke and that their chanting of "CIA, go Away" could be heard. Larry also reported that the seventy attending his briefing was the largest number ever to attend a briefing at the school by an employer." A burning question is whether "Larry" ever tried to recruit a young Barack Obama, Jr. at Occidental and whether he was successful at the enthusiastically pro-CIA campus in 1979.

The goal of the CIA's infiltration of leftist movements through Obama's post-Columbia "leftist outreach" employer, BIC was to carry out the tactics championed by former OSS and CIA officer Herbert Marcuse, a German-born Jew and self-proclaimed "Hegelian" and "Marxist." Marcuse's agenda included what Yuri Zhukov wrote in *Pravda* on May 30, 1968: "radical and global negation of all the elements constituting [the industrial socialist society], including Communist Parties." Marcuse, as Zhukov wrote, sought to "cast doubt on the chief role of the working class in the struggle for progress, democracy, and socialism."[243]

President Obama's "liberal" policies succeeded in destroying the progressive left in the United States, including the labor union movement and the social security and welfare programs instituted by the Franklin Roosevelt, Harry Truman, John F. Kennedy, and Lyndon Johnson administrations. Obama was groomed by the CIA to do what no Republican or conservative politician could ever do: destroy the American middle class and the American social safety net – and accomplish these deeds from a contrived "leftist" position. Obama has accomplished his task.

Obama's "radical" campus activities mirror those of University of Paris sixties student radical Daniel Cohn-Bendit, who led "Maoist" and "Trotskyite" student riots while on a stipend from the West German government. Cohn-Bendit's activities on behalf of the CIA and the French extreme right were revealed by French General Confederation of Labor Benoit

---

[243] Yury Zhukov, "Marcuse: False Prophet of Decommunized Marxism," *Pravda*, May 30, 1968.

Franchon on May 27, 1968, while addressing workers at a Renault automobile plant, "Now, the whole gang of them are only concerned to see that it 'boils.' They praise in every manner the enthusiasm of young people, but really are preparing to ensnare and confuse us." [244]

One of the CIA tasks of the French student protesters in Paris in 1968 was the derailing of the Paris peace talks between the United States and North Vietnam. The leftist "fifth columnists" were, thus, responsible for continuing the Indochina war well into the Nixon administration. Just as with his French "radical" predecessors, Obama came into office on a wave of American anti-war feelings and then not only continued the U.S. military presence in Iraq but boosted it in Afghanistan and Yemen.

Obama's membership in a Marxist Club at Occidental, one of the CIA's favorite campuses for recruiting agents, fit a pattern of CIA meddling in student organizations, particularly leftist ones like Students for a Democratic Society and the National Student Association, across the nation. Obama's alma mater, Columbia, has a long association with U.S. intelligence that even predates the CIA. The Russian Institute of Columbia University was the brainchild of Professor Gerold T. Robinson in 1944 while he was on loan from Columbia to the OSS. The institute later trained many Slavic language linguists for the CIA's Radio Free Europe and U.S. Air Force personnel who flew signals intelligence missions against the USSR, Hungary, and Albania. Columbia also excelled in training CIA operatives for Ann Dunham-type "field work," in South Vietnam, Thailand, Bolivia, and

---

[244] Klaus Mehnert, *Moscow and the New Left*, Berkeley: University of California Press, 1975, p. 149.

Guatemala – all targets for CIA anti-communist activities.

In 1967, the year Obama's mother whisked him off to post-coup Indonesia, the CIA was revealed to have had several U.S. college students studying abroad on summer studies programs acting as agents. The Independent Research Foundation, co-founded by "leftist" feminist Gloria Steinem, was revealed to have been a CIA front tasked with attending World Youth Festivals and compiling dossiers on attendees.

Columbia's School of International Affairs (SIA) conducted detailed studies of socialist countries, including the USSR, that were extremely similar to those produced by BIA. Columbia also maintained close links with the Pentagon and the National Security Agency through its support for the Institute for Defense Analysis (IDA).

Obama's "faux" journalism work for BIC was authorized by both the CIA and the company's management. Before the post-Watergate restrictions on CIA activities, CIA agents were able to recruit journalists, usually "stringers" without Langley's approval. That changed after the Frank Church and Otis Pike congressional hearings. Somewhere in the bowels of Langley may be CIA-BIC agreements on the use of BIC personnel as CIA assets or agents. And those files may contain the name or names "Barry Obama," "Barry Soetoro," "Barack Obama," or "Barack Sutoro." Obama's other alma mater, Harvard, also maintained close ties with the CIA.

The FBI also had a penchant for hiring informers in liberal and black communities like south Chicago. Informers were screened in files known as PSIs and PRIs: potential security informant and potential racial informant and were paid a stipend. After being approved, PSIs and PRIs became "reliable informants" and were assigned a cover name, an informant number, and a regular salary. A scan of the FBI's files for anyone of Obama's appellations during his time in south Chicago may reveal one or more of such informant files.

The Rockefeller family was fond of funding a number of left-wing organizations. Groups devoted to the anti-nuclear movement were linked to the Rockefeller Family Fund-supported Corporate Data Exchange. Inc. (CDE), a BIC-like "research organization" albeit a tax-exempt one, founded in 1975 to "investigate economic decentralization and corporate control," according to an April 21, 1983, article in the *Pittsburgh Tribune-Review* titled "Foundations Bankrolling Anti-Nuclear Causes." Three of the CDE's founders were associated with intelligence-gathering for the North American Congress on Latin America (NACLA), a progressive organization that is ostensibly opposed to U.S. interventionism in Latin America.

The CIA archives contain an undated paper titled "The Agency and the Young Employee," that describes the CIA's outreach to young people: "The young Agency employee or potential employee shares common experiences with his counterparts in the sub-culture and, although he may not have been in most instances an active participant in this counter-culture, he has been in close touch with it and its views." The tract continues, "menial work – until he 'knows the business' – is anathema and is met with derision. He similarly views long periods of training, job orientation, and job rotation as wasteful of his time . . . The CIA is just beginning to see the influx of the new generation . . . They can be a great asset to the present and future of CIA."[245]

---

[245] CIA, "The Agency and the Young Employee," undated.

Indeed, with Barack Hussein Obama, Jr., he was a great asset and continues to be one for the CIA.

One person who may have been very instrumental in cleaning up Indonesian state files and archives of any information that could be damaging to Obama's family, including Lolo Soetoro, is American Samoa delegate to the House of Representatives Eni Faleomavaega. During the first week of July 2007, while Obama's candidacy for president had, on the surface, as much chance as that of Dennis Kucinich or Chris Dodd, Faleomavaega visited Jakarta as part of a congressional delegation for talks with Indonesian leaders, including President Susilo Bambang Yudhoyono.

Faleomavaega was looking for concessions for the plight of his fellow Pacific islanders, the people of Indonesian-occupied West Papua. However, Faleomavaega also wanted access to Indonesia's files on the Obama and Soetoro families – in what amounted to a "clean-up" operation for his friend Obama. The official reason given was the files were needed for the U.S. National Archives. Yet, in July 2007, it was Hillary Clinton who was considered the "chosen one" for the Democrats. Certainly, no one paid a visit to Zagreb, Croatia looking for documents for the U.S. National Archives in the event Kucinich, of Croatian ancestry, was elected president. However, in July 2007, there appeared to be a foregone conclusion that Obama would become the next President of the United States and that Indonesian files had to be picked clean. For Faleomavaega, he got nothing for his West Papuans or his clean-up operation on behalf of the CIA and, with the Republican take-over of the House, he lost his vote in committee, as well.

Obama's mother's employer and the CIA

Ann Soetoro's employer in Indonesia, the Ford Foundation, had a long-standing relationship with the CIA. It should be recalled that while ostensibly working on micro-financing and rural development projects in Indonesia, Dunham's grant paymaster was Peter Geithner, the father of Obama's Treasury Secretary.

The rural development project funded by the Ford Foundation had long been a cover for U.S. intelligence activities in Indonesia. An Indonesian Permanent Mission to the UN bulletin dated November 19, 1959, states that a Ford Foundation grant funded the Village Community Development Bureau's work with "development projects in line with village custom and tradition."

The Ford Foundation helped establish two Cold War institutes at Columbia University and Harvard, two universities where Obama graduated. In the post-World War II years, Ford Foundation money helped create the Russian Institute at Columbia and the Russian Research Center at Harvard to promote the study of Soviet and Russian history and politics for a cadre of CIA Kremlinologists. Recall that Dunham and Obama, Sr. met at a Russian language class at the University of Hawaii in 1960.

The Ford and Rockefeller Foundations continued to fund Columbia's Soviet studies programs through the early 1980s, while Obama was allegedly a student enrolled in a Soviet studies program taught by Zbigniew Brzezinski, the former National Security Adviser under President Carter.

The Ford Foundation also funded CIA-directed propaganda campaigns around the world. In 1967, Shepherd Stone, born Shepherd Arthur Cohen, a former

New York Times reporter and director of international affairs for the Ford Foundation, became president of the International Association of Cultural Freedom (IACF), which saw its name change from the Congress of Cultural Freedom after its direct funding from the CIA ceased.

Much like Barack Obama's post-Columbia employer, BIC, the Ford Foundation, through groups like the IACF, curried links with some of Europe's main leftist political parties, including the British Labor Party, the West German Social Democrats, and the French Socialists.

However, not every world leader was lulled into a false sense of security by the Ford Foundation. A formerly SECRET CIA "Current Intelligence Weekly Summary," dated April 20, 1962, reports that Burmese strongman Ne Win ordered "the Asia Foundation and Ford Foundation to wind up their activities" in Burma. The CIA report attacks Ne Win for his decision to toss out both CIA-linked organizations, stating, "Ne Win is a narrow nationalist with a suspicious conspiratorial outlook, a short temper, and a tendency toward snap decisions."[246]

Columnist Murray Kempton, writing in the October 3, 1967, *New York Post* lambasted Stone, the IACF, and the Ford Foundation for their close links to the CIA. Kempton wrote, "One standard apology for the CIA used to be that its subsidies were a considerable force for cultural progress, and that it could not really be distinguished from, say, the Ford Foundation. This is a sounder comparison than one would have thought possible before reading the annual report of the Ford Foundation, after which it is difficult with confidence to

---

[246] CIA, "Current Intelligence Weekly Summary," April 20, 1962.

distinguish the international activities of the Ford Foundation from those of the CIA."[247]

Kempton cited the Ford Foundation's $8 million grant to MIT's CENIS, adding that the center was established with CIA funds.[248] In 1966, one of the architects of the Cold War policies of Presidents Kennedy and Johnson, McGeorge Bundy, took over as the President of the Ford Foundation. Bundy also worked with the Council on Foreign Relations and CIA officers Allen Dulles and Richard Bissell to create a carve-out in the post-World War II Marshall Plan that covertly steered aid money to anti-Communist groups in Italy and France. After President Kennedy's assassination in 1963, Bundy began directing U.S. covert operations as chairman of the super-secret "303 Committee" in the Johnson White House.

Bundy signed a Secret memo on February 27, 1961, in which the Sprague Committee report on U.S. Information Activities Abroad was circulated to senior officials. The Sprague Committee, chaired by Mansfield D. Sprague of CIA-rife New Canaan, Connecticut, was commissioned by President Eisenhower and included Allen Dulles, CIA director, and the committee's executive director, Waldemar A. Nielsen, who was "loaned" by the Ford Foundation. The committee recommended integrating "psychological factors" into the United States "informational system."

The CIA's funding of foundations such as Ford and Rockefeller was so prevalent during the 1960s, New York Congressman William Fitts Ryan of New York introduced legislation in 1967 that would have

---

[247] Murray Kempton, *New York Post*, Oct. 3, 1967.
[248] *Ibid.*

prohibited the CIA from "granting, contributing, lending, or otherwise paying, directly or indirectly, any of its funds to any foundation or philanthropic organization, labor organization, publishing organization, radio or broadcasting organization, or educational institution – including organization composed of students or faculty members – incorporated in the United States."

In a case eerily reminiscent of the post-gall bladder surgery death of Pennsylvania Democratic Representative John Murtha in February 2010, in September 1972, Ryan died suddenly following surgery on an ulcer and after he cast a vote against new Vietnam War appropriations.

Ryan was particularly incensed over the CIA's use of the National Student Association (NSA) and its global counterpart, the International Student Conference (ISC), to recruit agents. In fact, the Airlift Africa project that brought Obama, Sr. to the University of Hawaii appears to have been part of a larger CIA program to use the NSA and ISC to recruit young college students into its ranks. The CIA funded technical assistance, education, and student exchange programs, via the NSA and ISC, with Third World nations like Kenya and Indonesia, the home countries of President Obama's father and step-father, respectively.

Although Airlift Africa received a $100,000 grant from the Joseph P. Kennedy Foundation to pay for African students personally selected by the CIA's Kenyan nationalist asset, Tom Mboya, a mentor of Barack Obama, Sr., to travel to the United States to study at various colleges (Obama, Sr. was the first African student to attend the University of Hawaii), the CIA used a series of front foundations to launder money for such projects. The chief CIA fund used for such purposes in the early 1960s was the New York-based J. M. Kaplan Fund. J.M. Kaplan was the president of the Welch's Grape Juice company. The CIA used a network of other funds to pass money through the Kaplan Fund. These funds included the Borden Trust of Philadelphia, the Price Fund of New York, the Edsel Fund of San Francisco, the Beacon Fund of Boston, and the Kentfield Fund of Dallas.

The CIA funneled money through scores of organizations from a number of non-profit foundations. The CIA front organizations established for Africa included the African-American Institute (AAI) – which partly funded Barack Obama, Sr.'s scholarship at the University of Hawaii, American Society of African Culture (AMSAC), African American Labor Center, East African Institute of Social and Cultural Affairs, East African Publishing House, Jomo Kenyatta Educational Institute, Kenneth Kaunda Foundation, and Milton Obote Foundation.[249]

The African-American Institute opened it doors at 345 E, 46th Street in New York with Waldemar Nielsen, a veteran of the Ford Foundation and Council on Foreign Relations, at its helm.

Other groups funded by the CIA included the American Council for International Commission of Jurists, American Friends of the Middle East (disestablished after the Israel Lobby in the United States complained it tilted too favorably toward the Arabs), Association of Hungarian Students in North America, Committee for Self-Determination, Committee on International Relations, Fund for International Social and Economic Education, Independent Research Service, Institute of International Labor Research,

---

[249] Africa Research Group, *op. cit.*

International Development Foundation, International Marketing Institute, Paderewski Foundation, Pan American Foundation, United States Youth Council, and the Philadelphia Education Fund for the Nordic Arts.[250]

In addition to the previously cited foundations, other financial conduits for CIA funding included: the Andrew Hamilton Fund; Benjamin Rosenthal Foundation; Broad-High Foundation; Catherwood Foundation; Chesapeake Foundation; David, Joseph, and Winfield Baird Foundation, Dodge Foundation; Florence Foundation; Gothan Fund; Heights Fund; Independence Foundation; J. Frederick Brown Foundation; Jones-O'Donnell Foundation; Littauer Foundation; Marshall Foundation; McGregor Fund; Michigan Fund; Monroe Fund; Norman Fund; Pappas Charitable Trust; Price Fund; Robert E. Smith Fund; San Miguel Fund; Sydney and Esther Rabb Charitable Foundation; Tower Fund; Vernon Fund; Warden Trust; and Williford-Telford Fund.[251] Another CIA pass-through was the Appalachian Fund, which in 1964 provided $20,000 to the Rabb Foundation that, in turn, passed the money to the American Society of African Culture.[252]

The Warden Trust of Cleveland provided a grant for the American Newspapers Guild to fund an African Journalism Institute. The CIA was suspected as the original financial source for the grant. The Andrew Hamilton Fund was also believed to be funneling CIA

---

[250] James Hepburn, Farewell America, Vaduz, Liechtenstein: Frontiers Publishing Company, 1968, p. 314.
[251] Ibid., p. 315.
[252] Congressional Record, March 9, 1967.

money through the Guild for special journalism projects.[253]

The Price Fund was involved in funneling CIA funds to ostensibly leftist organizations in Africa. The Price Fund and the International Development Foundation to anti-apartheid movements in Africa. The Africa Bureau, a London-based anti-apartheid group, received CIA funding. The African-American Institute funneled CIA money to the anti-apartheid United States-South Africa Leadership Exchange Program (USSALEP). USSALEP would later receive funding directly from USAID and the National Endowment for Democracy (NED) and, in turn, would provide millions of dollars in support to the African National Congress (ANC) of South Africa and the largely Zulu Inkatha Freedom Party.[254]

The Fairfield Foundation funneled CIA money to the Congress for Cultural Freedom (CCF), which supported a variety of magazines around the world, including the British monthly *Encounter*. After CCF was exposed in 1967 as receiving money from the CIA, it changed its name to the International Association for Cultural Freedom and named as its director Shepard Stone, the international affairs director for the Ford Foundation. Another mysterious CIA foundation was the San Jacinto Foundation, located in the offices of F. G. O'Connor in the San Jacinto Building in Houston. When a *Ramparts* reporter asked Mr. O'Connor about the foundation, he replied, "It is a private, closed

---

[253] Orr Kelly, "Guild Chief 'Vaguely' Aware CIA Might be Source of Aid," *Washington Star*, February 20, 1967.

[254] Richard Cummings, "A Diamond is Forever: Mandela Triumphs, Buthelezi and deKlerk Survive, and ANC on the U.S. Payroll," *International Journal of Intelligence and Counterintelligence*, Summer, 1995.

foundation, never had any publicity and doesn't want any."[255]

In 1958, a CIA-linked group called the Western Regional Assembly met at Lake Arrowhead, California in a seminar titled "The United States and Africa." Among those in attendance was Walter P. Coombs, the executive director of the Los Angeles World Affairs Council; Arthur N. Young, Trustee of Occidental College; and Frank LaMacchia, identified as "economic officer, American Consulate General, Nairobi, Kenya."[256] However, "Who's Who in the CIA" identified LaMacchia as a CIA officer assigned to Nairobi, as well as Salisbury, Southern Rhodesia, Seoul, and Baghdad.

The Lake Arrowhead conclave was told that for Africa's emerging nations, "furtherance of education on the college level is important, and the number of scholarships for Africans to American institutions of higher learning should be increased." In 1959, the CIA, likely though LaMacchia in Nairobi, and Mboya, kicked off Airlift Africa that saw 230 African students airlifted to the United States, including Barack Obama, Sr., via funding from the Kennedy Foundation and the African-American Students Foundation.

The Lake Arrowhead attendees also heard the Assistant Secretary of State for African Affairs, Joseph C. Satterthwaite, warn, "persistent and ingenious Communists, skilled in subversive and revolutionary tactics, must be reckoned with" in Africa. The Airlift

---

[255] *Ibid.*
"The United States and Africa, Western Regional Assembly, Lake Arrowhead, California.

Africa project was a form of reckoning with the pro-Communists in Africa.

The CIA's program of aiding private foundations in educating America's brand of next generation African leaders was explained in an academic article by Richard M. Hunt found in the CIA's archives. Hunt wrote, ". . . the new pattern of CIA funding emphasized assistance to private American institutions which were already supporting foreign students, journalists, lawyers, and trade unionists. Respectable groups like the Asian Foundation, African-American Institute, American Friends of the Middle East, and the American Newspaper Guild were typical beneficiaries. Once again, it was probably true that the decision to channel CIA money in this way developed as a response to prior Soviet initiatives. In many countries of Africa, for instance, scholarships for study in the Soviet Union had been offered to politically susceptible Africans. Patrice Lumumba 'Friendship' University in Moscow had been designed for just the purpose of educating incipient foreign leaders in Communist doctrines. Accordingly, practically all of these new types of CIA-aided organizations established academic scholarships and professional training programs for foreign leaders whose political loyalties had not been compromised by Communist blandishments. The reason why private American foundations were selected for this task could probably be traced back to the desire of CIA officials to protect individual foreign recipients. Most grantees came from the non-aligned nations where the fears of neo-colonialism prohibited the direct acceptance of United States government funds."[257]

---

[257] Richard M. Hunt, "The CIA Exposures: End of an Affair," *The Virginia Quarterly Review,* undated article in CIA archives.

One of the Kenyan politicians who LaMacchia and Mboya kept a close eye on was Kenyan left-wing nationalist leader Oginga Odinga, whose son Raila Odinga became Kenya's Prime Minister and who is a distant cousin of President Obama. Oginga Odinga, a Luo like Mboya and Obama, Sr., had cultivated close relations with Soviet bloc countries and he was dispatching Kenyan students to the East bloc for college educations.

In his request to extend his alien student visa, Barack Obama, Sr. stated he was, in addition to working for Dole Corporation in Honolulu, on a scholarship from the African American Institute, created in 1954 by the CIA. According to a document in the CIA files, "In 1954, it was the CIA that put the African American Institute on a solid financial footing, in close cooperation with the American Metal Climax Corporation, the African mining concern whose chairman became AAI's big angel."[258] The company changed its name to AMAX, Inc., merged with Cyprus Minerals Company to become Cyprus Amax Minerals Company, became a subsidiary of Phelps Dodge as Climax Molybdenum and eventually became a subsidiary of Freeport McMoran.

AAI, like BIC, presented a "liberal" side of the CIA to impressionable African leaders. And like BIC, AAI's headquarters across the street from UN headquarters in New York. AAI also worked closely with Ann Dunham's employers, USAID and the World Bank. AAI influenced, through published articles, the perception of people in the United States and abroad on issues pertaining to Africa. Publications that served as echo chambers for the CIA included *Africa Report,*

---

[258] Africa Research Group. *op. cit.*

Africa Forum, and articles distributed by the Foreign News Service, Inc.[259]

On August 17, 1962, Obama, Sr. listed the Koinonia Foundation, a Christian missionary organization established in the 1950s, as his mailing address in the United States. Where the Immigration and Naturalization Service (INS) requested Obama, Sr.'s mailing address, with number and street. Obama listed it as Post Office Box 5744, Pikesville, Baltimore 8, Maryland, clearly not a street address.

Although Koinonia, which is a Greek word meaning sacred fellowship and communion, started out as a Christian missionary fellowship, it later claimed it was no longer exclusively Christian. In the 1960s, Koinonia became a learning center for such non-Christian practices as yoga, art dancing, and even more curiously, psychology. Koinonia's Grants Review Committee was later listed at a street address in Westminster, Maryland, not far from Baltimore, but its national headquarters moved to Grand Rapids, Michigan, after an interlude in Alexandria. Virginia.

Koinonia has claimed to be particularly active in East Africa, including Rwanda; China, and Haiti. The foundation has also been involved in projects in Ethiopia, Nicaragua, and the Democratic Republic of Congo.

In 1958, Koinonia's executive director, Murray Glenn Harding, attended a high-level national security seminar, the proceedings of which are in the CIA's archives. The seminar, titled "Foreign Aspects of U.S. National Security," was sponsored by the White House. The seminar, held on February 25, 1958, provided a

---

[259] Hepburn, *op. cit.*, p. 315.

number of top-shelf speakers. Harding heard the speakers on the needed directions for U.S. national security policy. Speakers included President Dwight Eisenhower, former President Harry S Truman, Secretary of State John Foster Dulles, Eisenhower Democratic opponent in 1952 and 1956 Adlai Stevenson, former Secretary of State Dean Acheson, Vice President Richard Nixon, Undersecretary of State Douglas Dillon, Secretary of Defense Neil H. McElroy, CIA director Allen Dulles, Senate Majority Leader Lyndon B. Johnson (the major promoter of Hawaii's East-West Center), Chie Justice Earl Warren, 1948 Republican presidential candidate Thomas E. Dewey, House Speaker Sam Rayburn, House Minority Leader Joseph Martin, Senate Minority Whip Everett Dirksen, Minnesota Governor Orville Freeman (who would later head Business International Corporation), Senator Prescott Bush, MIT's CENIS's Walt W. Rostow, President of American Coldset Corporation Maurice Tempelsman, rocket scientist Werner von Braun, and Representatives George McGovern and Melvin Laird.

Eisenhower, referring to newly-independent and soon-to-be-independent countries, said the U.S. would help countries resist "Russian loans and credits" and ultimate Soviet economic and political control. It certainly appears that Barack Obama Sr.'s benefactor in Baltimore would not have his prized Kenyan student and intelligence asset picking pineapples in Hawaii for Dole at $1.33 an hour.

Koinonia's executive secretary for a period of time was Ann Pherson, whose husband, John R. Pherson, worked for the CIA in, among other locations, Cyprus, from 1968 to 1971.[260]

---

[260] *Washington Post*, "Ann Pherson dies at 80," June 25, 1999.

The Koinonia Community in Nairobi was shaken by sexual abuse allegations swirling around Father Renato Kizito, an Italian priest who previously served in Zambia until the end of the 1980s. In Kenya, the Koinonia Community is described as a Christian relief project helping street children, mostly young boys. Kizito was accused of sexual assault and sodomy of young boys at Koinonia.[261]

One of the agencies that worked closely with the CIA to fund anti-communist student activities abroad was USAID, one of Ann Dunham's employers in Indonesia. The CIA student operations were conducted through Langley's Covert Action Division Number Five, nested within the Plans Division. One of the chief missions of the CIA's foreign students was to infiltrate leftist student movements to either disrupt or recruit.

The Richard Parsons Project

According to top Democratic Party sources, some with long years of political experience at the national level and in the highest levels of government, there was one adviser to President Obama who had his ear even more than then-chief of staff Rahm Emanuel. That man was Richard Parsons, a graduate of the University of Hawaii and the chairman of Citigroup. Until 2007, Parsons also served as chief executive officer of media giant Time Warner.

Democratic Party sources revealed that Parsons knew Obama's mother, Ann Dunham, at the East-West Center at the University of Hawaii, the CIA front

---

[261] *Spiegel Online*, "Church shaken by sexual abuse allegations in Africa," August 11, 2011.

operation to influence and train a new generation of political leaders in the Asia-Pacific region. Parsons graduated from the University of Hawaii in 1968, one year after Ann Soetoro's graduation. Parsons also met his wife, Laura Ann Bush, at the university and they married in 1968.

The Rockefellers had a particular interest in Indonesia. Michael Rockefeller, the youngest son of Nelson Rockefeller, was reportedly on more than a mere nature expedition when he disappeared without a trace in Netherlands New Guinea in 1961. The Kennedy administration had secretly been negotiating the New York Agreement between the Netherlands and Indonesia that would transfer sovereignty of the mineral-rich colony from the Dutch to the Indonesians in 1962.

A deal was also worked out between National Security Adviser McGeorge Bundy and Freeport Sulphur (later Freeport McMoran) to open up West New Guinea to Freeport gold mining operations. After the CIA ousted Sukarno in 1965, the new Suharto government quickly signed a mineral rights deal with Freeport for mining in West New Guinea. Later, Rockefeller man Henry Kissinger would join the board of Freeport McMoran. Kissinger was the architect of the bloody Indonesian invasion and occupation of newly-independent Portuguese Timor (now East Timor) in 1975. It also turned out that Obama's step-father, Soetoro, was dispatched to West New Guinea to put down natives who believed their land was stolen from them by Indonesia after they were to be given the right of self-determination.

Parsons has had a long relationship with the Rockefeller family. Parson's father was reportedly a gardener for the Kykuit Rockefeller Estate in Westchester County, New York. The young Parson's career was helped along with the assistance of then-New York Governor Nelson Rockefeller. After earning his law degree at Union University's Albany Law School, he became a legal counsel to Rockefeller in Albany. Following that stint, Parsons ended up as a managing partner of the Manhattan law firm, Patterson, Belknap, Webb & Tyler. There, Parsons worked with Rudolph Giuliani. Parsons looked after the legal affairs of Nelson Rockefeller's widow, Margaretta "Happy" Rockefeller, after the former Vice President died at a Manhattan townhouse he owned after suffering a sudden heart attack in 1979 during what many believe was an extramarital tryst with an aide, Megan Marshack.

GOP insiders revealed that it was Parsons and Greg Craig, who was President Obama's counsel and represented John W. Hinckley, Jr. after his attempted assassination of President Reagan in 1981, who helped engineer Nelson Rockefeller into the vice presidency after Gerald Ford became President after Richard Nixon's resignation in 1974. Rockefeller was always miffed at Nixon for not being chosen as his running mate in 1968. But Nixon, who despised Rockefeller but was forced to take on Rockefeller foreign policy adviser Kissinger as his national security adviser, figured with Rockefeller as his Vice President, Nixon would be fair game for just about anything. Instead, Nixon chose little-known Maryland Governor Spiro Agnew as his running mate. After Agnew resigned amid a bribery scandal in 1973, Gerald Ford became Vice President. When Nixon resigned in 1974 and Ford assumed the presidency, Rockefeller was chosen as the Vice President.

Nelson Rockefeller had always wanted to be president. In 1975, he almost had his chance when two women, Lynette "Squeaky" Fromme and Sarah Jane

Moore came dangerously close to assassinating President Ford. Rockefeller wanted to continue on the Ford ticket in 1976 but there was another wealthy GOP family with presidential ambitions that had other ideas. George H. W. Bush conspired to have Rockefeller dumped from the GOP ticket, however, he did not get his wishes to replace Rockefeller as Ford's running mate. That slot went to Kansas Senator Bob Dole. As 1980 approached, it was Rockefeller's last chance at the presidency. Rockefeller was 70, normally considered too old for a presidential run. However, Ronald Reagan was only a year younger, 69. Rockefeller also entertained the notion of running with Reagan in order to protect the interests of the group Reagan constantly attacked: the New York-based Trilateral Commission, a Rockefeller family creation.

But once again, the other powerful GOP family had different ideas. It would be George H. W. Bush who would run with Reagan with a deal to have Ford on the ticket with Reagan abandoned at the eleventh hour at the 1980 GOP convention. There is a belief that Nelson Rockefeller's sudden heart attack may have been spurred on with a bit of assistance in the form of a drug he was given. However, no one will ever know for certain. There was no autopsy on Rockefeller's body and he was cremated. Nevertheless, as he entertained a return to the national stage in 1978 and 1979, Rockefeller aides Parsons and Craig were busy pushing his interests.

Parsons became chairman of Dime Savings Bank on the recommendation of Harry W. Albright, Jr., a former aide to Rockefeller and New York state banking regulator. In 1989, Parsons supported Republican New York mayoral candidate Rudolph Giuliani over

Democratic candidate David Dinkins, who was elected to become New York's first African-American mayor.

In 1991, Nelson Rockefeller's brother, Laurance Rockefeller, recommended that Parsons be appointed to the board of Time Warner. In 2001, Parsons became chief executive officer of AOL Time Warner, after the merger with the Internet firm.

Parsons served as co-chair of President George W. Bush's commission on Social Security reform. He also works closely with David Rockefeller and New York Mayor Michael Bloomberg. Parsons also served on an economic advisory team under President Obama.

Part of the reason why Obama was not critically treated by the media was the fact that Parsons exercised control over a vast array of the corporate media, including CNN, *Time* magazine, *Money, People*, and *Fortune* magazines, and, at the time, AOL.

But more importantly, Parsons, according to Democratic Party sources, has ensured that Obama maintained his policy of looking forward and not to the past. Parsons, who is a friend of former Bush policy adviser Karl Rove, has convinced Obama that there should be no criminal investigations by the Justice Department of Rove or other top Bush administration officials from everything from political prosecutions of former Alabama Democratic Governor Don Siegelman, whose bribery conviction appeal was rejected by the Supreme Court in June 2012, and Rove's involvement in election fraud to the CIA's rendition and torture programs. Parsons was quickly named as a member of the economic advisory team that met with President-elect Obama just two days after the 2008 election.

GOP sources claimed that Parsons represented the interests of the Rockefeller family and the Council on Foreign Relations in his numerous meetings with Obama, described as one-way communications that ensured that Obama would carry out the wishes of the Rockefellers and their business friends. One of those demands may have played out in Alabama, where Parsons and fellow African-American, Democratic Alabama Representative Artur Davis, who, in May 2012 switched parties from Democratic to Republican, reportedly prevailed upon Obama and his Attorney General, Eric Holder, to appoint Montgomery attorney George Beck to replace U.S. Attorney Leura Canary as U.S. Attorney for the Middle District of Alabama.

Alabama was also a major center for covert CIA operations during the Iran-contra affair and Republicans, as well as those special interests associated with Obama, felt it best to leave certain closets closed. Canary, as part of the Rove operation, targeted Siegelman in a purely political prosecution. Beck, who was associated, according to informed Alabama political sources, with CIA-tainted Alabama Republican Governor Bob Riley, would continue the prosecution of Siegelman and ensure that there would be no federal criminal investigation of Rove's past illegal political activities in the state's elections and other "irregularities." In addition, Beck was also the attorney for Nick Bailey, one of the chief witnesses against Siegelman. Beck permitted federal investigators to question Bailey some 70 times and he raised no objections to the questioning being conducted in a purely civilian matter at Maxwell Air Force Base, a military compound outside of Montgomery.

The Rockefellers were at the forefront of Hawaii's booming real estate development in the 1960s. The Rockefellers also had controlling interest in Hawaii's major bank, the Bank of Hawaii, or "Bank OH" as it was called by the local Hawaiians. The bank held millions of dollars in escrowed building and construction accounts, payable to builders after the completion of hotel and other projects. The "grand dame" of "Bank OH" was Madelyn Dunham, Obama's grandmother. Madelyn Dunham was also "Bank OH's" vice president in charge of the escrow accounts. Obama's mother,

The micro-loan banking project of Ann Dunham, which provided small loans to Third World farmers and artisans, had another, more secretive future purpose. The micro-loan system, spurred on by the Rockefellers and their Wall Street pals, would lay the groundwork for the future transfer of millions of jobs from American workers to cheap labor markets in the Third World.

"Svengali" has evolved from George du Maurier's fictional character to mean someone who is a highly influential adviser to a political leader but accountable to no one. Richard Parsons channeled the wishes of the Rockefellers and other Wall Street barons to Obama. With Obama listening more to Wall Street – through Parsons – than Main Street, he and his party lost the support of many traditional Democratic supporters, including the labor unions.

To provide additional context to the idea that Obama was controlled by more powerful and clandestine special interests, an informed source in Washington, DC pointed out that Greg Craig would have been involved in such a high-level matter as the Presidential intrigue wrapped around the Watergate scandal in 1974. Craig graduated from Yale in 1972. Joining the powerful Washington law firm of Williams and Connolly in 1972, Craig was part of a team with a senior partner, perhaps even his mentor, the CIA-connected Edward Bennett Williams. Two-year associates usually don't operate solo at such a level.

250

251

252

Chapter Ten – Stanley Ann Dunham and the Misery Industrial Complex

On CIA meddling in U.S. campus activities: *It is one of the saddest times, in reference to public policy, our Government has had.* – Vice President Hubert H. Humphrey.

The world of non-governmental organizations (NGOs) and U.S. government-run foreign assistance programs in which President Obama was raised has long been dominated by the CIA. Agencies like USAID and contractors and organizations that feed off of it represent what can best be described as the "misery industrial complex." It is against this backdrop of U.S. intelligence and foreign aid programs that Obama's continuation of Bush-era covert and overt intelligence operations abroad must be seen. Obama's mother, father, and step-father directly benefited from U.S. government assistance programs in countries where the CIA backed despotic regimes, lavishing them with hundreds of millions of dollars of assistance. This chapter explains President Obama's current foreign policy and his love affair with intelligence and the CIA. He and his family are products of the "misery industrial complex" through which the CIA maintains a tight grip on all facets of the U.S. foreign policy apparatus.

Obama's mother, Ann Dunham, worked on micro-financing projects for USAID and the Ford Foundation, which helped prop up dictatorships in Indonesia and Pakistan. After Suharto seized power in 1965, USAID returned to Indonesia, with Ann Soetoro as one of its chief employees, to help Suharto create the

253

New Order (Orde Baru) that would usher in decades of fascist and kleptocratic rule. Suharto established the Bureau of Logistics (BULOG) that steered USAID-provided rice and other food staples to Suharto's business cronies. In fact, U.S. the Food for Peace program saw money gained by foreign governments from the sale of commodities like rice, beans, and wheat deposited in "counterpart funds" that were later used to purchase weapons. The misuse of Food for Peace was not only endemic in Indonesia but also South Vietnam, South Korea, Cambodia, Turkey, Greece, Spain, and Taiwan.[262]

Suharto also relied on a group of U.S. economists, including Obama's mother, to re-engineer Indonesia's socialist economy. The group was called the "Berkeley mafia" and it ensured that Indonesia was compliant with dictates of the World Bank, International Monetary Fund, and large Western commercial banks. It is a family history that Obama refuses to comment on and one that is certainly nothing to be proud of.

While USAID was moving into Indonesia in 1965, USAID contractors flying for the CIA airline, Air America, were dropping off weapons and picking up drugs in Laos and dropping off the contraband in Thailand and South Vietnam.

One of the covert CIA operations that Obama continued was the use of USAID as a front for destabilizing foreign governments.

One USAID contractor, Development Alternatives, Inc. (DAI) of Bethesda, Maryland, was caught red-handed providing assistance to opposition forces in Cuba and Venezuela. DAI contractor Alan

---

[262] "Food for War," *Des Moines Register*, July 29, 1972.

Gross was arrested in Cuba in December 2009. Gross claimed to be installing Internet and other communications networks for the Jewish community in Cuba, however, leading members of that community reported they had never heard of Gross. The Cuban leadership, believing Gross to be a spy, ultimately sentenced him to a fifteen-year prison term. Shortly thereafter, former New Mexico Governor Bill Richardson went to Cuba seeking Gross's release.

USAID has long been involved in trying to oust the Castro government in Cuba, funneling money through the Cuban-American National Foundation, the Center for a Free Cuba, and even a German foundation, the Konrad Adenauer Stiftung, an adjunct of Chancellor Angela Merkel's Christian Democratic Party.

DAI was heavily involved with USAID's Office of Transition Initiatives, which transfers U.S. funds to opposition parties, labor and student movements, and other groups that are pro-American. DAI, under USAID contract, was caught providing U.S. funds to Venezuelan labor unions and media outlets that supported the CIA-led coup against Venezuelan President Hugo Chavez in 2002.

In Haiti, USAID, acting at the behest of the CIA, funded political opposition to President Jean-Bertrand Aristide, ousted in CIA-backed coups in 1991 and 2004. After Aristide's return to power in 1994, USAID money used to oppose Aristide was funneled through a "Project Democracy." Today, USAID is providing dubious small and micro-financing loans to small businesses in Haiti. The legacy of the micro-loan scheme created, in part, by Obama's mother continues in the earthquake-ravaged nation.

Ann Dunham/Soetoro served on the Executive Committee of Women's World Banking, which included as members Muhammad Yunus, the managing director of Grameen Bank of Bangladesh, and Ellen Sirleaf-Johnson of Liberia. Yunus was awarded the Nobel Peace Prize in 2006 for his championing micro-financing and Johnson-Sirleaf was elected President of Liberia in 2005 and received the Nobel Peace Prize in 2011, as controversial a move as was the awarding of the 2009 Peace Prize to Ann Dunham's son, Barack Obama.

The world was shocked that a new president of the United States would be awarded the Nobel Peace Prize. However, looking at all of Obama's other easy breaks, it was not a stretch to believe the "aspirational" award to Obama had been cooked up by the CIA. In 1989, the Dalai Lama of Tibet was awarded the Nobel Peace Prize, even though he had been on the CIA's payroll since 1958, the same year the CIA ensured the Nobel Prize for Literature was awarded to the banned Soviet author Boris Pasternak for *Dr. Zhivago*. Only after direct lobbying of the Swedish Nobel Academy by the CIA was Pasternak awarded the Nobel Prize, passing over two more well-known authors, Alberto Moravia of Italy and Karen Blixen of Denmark.

Ann Dunham helped to lay the groundwork for the UN's Fourth World Conference on Women in September 1995. Present at the Beijing conference were Yunus, Johnson-Sirleaf, and First Lady Hillary Rodham Clinton, who addressed the delegates. By September 1995, Ann was seriously ill with uterine cancer. She died in Hawaii in November 1995.

Chief Obama campaign backer George Soros maintained a close links with Johnson Sirleaf, a former Vice President of Equator Bank in Washington, DC. Equator Bank was later bought by HSBC, which was a key financial partner of Soros.

Yunus was fired as the head of Grameen Bank by the Bangladesh government after charges were leveled that he misappropriated Norwegian aid money, charged usurious interest rates of between 30 and 200 percent, and engaged in fraud in a village phone system owned by Grameen Bank. The Obama administration quickly condemned the Bangladesh government's firing of Yunus. Bangladesh Prime Minister Sheikh Hasina Wazed charged Yunus with "sucking blood from the poor in the name of poverty alleviation."[263]

Bolivian President Evo Morales tossed USAID out of his country, charging it with acting with the CIA to destabilize Bolivia and bring about a coup. To this day, USAID is providing hundreds of thousands of dollars in aid to groups trying to undermine Nicaraguan President Daniel Ortega.

During his ten-year rule, Peruvian President Alberto Fujimori and his intelligence chief, Vladimiro Montesinos, thought to be a CIA asset, reportedly received USAID funds to put down the Shining Path and Tupac Amaru guerrilla movements.

Continuing USAID and CIA covert ops in Pakistan and Indonesia

Private military contractors working for the ex-Blackwater, morphed into Xe Services and thereafter, Academi Inc., were reported to have been posing as USAID employees in Pakistan. The Pakistani press

---

[263] Lydia Polgreen, "Nobel Laureate Loses Last Legal Battle to Save Job at Bank," *New York Times*, April 5, 2011.

reported that USAID was bypassing the Pakistan ministries of Education and Information and providing direct educational assistance to Pakistani students. One USAID program in the Federally-Administered Tribal Areas (FATA) of Pakistan resulted in some $45 million disappearing down a virtual black hole.

In the 1980s, when Ann Dunham and Barack Obama, Jr. spent time in Pakistan, USAID opened up a major office in Islamabad that distributed "non-lethal aid" to Afghan mujaheddin refugees in Pakistan, particularly in Peshawar. Some of the USAID assistance was also reportedly used to buy weapons for the Afghan mujaheddin but some of the weapons ended up in the hands of Pakistani Muslim radicals intent on ousting Pakistani dictator Muhammad Zia-ul Haq. Other USAID money ended up paying for expensive automobiles for leading Afghan mujaheddin commanders in Pakistan. Zia-ul Haq, his top generals, U.S. ambassador Arnold Raphel, and the head of the U.S. military aid mission in Islamabad General Herbert Wassom were killed in the suspicious crash of their C-130 aircraft in August 1988. A board of inquiry concluded that poisonous gas was released inside the aircraft causing it to crash after take-off in Bahawalpur.

The June 18, 1998, *The Jakarta Post* reported that USAID programs in Indonesia continued to be fronts for CIA activity. Specifically, the paper said two Indonesian NGOs, the Indonesian Environmental Forum and the Indonesian Biodiversity Foundation, were charged with accepting money from USAID but should have known that the aid did not come "free of charge" and was linked to the CIA.[264]

---

[264] *Jakarta Post*, June 18, 1998.

In 2002, USAID in Palestine, where DAI was also active, demanded detailed personal information on all the members of NGOs that received American funding. The Palestinian press reported that the information, including personal political opinions of NGO members, was to be turned over to the CIA and eventually, Mossad, to apply pressure on the NGOs to comply with U.S. and Israeli policies.

For years, USAID operated in Manila from the J. Walter Thompson advertising agency building at the Ramon Magsaysay Center on Roxas Boulevard in the Malate district of the city. In 2000, the offices moved to the Makati district of the city but the building that housed USAID was always known to locals as the "CIA building." The building, owned by the Ramon Magsaysay Foundation, in honor of the Philippines President who died in a 1955 plane crash, was built in 1959 with a loan from the Rockefeller family. The Rockefellers also provided grants to the Magsaysay Foundation. Magsaysay was a favorite of the CIA, which funded the Philippines National Movement for Free Elections (NAMFREL) to "monitor" the 1951 presidential election to ensure Magsaysay's victory. NAMFREL, which continued to receive CIA funding through USAID, NED, and Asia Foundation, monitored the 1986 election and used the questionable results to force President Ferdinand Marcos from office.

In 2004, USAID was charged by Philippines opposition parties with using CIA agents to "monitor" elections in the country. The deal to permit USAID observers was signed by President Gloria Macapagal-Arroyo. The head of the left-wing Anakpawis Party, Congressman Crispin Beltran charged that foreign intelligence agents brokered an official agreement with the Comelec (election commission) to interfere in the election on behalf of Macapagal-Arroyo. On May 20, 2008, Beltran, known to his followers as "Comrade Bel," died after he fell from the roof of his home.

The CIA-linked Asia Foundation, which worked closely with the CIA-funded East-West Center at the University of Hawaii in Manoa, was linked closely to USAID covert programs in Laos, Indonesia, the Philippines, South Vietnam, Thailand, Palau, Malaysia, and other Asian-Pacific nations. In Laos and Thailand, USAID officials provided counter-insurgency military training to Laotian and Thai special forces. In 1970, Dan Mitrione, a USAID official who was working for the CIA training Uruguayan special police on torture tactics, was kidnapped and killed by Tupamaro guerrillas.

In 1988, USAID opened a huge compound in a suburb of San Jose, Costa Rica that many Costa Ricans charged was the CIA headquarters for the "parallel state" established by the CIA in Costa Rica to support the contra-led civil war in neighboring Nicaragua. USAID also pumped millions of dollars in loans, some at zero percent, to private banks in Costa Rica to undermine the state banking system.

In 1995, U.S. Representative Mel Reynolds (D-IL), who was convicted of having sex with an underage female campaign worker, was also revealed as working for U.S. intelligence in the 1980s, via employment with USIA and USAID in Africa, particularly in Sudan. Reynolds, an African-American, also spent time in Israel under USIA cover.

President Obama continued USAID's involvement in CIA-directed programs in former Soviet states, including Georgia, Ukraine, and Kyrgyzstan. In so doing, USAID complements the destabilization efforts of George Soros and his network of NGOs. Soros was a major financial backer of Obama's presidential campaign. In 1999, Croatian media reported that USAID was working through various NGOs, some connected to Soros, to oust the ailing Croatian President Franjo Tudjman. The paper *Vjesnik* charged that USAID, as well as the U.S. Information Service (USIS), were used as ''tampons between the American non-governmental agencies and American state bodies." The paper said the USAID program to aid Tudjman's opposition was run by the CIA and coordinated by the U.S. ambassador in Zagreb, William Montgomery.

In a 2008 Russian documentary film, "Technology of Modern Coup," Bermet Akayeva, the daughter of ousted Kyrgyz President Askar Akayev, ousted in the 2005 Tulip Revolution, stated, "USAID is very actively financed by the Soros Foundation, by the National Democratic Institute and some kind of training is carried out constantly. However, it is difficult to describe USAID as an NGO given that it is under the U.S. Department of State. They work very actively." Akayeva said there were rumors in Kyrgyzstan that the U.S.-backed coup plotters distributed narcotics to rioters who participated in the coup.

In the north Caucasus, NGOs supported by USAID, have been accused by Russian authorities of having links to Chechen terrorists.

In 2002, Eritrea expelled USAID from the country, accusing it of working with the CIA to overthrow the government and assisting Ethiopia, which had engaged in a border war with Eritrea.

USAID in Africa: involvement in political assassinations and corruption

In 2009, Susan Tsvangirai, the wife of Zimbabwean Prime Minister Morgan Tsvangirai, was killed in an automobile accident in which the Prime Minister was injured. The truck that struck their automobile was bought with USAID funds and bore a U.S. embassy license plate. USAID denied it had anything to do with the truck. Public Works Minister Theresa Mokone, a friend of Mrs. Tsvangirai, likened the crash to the mysterious auto accident that killed popular and incorruptible Tanzanian Prime Minister Edward Sokoine in 1984. Sokoine was the designated successor to President Julius Nyerere, who antagonized the CIA by his close ties with the Soviet Union and China. Sokoine created a number of enemies among the elite class when he ordered the assets of embezzlers and smugglers seized. USAID, at the time of Sokoine's possible assassination, was heavily-involved in Tanzania.

In Zaire, millions of dollars in USAID money was diverted by CIA-backed dictator Mobutu Sese Seko to amass his personal fortune making him one of the world's wealthiest leaders. Other USAID funds for Zaire were diverted to help the Angolan rebel forces of UNITA leader Jonas Savimbi, in violation of U.S. law prohibiting aid to Angolan rebel groups. The covert aid program to UNITA was started in 1976 by Gerald Ford's Secretary of Defense, Donald Rumsfeld. Similarly, during the Reagan administration, USAID money was funneled through the National Endowment for Democracy to the Nicaraguan contras, again in violation of a specific law prohibiting such assistance.

During the late 1970s and 80s, USAID-funded "researchers" established links with African liberation movements, particularly the African National Congress of South Africa and the Zimbabwe African National Union-Patriotic Front (ZANU-PF) of Zimbabwe. Actually, these programs were CIA activities using "leftist" academics to spy on the nationalist movements.

The operations were concentrated in Harare, Zimbabwe and Cape Town, South Africa, and cities that had a large expatriate African student community, including London and Melbourne and Perth, Australia.

USAID and the oil industry

In 1998, USAID participated in a closed-door meeting between major oil companies and the CIA, National Security Council, and three State Department officials, Stuart Eisenstat, Thomas Pickering, and Susan Rice (Obama's ambassador to the UN) . The topic was exploitation of Africa's oil resources and the senior executives of Exxon, Mobil, Chevron (where Condoleezza Rice was a board member), and Texaco were present along with Department of Energy and Petroleum Finance Corporation officials.

In 2000, the CIA and USAID worked jointly through a private military company, Military Professional Resources, Inc. (MPRI) to train the Nigerian army in tactics to combat secessionists in Nigeria's oil-rich Niger Delta region. The CIA also commissioned the services of a private business intelligence and risk firm, Evidence-Based Research (EBR) of Vienna, Virginia, which appears to be a very similar operation to the CIA front BIC, to conduct an assessment of the tribal revolt in the Niger Delta region, referred to by the CIA as a "semi-riot zone." EBR was formed in 1987, a year after Business International was sold to the Economist Intelligence Unit in London.

A formerly SECRET CIA Intelligence Assessment, dated June 1983, and titled "Indonesia: Deteriorating Prospects for Energy Diversification," [Appendix 27] warns of a drop in Indonesia's oil export capacity. The CIA, along with USAID and the World

263

Bank/IMF, had invested heavily in Indonesia, most importantly, to secure the nation's oil supply for the United States and its allies.[265]

After helping Suharto seize power, Soetoro became an official of the Indonesian state-owned oil company, Pertamina, and Mobil Oil. The CIA assessment states: "Huffco and Mobil, two U.S. firms, rapidly developed natural gas exports for the Japanese market in the past decade in partnership with Pertamina." The memo states that this development, as well as coal, hydro, and geothermal, was carried out with strong financial and technical assistance from the World Bank and foreign aid donors like USAID. Huffco is Huffington Oil, founded in 1956 by Texas oil man Roy M. Huffington, the father of former Representative Michael Huffington (R-CA), a former vice chairman of Huffco and the ex-husband of Arianna Huffington, founder of the *Huffington Post*. The Huffingtons divorced in 1997 and a year later Michael Huffington announced that he was gay. More noteworthy is the fact that Roy Huffington, who died in 2008, was a seven-year chairman of the Asia Society, linked to the East-West Center in Hawaii, where Obama's father and step-father resided, and the CIA.

Case Study on how USAID was used by the CIA for political purposes

A case of how the CIA used USAID to prevent a left-wing political party to winning at the polls is Mauritius. In a formerly Secret CIA Intelligence Memorandum,

---

[265] CIA, "Indonesia: Deteriorating Prospects for Energy Diversification." Intelligence Assessment, June 1983.

dated June 1982, and titled "Mauritius: Moderate Government Threatened at Polls," [Appendix 28] the CIA discusses the use of USAID money to prop up the pro-Western Labor government Prime Minister Seewoosagur Ramgoolam at the expense of the leftist Militant Mauritian Movement (MMM) of Paul Berenger.

Ramgoolam was forced to adopt economically destructive austerity measures dictated by the IMF that resulted in high unemployment, wage reductions, and currency devaluation. The beneficiary of the economic downturn would have been Berenger and his socialist MMM. But the CIA and USAID intervened to send aid money to Ramgoolam. The CIA memo states: "Labor is attempting to limit the political fallout from the restrictive measures and regain the political initiative by the announcement in mid-May of . . . a large public works program that would employ 8,000 people. The funds for the program are derived from the USAID "Food for Work" agreement."[266]

The importance of Ramgoolam to the CIA was his quiet support for the U.S. military base on Diego Garcia, a British island in the Indian Ocean over which Mauritius officially claimed sovereignty. The Pentagon also intervened in the Mauritian economic situation by agreeing to employ Mauritian workers on Diego Garcia. Ramgoolam also succeeded in getting an agreement for the United Kingdom to compensate 1200 Diego Garcians who were removed from the island to Mauritius in 1971 to make way for the military base.

---

[266] CIA, "Mauritius: Moderate Government Threatened at Polls," Intelligence Memorandum, June 1982.

USAID funds were used by the CIA to prevent the nightmare scenario for the agency. The memo states: "An MMM victory would be a political victory for the Soviets, shifting Mauritius from a pro-Western to an non-aligned or even pro-Soviet position. [sentence redacted]. Based on MMM rhetoric, however, Moscow has reason to believe that an MMM regime would deny the Western powers the limited, though useful, military access they now enjoy on Mauritius. An MMM regime would be a valuable ally in Moscow's campaign for an Indian Ocean zone of peace and against the US military presence on Diego Garcia."[267]

The CIA also believed the MMM to be influenced by Libya, which it accused of stirring up Mauritian Muslim youth. However, MMM leader Berenger was, at the time, the prominent Christian political leader in Mauritius. The CIA memo states "The Libyans have been rumored to be storing weapons in the Seychelles for the MMM, according to the US Embassy in Seychelles."[268]

The CIA memo states that an MMM victory would reduce the Hindu community's influence. Mauritian politics was dominated by Hindus of Indian origin. The CIA also believed that the MMM would invite Cuban medical doctors and teachers to the island nation.[269]

The CIA memo also reveals that South Africa's apartheid regime was assisting Ramgoolam's re-election campaign costs to avert an MMM victory.[270]

---

[267] *Ibid.*
[268] *Ibid.*
[269] *Ibid.*
[270] *Ibid.*

President Obama's entire career and family history strongly suggested that the person who became the chief executive of the United States had a crass view of the world's downtrodden peoples. Years of exposure to CIA operatives operating under corporate, USAID, World Bank, micro-financing schemes, NGO, and diplomatic cover extended the U.S. Intelligence Community's massive control over America's foreign and domestic policies and that influence permeated the past activities of Obama and his family at home and abroad.

268

Chapter Eleven – The Captain America Recruiting Program

On the proposal to create the CIA in 1947: *the powers of the proposed agency seem almost unlimited and need clarification.* – General George C. Marshall.

In 1965, the year President Obama's stepfather, Lieutenant Colonel Lolo Soetoro, henchman for General Suharto's CIA-led coup against the Sukarno government in Indonesia, left the University of Hawaii's East-West Center to serve Suharto in helping the CIA's coup, the CIA and right-wing Time-Life maven Clare Boothe Luce was putting together the "Cold War College" to train young men and women to suppress popular leftist movements in non-aligned Third World nations. The college never materialized. However, as described in this chapter, there were other avenues to recruit enthusiastic stalwarts into the ranks of the U.S. intelligence community.

The Cold War College was to be part of Luce's Freedom Studies Center, an anti-Communist operative training center established with the assistance of 63 higher education institutions and other organizations in 1966 to counter what Luce called "various schools run by the Communist Party, the Black Panthers, and other revolutionary groups." The Freedom Studies Center was known as a graduate center of excellence for "psycho-political warfare."[271]

---

[271] Samuel Yette, "Ex-FBI Agent Heads Academy to Fight Reds," *Baltimore News American*, November 3, 1971.

Luce ran the Freedom Studies Center from her Longlea Farm estate in Boston, Virginia (the farm was later sold to the secretive right-wing Catholic sect Opus Dei). Although the center received no federal funds, its first seminars attracted such speakers as Army chief of staff General William Westmoreland, former CIA director Allen Dulles, and Richard Ichord, chairman of the House Internal Security Committee. The center also counted among its advisory board members Vice President Spiro Agnew, Transportation Secretary John Volpe, Housing and Urban Development Secretary George Romney, Interior Secretary Rogers Morton, as well as Senators Karl Mundt, Harry F. Byrd, Mark Hatfield, Strom Thurmond, Thomas Dodd, and Russell Long, Governors John Dempsey of Connecticut, Warren Knowles of Wisconsin, and Jack Williams of Arizona, and Illinois Representatives Dan Rostenkowski, Roman Pucinski, and Edward Derwinski.

Three Illinois education officials were also members of the Freedom Studies Center board: Ray Page, superintendent of public instruction for the state of Illinois, and Robert Hanrahan, Superintendent, Cook County schools, and Benjamin Willis, retired general superintendent of Chicago schools. CIA archives contain various documents on the Freedom Studies Center and the proposed "Cold War College." [Appendix 31]

Had President Lyndon Johnson not named him the head of the Pentagon's counter-insurgency effort in Indochina, the "Cold War College," also to be known as the "United Freedom Academy," would have been run by General Edward Lansdale, who planned to run the "college" as a center for "psycho-political warfare."

Lansdale envisaged sending "freedom teams" of American young men and women who were Cold War "college" graduates to "change the course of history in favor of freedom." It was just the type of work engaged

270

in by Obama's mother, Ann Dunham, in post-Sukarno Indonesia, and his grandfather, Stanley Armour Dunham, in laying the groundwork for young Third World nationals to study in Hawaii during the height of the Cold War.

Lansdale was a model hero in William Lederer's co-authored book. *The Ugly American*. Obama's grandfather enjoyed taking his young grandson to Lederer's Bar in Honolulu, a bar that likely saw Lansdale as a patron on more than one occasion.

It is also noteworthy that one of the Freedom Center's directors was retired General Lawrence H. Whiting, Vice Chairman of the Board of the American Furniture Mart in Chicago [Whiting was not a real general but had been a "special consultant" to the War department in World War II and appears to have self-adopted the title of "general."]. Another board member for the center was Frank Vignola, President of Vignola Furniture Company. Obama's grandfather, Stanley Dunham, claims to have been a furniture salesman, including for non-existent Pratt Furniture in Honolulu. Obama's mother's application for U.S. passport renewal, filed in Jakarta, Indonesia on August 13, 1968, lists her father's place of employment as the Bank of Hawaii, [Appendix 32] the same employer as Obama's grandmother, Madelyn Dunham.

As pointed out previously, Madelyn's vice president duties for the bank entailed handling the escrow accounts for CIA slush payments to America's favorite dictators in Asia, including Suharto, Park Chung Hee in South Korea, Chiang Kai-shek in Taiwan, Lon Nol in Cambodia, and Ferdinand Marcos in the Philippines.

In fact, Hawaii was the asylum location of preference for such deposed American allies in Asia, including South Korea's Syngman Rhee, Lon Nol, and Marcos.

The Freedom Studies Center was headed by John Fisher, a former FBI agent under J. Edgar Hoover, who was another center supporter. Fisher became the head of security for Sears, Roebuck & Company in Chicago to bust up communist infiltration of Sears's affiliated labor unions. Fisher later worked for the right-wing American Security Council, a corporate entity that fought against communist influence in the United States and abroad.

In a November 18, 1970, appeal for corporate support, Luce stated that "the Freedom Studies Center wants to begin to enroll 40 full-time students in a pilot leadership training program. Next year we hope to have 100 students and reach the level of 400 students soon thereafter." Luce added, "as part of this training, students will work on actual projects underway at the American Security Council, the Institute for American Strategy, and the Council on National Security."[272]

Although Luce's college never got off the ground, the CIA increased its recruitment programs at its favored colleges, including Obama's two almae mater, Occidental in Los Angeles and Columbia University in New York. Obama's post-Columbia employer, BIC, increased its own presence within leftist student organizations, including Students for Democratic Society (SDS). In Luce's November 18, 1970, letter, she warned about leftist infiltration of U.S. urban centers: ". . . of Castro's 42 training centers in Cuba for exporting revolution to all the Americas, two are devoted exclusively to training leaders for urban guerrilla warfare in the United States! Just one of these has already trained 902 revolutionaries like S.D.S. leader

---

[272] Clare Boothe Luce letter, dated November 18, 1970, maintained in CIA archives.

Mark Rudd, and Black Panther leader Stokely Carmichael."[273]

The Luce plan followed the exposure in 1967 of the CIA's covert funding, since at least the early 1950s, of the National Student Association in a program to influence the work of the organization, which was composed of university and college student government bodies. The major target for the CIA was leftist and politically-active American college students attending international symposia to counteract domination by communist and socialist student representatives. The CIA's funding of the National Student Association was also a classic move to dominate two opposing groups, the National Student Association on the left and the Young Americans for Freedom on the right, for maximum political advantage and control. The CIA later infiltrated, along with the FBI, the anti-Vietnam War Students for Democratic Society (SDS). Ann Dunham, Barack H. Obama. Sr., and Lolo Soetoro were all attending the University of Hawaii at the height of the CIA's infiltration of college campuses and the Oahu campus was a major target for such infiltration activities through a host of channels.

Some would scoff at the notion of a free-spirited and liberal-oriented Ann Dunham being a willing agent for the CIA. However, the name Allard K. Lowenstein should be recalled when it comes to young, leftist student leaders being co-opted by the CIA. Lowenstein, who was the head of the National Student Association and would later become a Democratic member of the U.S. House of Representatives from New York, was called a "pied piper" for the American pro-civil rights

---

[273] *Ibid.*

and anti-apartheid youth movement.[274] In 1962, Lowenstein was recruited by the CIA to act as a liaison with the African National Congress (ANC). CIA support for Lowenstein's South Africa operations was funneled through the American Society for African Culture. Lowenstein managed to save ANC leaders Nelson Mandela and Walter Sisulu from the gallows. With Mandela's and Sisulu's life terms in prison rather than their executions by South Africa's apartheid government, the CIA was able to neutralize the ANC without a bloody finger pointing at Washington. Later, Lowenstein worked closely with his old friend, longtime CIA official Frank Carlucci, to maintain CIA influence over South West Africa People's Organization (SWAPO) senior official Theo-Ben Gurirab. In 1980, while Obama was being groomed by the CIA at Occidental in a manner very similar to the agency's sponsorship of Lowenstein's student activities in Africa, Lowenstein was assassinated by Dennis Sweeney, a former civil rights worker in Mississippi.[275] In many ways, Lowenstein was the CIA's blueprint for other so-called "progressive" leaders of the left, including Barack Obama, Jr.

At the height of its student and academia infiltration program, the CIA was operating from several stations around the world from which it could oversee its program of co-opting student meetings, academic conferences, and other symposia. In 1958, Paul Sigmund, a Princeton political science professor, co-founded the CIA-supported Independent Research Service, which was responsible for amassing dossiers on World Youth Festival participants. The Independent

---

[274] Hugh Wilford, The *Mighty Wurlitzer: How the CIA Played America*. Cambridge: Harvard University Press, 2008, p. 131.
[275] Cummings, *op. cit.*

Research Service was co-founded by feminist icon Gloria Steinem, who admitted to *The New York Times* in a February 21, 1967, article that the CIA was a major source of funds for the group.[276] During the Cold War, World Youth Festivals were accused of being Communist propaganda tools, since most of the conferences were held in Communist capitals, including Moscow, East Berlin, Warsaw, Bucharest, Prague, Budapest, Pyongyang, Havana, and Sofia.

However, there was no credible evidence that any student dissidents and radicals were controlled by Communist governments. In fact, the CIA's infiltration program directed against colleges and universities was primarily for the purpose of recruiting agents and informants. In 1968, an internal CIA 41-page study titled "Restless Youth" concluded that "there is no convincing evidence control, manipulation, or significant financial support of student dissidents by any international Communist authority." The report also determined that most student radicals rejected Communist authoritarianism and that the Soviets would have to "cope with young people who are alienated by the more oppressive features of Soviet life."[277] The CIA's report should put to rest any notion that Ann Dunham or her son, Barack Obama, Jr., were committed Marxists or Communists. To the contrary, they both fit the bill for CIA student recruits and informants.

The year 1973, just as the allegations of CIA wrongdoing associated with the Watergate scandal reached the public eye, saw the activities of CIA fronts like BIC reach a crescendo. In 1973, the CIA operated

---

[276] John Cavanagh, Sally Frank, and Laurie Kirby, *op. cit.*
[277] C. Robert Zelnick, "CIA student study of '68 raises new questions," *Christian Science Monitor*, May 7, 1968.

from the following stations around the world, many
where BIC also maintained a significant presence:

<u>SOVIET BLOC</u>
Bulgaria, Sofia
Czechoslovakia, Prague
Germany, Berlin
Hungary, Budapest
Poland, Warsaw
Romania, Bucharest
USSR, Moscow

<u>EUROPE</u>
Austria, Vienna
Belgium, Brussels
  U.S, Mission to NATO
  U.S. Mission to the European Communities
Denmark, Copenhagen
England, London
Finland, Helsinki
Germany, Bonn
  Munich
Iceland, Reykjavik
Ireland, Dublin
Italy, Rome
Luxembourg, Luxembourg
Malta, Valletta
Netherlands, The Hague
Norway, Oslo
Portugal, Lisbon
Spain, Madrid
Sweden, Stockholm
Switzerland, Bern
  Geneva
Yugoslavia, Belgrade

PACIFIC

Australia, Canberra
  Melbourne
Philippines, Manila
New Zealand, Wellington

FAR EAST

Burma, Rangoon
Cambodia, Phnom Penh
Formosa, Taipei
Hong Kong
Indonesia, Djakarta
Japan, Tokyo
Korea, Seoul
Laos, Vientiane
Malaysia, Kuala Lumpur
Singapore
Thailand, Bangkok
  U.S. Representative to SEATO
Vietnam, Saigon

CANADA, Ottawa

AFRICA

Algeria, Algiers
Botswana, Gaborone
Burundi, Bujumbura
Cameroun, Yaounde
Central African Republic, Bangui
Chad, Fort Lamy
Congo, Kinshasa
Congo, Brazzaville
Dahomey, Cotonou

Ethiopia, Addis Ababa
Gabon, Libreville
Gambia, Bathurst
Ghana, Accra
Guinea, Conakry
Ivory Coast, Abidjan
Kenya, Nairobi
Lesotho, Maseru
Liberia, Monrovia
Libya, Tripoli
Malagasy Republic, Tananarive
Mali, Bamako
Malawi, Zomba
Mauritania, Nouakchott
Mauritius, Port Louis
Morocco, Rabat
Mozambique, Lourenco Marques
Niger, Niamey
Nigeria, Lagos
Rhodesia, Salisbury
Rwanda, Kigali
Senegal, Dakar
Sierra Leone, Freetown
Somalia, Mogadishu
South Africa, Pretoria
Sudan, Khartoum
Swaziland, Mbabane
Tanzania, Dar es Salaam
Togo, Lome
Tunisia, Tunis
Uganda, Kampala
Upper Volta, Ouagadougou
Zambia, Lusaka

NEAR EAST AND SOUTH ASIA

Afghanistan, Kabul
Bangladesh, Dacca
Ceylon, Colombo
Cyprus, Nicosia
Egypt, Cairo
Greece, Athens
India, New Delhi
Iran, Tehran
Iraq, Baghdad
Israel, Tel Aviv
Jordan, Amman
Kuwait, Kuwait
Lebanon, Beirut
Nepal, Katmandu
Pakistan, Islamabad
Saudi Arabia, Jidda
South Yemen, Aden
Syria, Damascus
Turkey, Ankara

ARA [Inter-American Affairs]

Argentina, Buenos Aires
Bahamas, Nassau
Barbados, Bridgetown
Bolivia, La Paz
Brazil, Rio de Janeiro
Chile, Santiago
Colombia, Bogota
Costa Rica, San Jose
Dominican Republic, Santo Domingo
Ecuador, Quito
El Salvador, San Salvador
Guatemala, Guatemala

Guyana, Georgetown
Haiti, Port au Prince
Honduras, Tegucigalpa
Jamaica, Kingston
Mexico, Mexico City
Nicaragua, Managua
Panama, Panama
Paraguay, Asuncion
Peru, Lima
Trinidad, Port of Spain
Uruguay, Montevideo
Venezuela, Caracas[278]

Although the "Cold War College" never materialized, the CIA's Cold War college recruitment programs at the University of Hawaii helped groom CIA agents-of-influence Stanley Ann Dunham, Barack H. Obama, Sr., and Lolo Soetoro Mangunharjo. Langley's recruiters at Occidental also nurtured a young and, according to his classmates, a very effeminate, lazy, and pot-smoking Barack Obama, Jr., whose only real friends were a handful of Pakistani students, including his roommate Imad Husain. In 1979, as the Soviets were consolidating their hold on Afghanistan, someone with Obama's family CIA connections, as well as his Pakistani connections, was a prime candidate for recruitment. As Black Panthers and El Rukn gang members began to reach out to countries like Libya in the mid-1980s, Barack Obama, Jr. came to the rescue, practically parachuting into south Chicago from BIC's swank offices in Manhattan, to become a "community organizer," or more precisely, a "snitch."

---

[278] CIA Project Processing Worksheet, June 1973.

In 1979, when Obama enrolled at Occidental, the issue of CIA recruitment of U.S. and foreign students attending U.S. universities and colleges was a major issue. Morton Halperin, a former adviser to the Defense Department during the Johnson administration and a Henry Kissinger subordinate in the Nixon administration's National Security Council, stated that college professors were often openly solicited by the CIA to recruit students. Halperin also said that the CIA was "interested in students from all countries" and that "there is an open-ended generalized interest in recruiting students from all over the world." Halperin added that there was a CIA station in the Bay area [San Francisco] which was "covert, secret, in constant communication with Washington and the various universities in the area." "It is very hard to find these people," he stressed.[279]

In 1979, after the abuses of the CIA were exposed by the Church and Pike Committees of Congress, the CIA announced it would continue to secretly recruit agents from U.S. college campuses. Princeton University was one such campus. In 1967, Princeton's Career Services director, Newell Brown, admitted, "We are aware of the kinds of people the CIA looks for and when we run into the type we tell them to send a resume."[280]

Barack Obama. Jr.'s and his mother's respective affiliations with the CIA occurred at the zeniths of the CIA's college recruitment efforts, time periods when campus officials actively supported the CIA's "talent spotting" at Occidental and the University of Hawaii.

---

[279] Mark Nassutti, "CIA accused of covertly recruiting students," *The Stanford Daily*, February 20, 1979.
[280] John Cavanagh, Sally Frank, and Laurie Kirby, *op. cit.*

In 1978, a panel was held in Hawaii on contacts between CIA agents and foreign-based journalists. The use of CIA agents as journalists' sources was a focus of the panel. The panel included Richard Halloran of *The New York Times*; Keyes Beech, Asia correspondent for the *Chicago Daily News*; and Dennis Bloodworth, Far East correspondent for the London *Observer*. The sponsor of the "Round Table on Asian News" panel was the University of Hawaii, which received a grant for the symposium from the Gannett Newspaper Foundation. The reporters all admitted to using CIA agents as sources.[281] There is little wonder why Obama always wanted to gloss over his work as an "editor" and "journalist" for BIC.

---

[281] Hank Sato, "Journalists Detail Contacts with CIA," *Honolulu Star-Bulletin*, February 25, 1978.

Chapter Twelve – Chicago: The CIA's Kind of Town

It was no secret that I was dissatisfied with the CIA – President Richard Nixon

Barack Obama's transfer from a potentially-lucrative future with BIC in Manhattan to south Chicago struck members of his family and some of his closest associates as odd. This chapter explains why Obama was needed in Chicago by his superiors. Chicago was considered by the CIA and FBI to be a hot-bed of black radicalism and potential terrorist activities. The CIA was anxious to dispatch their new recruit to field activity where Obama's unique name and background would be maximized in order to infiltrate the groups targeted by America's top intelligence and law enforcement agencies.

After leaving his cushy job with BIC in New York, Obama's arrival in the blighted south side of Chicago, where he began working for native New Yorker Jerry Kellman and his Development Communities Project (DCP), was a bit too little and much too late. The area's Wisconsin Steel plant had already closed down and unemployment had skyrocketed. Many observers wondered if Obama's arrival in Chicago from the plush offices of BIC in Manhattan was an attempt to "sheep dip" Obama to give him some "street creds" for future purposes. After all, Obama's only previous experience with non-profit activism was his short stint with Ralph Nader's Public Interest Research Group (PIRG) after graduating from Columbia. Obama's two major "success" projects in Chicago had nothing to do with permanently employing

283

idled workers: summer jobs for teens and asbestos removal from Altgeld Gardens, a dilapidated housing project built in the 1940s.

It was clear that Obama prepared carefully for his new role in Chicago, even altering his personality from the aloof professional at BIC to the hip African-American he would put on display in the slums of south Chicago. This personality change was noticed by a woman who knew Obama best, his mother. In Janny Scott's biography of Ann Dunham, a conversation between Ann and her colleague at Bank Rakyat Indonesia points to the angst Ann Dunham felt about Barack's personality change evidenced from his move from Manhattan to Chicago: "She (Ann) felt a little bit wistful or sad that Barack had moved to Chicago and chose to take on a really strongly identified black identity." Ann believed that Barack's new identity "had not really been part of who he was when he was growing up" and that Barack was "distancing himself from her."[282]

What Ann may or may not have known is that Barack Obama, as a recruit for a top-shelf CIA front company in Manhattan, would not cut the mustard in the tough streets of south Chicago. For Obama to blend in with the groups he was tasked with keeping a close eye on – namely, the Black Panthers, National of Islam, and El Rukn gang, he had to re-invent himself. Obama apparently put on such an excellent act of becoming a black radical, his mother even noticed the change, and she did not like what she saw. But Barack had always fit the bill for whoever in the U.S. intelligence community was passing him the orders from above.

---

[282] Janny Scott, *op. cit.*, p. 298.

The CIA's Operation CHAOS had targeted a number of domestic groups in a surveillance and disruption campaign. The groups included the Black Panthers and Nation of Islam.[283] A spokesman for an extreme right-wing group, the Minutemen's Robert Taylor, charged in 1971 that acts of violence blamed on the radical left were carried out by government agents intent on passing legislation restricting citizens' rights. Taylor charged that such black radical leaders as Stokely Carmichael and H. Rap Brown were actually working for the CIA. Taylor said his group "checked into the backgrounds of many other people prominent in the radical movement such as Abbie Hoffman and others of the Chicago Seven," adding "many of those individuals have parents who have State Department or a CIA background."[284]

Before going to work for BIC, Obama had reportedly traveled to Pakistan and India on his Indonesian passport during the time the United States was building up the mujaheddin forces in their war against the Soviets in Afghanistan. If Obama was working as a non-official cover (NOC) agent in Indonesia and South Asia, he would need a "career" to propel him into political office. After Obama's community organizing in Chicago, he was off to Harvard Law School but the grass roots network he was part of in Chicago would help propel Obama into the Illinois legislature, the U.S. Senate, and ultimately, the White House.

Why would the CIA be interested in someone like Obama? A May 11, 1965, memo for the record,

---

[283] Report to the President by the Commission on COA Activities Within the United States, p. 144.
[284] UPI, "Minutemen Hit Role of U.S. Agents," *Washington Post*, January 9, 1971.

given to this editor by a member of the [Martin Luther] King family, recounts a conversation between an individual whose name was redacted and the CIA's Morse Allen, [Appendix 13] the CIA's research director who was responsible for Project Artichoke and MK-ULTRA, two of the CIA's behavior modification programs . . . [285]

The most revealing part of the CIA memo is the following: "It is [redacted]'s belief that somehow or other Martin Luther KING must be removed from the leadership of the Negro movement, and his removal must come from within and not from without. [Redacted] feels that somewhere in the Negro movement, at the top, there must be a Negro leader who is 'clean' who could step into the vacuum and chaos if Martin Luther KING were either exposed or assassinated."[286]

There is an increasing belief among African-American leaders in the United States that Barack Obama was what the CIA had in mind for a "clean" leader for the African-American movement, someone who would even be acceptable as President of the United States.

Obama's time in Chicago coincided with the concentration of FBI and CIA assets on the city, particularly the south side, because of the presence of remnants of the Black Panther Party and the violent El Rukn street gang, which was accused by the Reagan administration of maintaining links to Libyan leader Muammar el Qaddafi in the mid 1980s, coincidentally, at the same time Obama was "community organizing" in

---

[285] CIA, Memorandum for the Record, May 11, 1965.
[286] *Ibid.*

the same neighborhood where the El Rukns were also active. A retired CIA officer revealed to the author on background that his brief included monitoring Qaddafi's overseas activities. The retired Clandestine Services agent stated unequivocally that there was absolutely no truth to the contention that Qaddafi was supplying weapons or any other material support to the El Rukns or Black Panthers.

The El Rukns also claimed to be community organizers. In essence, Obama's Development Communities Project had a more sinister competitor in the El Rukns. The El Rukns also had a property development and holding company, El Pyramid Real Estate and Maintenance Corporation located at 6417 South Kenwood Avenue in Chicago's south side. From this front operation, El Rukn leader Jeff Fort, aka Abdullah Malik, directed the El Rukn's drug, prostitution, and other criminal operations.

Whether or not Fort ever ran into Obama on the south side will not be known any time soon. Convicted of conspiring with Libya to carry out terrorist attacks in the United States, Fort was incarcerated at the Florence, Colorado Supermax prison where he was under a "no human contact" order. Fort received an 80 year prison sentence.

The CIA's and FBI's interest in south Chicago began in the late 1960s when FBI director J. Edgar Hoover feared that the dialogue between Fred Hampton's Black Panthers in Chicago and street gangs would result in a Black militant coalition. The Chicago FBI set out to create tension between the Black Panthers and another group, the Blackstone Rangers.

The Rangers were headed by Fort. On January 30, 1969, the head of the FBI's domestic intelligence operation, William Sullivan, ordered the Chicago FBI office to send the following letter to Fort in an attempt to stir up problems between the Rangers and the Panthers:

"Brother Jeff,
I've spent some time with some Panther friends *on the west side lately and I know what's been going on. The brothers that run the Panthers blame you for blocking their thing and their's* [sic] *supposed to be a hit out for you. I'm not a Panther, or a Ranger, just Black. From what I see these Panthers are out for themselves not black people. I think you ought to know what they're up to. I know what I'd do if I was you. You might hear from me again.*
A black brother you don't know"

The FBI managed to infiltrate one of its informants into the entourage of Fred Hampton, the Black Panther Illinois state chairman. On December 3, 1969, a SWAT team attacked Hampton's apartment, killing Hampton and then pumping a large amount of drugs into his stomach. Hampton was not a drug user.

The success of the FBI in its COunterINTELligence PROgram (COINTELPRO) operation against the Panthers would lay the grounds for the use of other community informants against black militant. In the 1980s, the CIA and FBI turned its attention to Black Ranger-turned-El Rukn leader Fort. Obama, with his credentials as a CIA NOC in Pakistan and New York under his belt, suddenly arrived on the scene in Chicago.

Infiltrating African Americans into the ranks of black radical groups was part of the playbooks of the FBI, CIA, and city police department intelligence units.

When one such African-American spy, known only as "Mr. Smith," was discovered working for the Houston Police Department, the head of the local Student Nonviolent Coordinating Committee Lee Otis Johnson said, "Man, we know who those cats [informers] are . . . We hold our strategy meeting on Sunday and a public meeting on Monday, and those cats don't know nothing about the strategy meeting. We know more about the police than they know about us."[287]

The comment was similar to those heard from members of the Black Panthers and Nation of Islam about Barack Obama and his actual employers in the 1980s. The CIA was particularly worried about links between the Black Panthers and black Marxist nationalists in the Caribbean, especially in Jamaica, Trinidad and Tobago, Guyana, and Barbados.

Obama's previous experience as an editor and reporter for the CIA's front company, BIC, in New York, may have also been useful in Chicago. The FBI and CIA had long been using Chicago reporters as confidential informants in the government's program that targeted black and anti-war groups for enhanced surveillance. In 1970, all four Chicago newspapers and a number of television stations were approached by federal agents demanding information on the Black Panthers and the Weathermen faction of the Students for Democratic Society,[288] members of which Obama established close contacts after arriving in Chicago.

---

[287] David Brand, "Undercover Cops: Police Intelligence Units Step Up Their Watch on the Racial Situation; Houston Department Places Informers in Black Groups; Negro Leaders are Critical," *Wall Street Journal*, September 10, 1968.
[288] "Will Reporters let the Feds use them as spies?" *Daily World*, February 7, 1970.

In the mid-1980s, there was a real fear by the FBI and CIA that Chicago was turning into a terrorist haven. On June 3, 1984, *The Chicago Tribune* carried the following story: "21 bombs trigger fears of more to come in Midwest." The story was about small bombs being discovered in Illinois, Wisconsin, and Minnesota, with Indiana, Iowa, Michigan, and North and South Dakota seen as future bomb targets.[289]

Headlines like the one above prompted the CIA and FBI to infiltrate as many agents into suspected radical groups in Chicago and the Midwest.

During the 2008 presidential campaign, former Manhattan Borough President Percy Sutton claimed he first heard about Obama in 1988 from Dr. Khalid Al-Mansour, a Black Muslim who inspired many of the

---

[289] Douglas Frantz and Philip Wattley, "21 bombs trigger fears of more to come in Midwest, *Chicago Tribune*, June 3, 1984.

290

founders of the Black Panther Party in the 1960s, including Fred Hampton. Mansour was apparently raising money for Obama's Harvard Law School education in 1988. The association between Obama and Mansour indicates that Obama did have a connection with a possible intermediary to the Black Panthers in Chicago at the same time the El Rukns were under CIA and FBI surveillance.

In 1988, Obama, who was also employed by the Gamaliel Foundation, a church congregation-based community development movement with operations in the United States, United Kingdom, and South Africa, left Chicago for Europe and Kenya. It is ironic that Obama was traveling the world and not campaigning for Democratic presidential candidate Michael Dukakis, who, after the Democratic National Convention, was shown as a potential victor over Vice President George H. W. Bush, who had been the CIA director in 1976.

In late 1988, Obama entered Harvard Law School. Obama has failed to reveal his transcripts from Harvard. Later, Sutton was reported to have retracted his story about first hearing about Obama from Mansour. However, that report turned out to be false as it emanated from Harlem sources who were opposed to the old guard New York black leaders like Sutton and Representative Charles Rangel. Mansour kept a low profile during the campaign in 2008.

Eventually, Obama moved back to Chicago from Harvard to begin his political career.

Multiple informed sources from four states revealed that Obama was compromised at the outset by U.S. government "handlers" who knew and continue to know about his past drug use and sexual predilections. In fact, the Chicago Police Department maintained an open case on Obama's activities with drugs and "morals" violations in the late 1990s while he was serving as an Illinois state senator from Chicago's south side. [290]

Two top Democrats, a former official with the Democratic National Committee and a former elected member of Congress, revealed to the author that Obama's 2004 U.S. Senate campaign in Illinois employed well-tested CIA tactics, often employed in elections abroad, to destroy his Democratic primary and Republican general election opponents.

The Obama campaign obtained the contents of sealed divorce records of Democratic primary candidate Blair Hull and Republican general election candidate Jack Ryan. After the content of the records were leaked to *The Chicago Tribune* by the Obama campaign, the Hull and Ryan campaigns imploded, paving the way for Obama to sail to electoral victory without having to defend his own rather sordid personal history in a heated campaign cycle. Obama's political guru David Axelrod was a reporter for the *Tribune* for eight years prior to becoming a political consultant. Axelrod left the first Obama administration to chair Obama's 2012 presidential re-election campaign from Chicago.

The first Obama victim was Hull, a multimillionaire former securities trader whose war chest made him the candidate to beat in the primary. A month before the March 16, 2004 primary, the *Tribune* leaked details of Hull's messy divorce. Since the records of his divorce from his second wife, Brenda Sexton, were sealed, Obama and other opponents called on Hull to release the records. After Hull and Sexton agreed to release the records, which indicated spousal abuse on the part of Hull, the candidate plummeted from first place in the polls to third. Obama won the primary in a landslide, capturing 52.8 percent, to 23.7 percent for Illinois Comptroller Dan Hynes, and 10.8 percent for Hull.

Launching a dirty tricks attack on a fellow Democrat was not Obama's first. Obama was elected to the Illinois

---

[290] Confidential source in Chicago.

State Senate in 1995 after he successfully challenged the nominating petition signatures of his three Democratic opponents, including incumbent state senator Alice Palmer. Invalidating the signatures of all his opponents, Obama was a single candidate on the ballot, ensuring his election to the State Senate.

State senator Palmer decided to run for Mel Reynolds's vacant Second District House seat. That opened the way for Obama to run for Palmer's then-open 13th district State Senate seat. Obama, who in June 1995 had assumed the chair of the Chicago Annenberg Challenge, along with its $49 million community chest to finance public school reform, had been a major backer of Palmer. Having just written *Dreams from My Father*, Obama was launching his political career.

Palmer, who lost the special Democratic primary to Jesse Jackson, Jr., decided to run again for her state Senate seat but it was too late. Obama had his eyes on that seat and easy work would be made of Palmer's plans.

With the U.S. Senate nomination under his belt, the next target was popular Republican candidate Jack Ryan. Ryan and Star Trek *Voyager* actress Jeri Ryan had divorced in 1999 and their divorce records, as were those of Hull and his ex-wife, were sealed. However, once again, details of the sealed Ryan divorce records were leaked to the *Tribune*. The Ryans demanded that the records remain sealed because of the harm the custody records would have on their 9-year old son. However, Los Angeles Superior Court Judge Robert Schnider disagreed and ordered the release of the records because the public interest over the privacy interests of the Ryans tipped "slightly to the public." Jeri Ryan was adamant that the records remain sealed because she was being subjected to stalker threats at the time.

Schnider received a public admonition from the California Commission on Judicial Performance on August 31, 2009: "In the commission's view, Judge Schnider's failure to properly discharge his duty to supervise [Family Law Department] Commissioner [Ann] Dobbs resulted in significant financial and emotional harm to family law litigants and seriously undermined the integrity of the judiciary."

Even before Schnider's ruling, sordid divorce record details emerged of Jack Ryan's alleged requests that his wife accompany him to perform publicly in bondage-oriented sex clubs in New York, New Orleans, and Paris. Schnider's later public admonition points to the lack of judicial integrity on his part and may help to explain the leak of the divorce records prior to his later ruling.

One of the Illinois Republicans who called for Ryan to fully disclose his divorce records was long-serving Representative Ray LaHood, a member of the House Permanent Select Committee on Intelligence. After LaHood pulled the GOP rug from under Ryan, other Illinois Republicans followed LaHood's lead, including House Speaker Dennis Hastert. LaHood was appointed Secretary of Transportation by President-elect Obama.

Ryan's campaign was doomed and Barack Obama was assured the U.S. Senate seat of departing Republican Senator Peter Fitzgerald. The Republicans dispatched Alan Keyes from Maryland to Illinois to take over the Republican Senate slot. Keyes was defeated by Obama by a whopping 70 to 27 percent rout in the November election.

Informed Democratic sources in Illinois told the author that one of the reasons Fitzgerald, who was also popular, declined to run for re-election was because of death threats against his son. Fitzgerald became the chairman of Chain Bridge Bank in McLean, Virginia, in the shadows of the CIA headquarters. As a Senator, Fitzgerald was the sole member who opposed a post-9/11 bailout of the airlines. After asking, "Who will bail out the American taxpayer?" the Senate approved the bailout 99 to 1.

However, things in Illinois would not be safe until one other nettlesome problem was eliminated as a threat: Illinois Democratic Governor Rod Blagojevich, who had ample political dirt on Obama and his brain trust of Rahm Emanuel – ultimately elected mayor of Chicago – Axelrod, and Chicago real estate tycoon Valerie Jarrett.

The decision was made to turn loose on Blagojevich the U.S. Attorney for Northern Illinois Patrick Fitzgerald, a longtime bag man for the CIA in New York, to indict and convict Blagojevich on corruption charges as he had done with Blagojevich's predecessor, Republican George Ryan. The plan was successful. After being convicted in a second trial, Blagojevich received a 14-year prison sentence.

The word from Democratic sources was that the Obama administration was a virtual mafia. One Democratic insider confided that it was known that Obama was recruited by the CIA, but the only detail that remained sketchy was when he was "talent spotted" by Langley. However, the insider maintained that Obama's entire Illinois political rise was accomplished with the CIA promoting Obama and derailing all of his opponents. The bottom line from the insider: "To cross them [the Obama White House] is to sign your own political death warrant – at least."

Jarrett, who became one of Obama's closest White House advisers, had a unique background in her own right. She was the daughter of Dr. James E. Bowman, a geneticist and pathologist, and Barbara Taylor Bowman, co-founder of Chicago's Erikson Institute, which specializes in early childhood development and education. Valerie was born in Shiraz, Iran in 1956, where her father worked from 1955 to 1961 as part of an International Cooperation Agency (ICA) program to help develop Iranian health and agriculture programs. Dr. Bowman served as the chair of pathology at Nemazee Hospital in Shiraz. Before being assigned to Iran, Bowman worked at the Fitzsimons Army Hospital in Denver.

ICA was the forerunner to USAID. Jarrett's parents and Obama's mother and stepfather had something else in common. They both worked in countries on behalf of U.S. agencies linked to the CIA subsequent to CIA-organized coups: the 1953 coup in Iran that ousted popularly-elected Prime Minister Mohammed Mossadeq and the 1965 coup in Indonesia that ousted democratically-elected President Sukarno. Jarrett became fluent in Farsi (Persian) and French.

No potential "Watergate"-level scandal is complete without a dead body and the Obama-Emanuel brewing political tempest in Chicago was not an exception. In 2009, the body of Chicago school board president and real estate developer Michael Scott was found in the Chicago River with a gunshot wound to the left side of his head. The Cook County Medical examiner quickly ruled Scott's death a suicide Chicago school board but police sources revealed that the death of Scott was a professional hit made to look like a suicide. Scott, along with some of Obama's close aides and friends, including Jarrett, stood to make potentially billions of dollars on land sales had Chicago won the 2016 Summer Olympics.

Richard Daley, Jr., who was never comfortable in spending tight city fund's in trying to snag the Olympics from the favorite, Rio de Janeiro, blamed the Obama White House of Jarrett, Axelrod, Emanuel, and Michelle Obama for the Olympics fiasco that saw President Obama personally visit Copenhagen to unsuccessfully pitch Chicago for the 2016 venue.

For Obama and Emanuel, the problem was that Daley and Blagojevich were holding some interesting cards in their showdown with the "Chicago Mafia" in the White House. In the end, Daley decided to forego another run for mayor of Chicago, opening up the way for Obama's chief of staff, Emanuel, to run for the office. As for Blagojevich, in June 2011, he was convicted by Fitzgerald's prosecution team for fraud committed while governor of Illinois. Blagojevich was sentenced to a 14-year prison sentence at the federal correctional institution in Littleton, Colorado, 102 miles north of the Florence Supermax federal prison, also known as the "Alcatraz of the Rockies," where convicted Chicago black militant Fort, who is also aware of Obama's early days in Chicago, is serving an 80-year sentence.

Obama was elected the first black president of the *Harvard Law Review* in 1990. Although Obama was quoted in *The New York Times* at the time, saying, "The fact that I've been elected shows a lot of progress . . . It's encouraging . . . But it's important that stories like mine aren't used to say that everything is O.K. for blacks. You have to remember that for every one of me, there are hundreds or thousands of black students with at least equal talent who don't get a chance."H

However, according to an African-American contemporary of Obama at Harvard in 1988, two years before Obama's election to head the *Harvard Law Review*, there was another portrait painted of Obama. The black Harvard student happened to hear a speech by the still virtually-unknown law school student on campus who was railing against black student activism on campus, cautioning those present that such activism was counter-productive. The Harvard student listened intently to the speech by Obama and turned to a colleague and inquired, "Who is that mulatto up there speaking against our interests?" The answer from the other student was, "That's Barry Obama." The last name was pronounced by some Harvard African-American students as "O-Bama," as in "ALA-bama," a reference to Obama's conservative views that accommodated white faculty and students on campus. The Harvard student replied to his friend, "that mulatto is going places with that attitude."

Chapter Thirteen – Back to the Future with Obama and the CIA

I am pissed off! . . . This is an act violating international law . . . It is an act of war . . . I don't like this . . . I don't like it one bit from the President or from you. – Senate Intelligence Committee Chairman Barry Goldwater in a letter to CIA director William Casey on discovering the CIA was secretly mining the harbors of Nicaragua.

Judging by the 2009 CIA- and Pentagon-supported coup d'etat against Honduran President Manuel Zelaya and the subsequent 2010 attempted coup against Ecuadorian President Rafael Correa, the Obama administration's Latin American foreign policy bears a strong resemblance to the policies of the Reagan and Nixon administration. It is Obama's background as the first covert U.S. intelligence agent to become president of the United States that has prompted him to adopt the worst attributes of his more imperialistic predecessors, including Reagan and Nixon.

This chapter reviews the similarities of Obama's foreign policy to the "gun boat" diplomacy of recent past administrations. Obama has made no secret of his personal dislike for Latin American leaders with strong revolutionary and progressive credentials, from Evo Morales of Bolivia and Hugo Chavez of Venezuela to return leaders of Nicaragua and Suriname who were the bane of the Reagan administration. In this respect, Obama's true CIA colors show through quite plainly.

During Ecuador's attempted coup that rebellious Ecuadorian police discussed killing Correa during their siege of the president at the Police Hospital in Quito.

299

This scenario bore an eerie resemblance to the Nixon administration's orchestrated attack on and assassination of Chilean President Salvador Allende, during the military coup of September 11, 1973. The CIA's overthrow of Allende was called Project Jakarta, named for the 1965 overthrow of Sukarno, and which was a blueprint for the coup in Chile.[291] Eerily, Obama's own early history was intertwined with the coup against Sukarno.

Recorded police transmissions during the Ecuador coup attempt provided evidence that some of the rebel police officers who besieged Correa at the hospital discussed killing him. Video recordings also showed retired Army Major Fidel Araujo, a supporter of Correa's pro-U.S. predecessor, Lucio Gutierrez, stirring up anti-Correa protesters. Most of Latin America's leaders called the rebellion against Correa an attempted coup. Secretary of State Clinton chose to call the coup a police protest. The Obama administration, which was unsuccessful in ousting Correa as it did Zelaya in Honduras in 2009, clearly suffered a major defeat in Ecuador. Organization of American States (OAS) Secretary General Jose Miguel Insulza termed the rebellion an attempted coup and Venezuela's President Hugo Chavez charged the CIA and the Obama administration with being behind the coup attempt. Chavez's charge was supported by the revelation that Zimbabwe's President Robert Mugabe, who was to travel to Quito from the UN General Assembly summit in New York, was warned not to go by the CIA, which had advance knowledge of the rebellion against Correa.

---

[291] Toohey and Pinwill, *op. cit.*, p. 102.

The CIA reportedly knew in advance that the coup against Correa would turn violent since Langley told Mugabe that his own safety would be in peril if he went ahead with his visit to Quito. The CIA warning to Mugabe was conveyed through Zimbabwe's Central Intelligence Organization (CIO). Mugabe quickly flew from New York to Harare, leaving members of his own delegation in the dark, according to the *Zim Daily*.

The CIA was known to have, along with Israel's Mossad, penetrated the Ecuadorian National Police, and CIA and Mossad fingerprints on the coup attempt became clearer by the day. The CIA and Mossad also conspired in the coup against Zelaya in Honduras.

Stung by the failure of the coup against Correa, Obama was forced to call the Ecuadorian leader and offer his support for Ecuador's "democratic institutions." Obama's hypocrisy in expressing support for Ecuador's president while not referring to the rebellion as a coup attempt was obvious. In the case of Honduras, Obama never expressed support for Zelaya or the country's democratic institutions because the U.S.-backed coup was successful. For Ecuador, Obama had to change his tune and offer Correa tepid support a week after the coup attempt.

Obama offered no support to Paraguay's progressive president Fernando Lugo after he was ousted in a Honduras-style CIA-backed "institutional coup" in June 2012. U.S. ambassor to Paraguay James Thessin held a secret meeting with Lugo while right-wing congressmen were voting to impeach the president. As is the Obama administration's modus operandi, the subject of the Lugo-Thessin meeting remains classified.[292]

---

[292] Associated Press, "Lugo allies criticize US neutrality on his

Considering Obama's snub of Suriname's President Desi Bouterse at a White House reception for world leaders in New York for the UN General Assembly summit, the Suriname leader was a sitting target for an Obama-sanctioned coup in Latin America. Bouterse's lack of an invitation to the White House reception at New York's Museum of Natural History came as a surprise to Bouterse's fellow Caribbean Community (CARICOM) leaders. Bouterse was the former military ruler of Suriname whose Mega Alliance party won the May 2010 general election. Bouterse was inaugurated on August 12, 2010. A little over a decade before, Bouterse was sentenced to prison *in absentia* by a Dutch court on charges of cocaine trafficking. Suriname law prohibited its citizens from being extradited to foreign countries.

However, it may not have been the criminal charges leveled against Bouterse in the Netherlands and in Suriname that had the Obama administration anxious to depose him. Bouterse was a primary target of the CIA during the Reagan administration because of his close ties to Fidel Castro's Cuba, the Sandinista government in Nicaragua, and the Marxist government of Grenada.

Bouterse originally took power in Suriname following a military coup in February 1980. Bouterse's government then declared Suriname a socialist republic. CIA director William Casey and his deputy, Robert Gates, who served as Obama's Defense Secretary, planned a coup to oust Bouterse from power. Casey and Gates cited Bouterse's close ties with Latin America's leftist governments, a program that bore a stark resemblance to the Obama and Hillary Clinton program

---

impeachment, but others' effort ailed to save him," *The Washington Post*, July 7, 2012.

to oust the leftist government of Honduras, followed by destabilization efforts in Ecuador, Bolivia, and other nations, including, once again, Suriname.

In December 1982, the CIA went ahead with plans to topple Bouterse. The CIA worked closely with Dutch intelligence to establish contacts with Bouterse's opposition in Suriname, including politicians, businessmen, and journalists. The Dutch provided assistance to former President Henck Chin a Sen and his Amsterdam-based opposition forces. The CIA plan included the landing of Surinamese rebels in Paramaribo, the Suriname capital, to seize power. There were also reports that the CIA planned to assassinate Bouterse during the coup, a direct violation of a White House executive order banning assassinations of foreign leaders. The CIA's chief in-country liaison for the coup was U.S. ambassador to Suriname Robert Duemling.

A formerly TOP SECRET CIA National Intelligence Daily, dated March 12, 1982, [Appendix 29] disclosed that the CIA was closely following an attempted coup against Bouterse by conservative military officers. The coup was launched on March 11, 1982. The CIA report stated: "Dissident military officers opposing the leftist trend of the military leadership launched a coup yesterday, but forces loyal to the government are still resisting. The group, calling itself the Army of National Liberation, is led by two officers who have been associated with conservative elements of the Surinamese society . . . Although the rebels have control of the Army's main barracks and ammunition depot in Paramaribo, government strongman Army Commander Bouterse and troops loyal to him apparently have taken up a defensive position in the capital's police camp some 6 kilometers away. Fighting subsided somewhat last night, with both sides claiming to be in control and appealing for support from military troops and citizenry. A large number of rank-and-file military, who had objected to Bouterse's leftist policies several months ago, probably will join the dissidents if Bouterse's position weakens further."

The failed coup attempt against Bouterse in March resulted in a CIA warning, contained in a CIA "Monthly Warning Assessment for Latin America" sent by the National Intelligence Officer for Latin America on July 29, 1982. [Appendix 30] The formerly Secret report stated, "State/INR summarized the growing danger that Castro will have a second Grenada-type success. Suriname's leader, Bouterse, visited Grenada for two weeks in May, met with Cubans there, met with Castro, is sending military and security personnel for Cuban training, has a very far left foreign minister, will receive Cuban assistance in foreign affairs, and will receive some Cuban weapons. There was no dissent that the situation is very bad. NIO/LA repeats a warning he has made for six months – that Suriname is on the way into the Cuban orbit through a Grenada-like subversive operation.[293] The warning was signed by Constantine Menges, a veteran CIA officer born in Ankara, Turkey after his family fled from Nazi Germany, Menges was Casey's National Intelligence Officer for Latin America who would later join the Reagan National Security Council and, after his retirement, join the neoconservative Hudson Institute and rail against the leftist government of Venezuela's Hugo Chavez and the threat from Iran. Menges died in 2004 and his career was praised by the neoconservative echo chamber in

---

[293] Memorandum for DCI from NIO/LA, dated August 4, 1982; DCI, National Intelligence Daily (Cable), TOP SECRET, March 12, 1982.

Washington. Even after the fall of the Communist bloc, Menges continued to warn of a "communist" threat to the United States from Russia and China.

The March 1982 coup in Suriname failed but the opposition would try again in December, only to be defeated a second time. The CIA's reference to "conservative elements of Surinamese society" is noteworthy. The Javanese community, with its strong presence in business, was opposed to Bouterse, who was from the more numerous and more leftist Creole African sector.

The CIA-Dutch plan was tipped off to Bouterse, possibly by the Brazilians who were opposed to a coup. Bouterse took swift retaliatory action. Although Bouterse was blamed for firebombing radio stations and a newspaper and union office in Paramaribo on December 8, 1982, there are suspicions that these may have been false flag operations carried out by the CIA to destabilize Bouterse. Key opposition figures, including two leaders of the Communist Party, arrested and they were executed on the evening of December 8 at Fort Zeelandia. Bouterse has denied ordering the executions. However, Bouterse still faces a criminal investigation for the executions but as President he now enjoys immunity from prosecution.

After the debacle in Paramaribo, the Senate and House Intelligence Committees blocked any further CIA actions to overthrow Bouterse and the CIA's plans for a Suriname coup were leaked to the media, including ABC News.

After the coup attempt against Bouterse, Cuba increased its aid to Suriname and helped to train Bouterse's personal security force. Bouterse veered further to the left and attended the non-aligned summit in New Delhi, flying first to Havana with Grenada Prime

Minister Maurice Bishop, then to Moscow, and on to New Delhi.[294] However, on October 23, 1983, after U.S. military forces invaded Grenada after the bloody coup against and execution of Bishop, Bouterse became alarmed at the Reagan administration's military aggressiveness. Bouterse expelled the Cuban ambassador, fired several pro-Cuban Suriname government officials, and terminated Cuba's assistance program, all with the approval of Duemling.

Suriname's third largest ethnic group is Javanese from Indonesia. In 1982, Obama's mother, Ann Dunham, who spoke Javanese, was well-entrenched with CIA programs in Java through her employment with USAID and the Ford Foundation, and who used her Indonesian last name, re-spelled Sutoro from Soetoro, would have been a valuable asset for the CIA's program to destabilize Suriname through its large Javanese minority. Curiously, Ann Dunham's employment contract with the Ford Foundation ended in December 1982, the same month that the CIA attempted to oust Bouterse. During her 1981-1982 contract with the Ford Foundation, Ann Dunham spent a lot of time liaising with the Ford Foundation's headquarters in New York, a city that was also a base for the Surinamese opposition.

In 1982, Obama, Jr. was in his last year at Columbia University in New York and in 1982 he went to work for BIC, which conducted outreach for the CIA to various leftist governments around the world, seeking to expand its intelligence contacts in otherwise hostile environments like that which existed in Suriname.

---

[294] Clifford Krauss, "Suriname Zigs Left, Zags Right," *The Nation*, February 11, 1984.

Although CARICOM leaders expressed shock that Obama would fail to invite Bouterse to the White House reception last month in New York, the nexus of Obama's work in 1983 for the CIA and his mother's possible ties to Surinam's Javanese community to assist in the coup against Bouterse may lie at the heart of Obama's disdain for the Suriname President. Considering Obama's adoption of Nixon- and Reagan-era coup policies in Latin America, Bouterse should consider himself the next target for an Obama-authorized coup in Latin America. Unlike the coup against Zelaya and the attempt against Correa, a coup attempt against Bouterse could carry with it a family vendetta from President Obama, himself.

The Obama administration not only maintained the Bush administration's policies, which sought to promote confrontation with the progressive bloc of Latin American nations, but actually hearkened back to the past imperialistic policies of the administration of Richard Nixon. During the Nixon administration, Secretary of State Henry Kissinger, who was also National Security Adviser, oversaw the bloody overthrow of Chilean Socialist President Salvador Allende on September 11, 1973 (which in Chile is a much more important "9/11" than what occurred in the United States in 2001 – although both can be considered rightist putsch coups d'état). After penning an agreement with Colombia's narco-fascist government that saw the establishment of seven new U.S. air and naval bases in Colombia, the Obama administration stood ready to see the election of a right-wing candidate to succeed Chilean Socialist President Michelle Bachelet in the January 2010 presidential election.

All the usual U.S. electoral contrivances appeared to be at work in Chile. Chiefly among them

307

was the National Endowment for Democracy (NED)-funded International Republican Institute (IRI), which champions right-wing political parties in Latin America and was at the center of coups and attempted coups in Haiti, Honduras, Venezuela, and Bolivia and elections in Panama, Nicaragua, Peru, Costa Rica, Paraguay, Guatemala, Mexico, and other countries on behalf of right-wing presidential candidates. On the board of the IRI were such right-wing notables as John McCain, L. Paul "Jerry' Bremer, neocon operative Randy Scheunemann, and Representative David Dreier (R-CA).

Operating alongside the IRI to influence the Chilean election were USAID, a virtual arm of the CIA, and the National Democratic Institute for International Affairs (NDIIA), on whose board and advisory board served such individuals as Madeleine Albright, Geraldine Ferraro, former Representative Martin Frost (D-TX), former Representative Stephen Solarz (D-NY), and former Representative Richard Gephardt (D-MO).

The NED funded both the IRI and NDIIA from U.S. taxpayers' money.

After helping to stir up labor and public service problems in Chile, particularly involving the privatization of mass transit in Santiago, the U.S.-led contrivance of governmental and non-governmental organizations, including those connected to George Soros's Open Society Institute, clearly favored the Harvard-educated billionaire right-wing candidate of the Alliance for Chile (APC), Sebastian Pinera, over his center-left main challenger former President Eduardo Frei Ruiz-Tagle. It was a mirror image of U.S. support for rightist presidential candidates in Mexico, Panama, Colombia, and other Latin American countries.

Pinera had been linked to a 1982 CIA bank operation in Chile involving the liquidated Talca Bank

308

and money laundering involving Chilean dictator General Augusto Pinochet. During his reign, Pinochet hid millions of dollars in foreign bank accounts, including many in the United States, particularly in Washington, DC's Riggs Bank, a bank that was closely connected to the Bush family before being acquired by PNC Bank.

The time frame for the Pinera revelations about CIA banking operations was important since it occurred one year before President Obama went to work for the CIA front in Manhattan, BIC. Obama was involved in writing specialized economic reports for the CIA front company for countries that included Chile. Although his role in the firm was downplayed, Obama at 22-years old, had his own office and secretary. And at 22-years old, Obama was meeting influential Japanese bankers and German bond traders. In fact, BIC had a close relationship with former West German Chancellor Helmut Schmidt, as well as former British Prime Minister Edward Heath, during the time that Obama worked for BIC.

BIC's links with Communist governments grew closer when countertrading, or sophisticated bartering deals, became the preferred method of trading between Western capitalist countries and nations with centralized planning economies. Trading houses such as Marc Rich, Cargill, Philipp Brothers, and the Man Group excelled at exchanging nontransferable currencies like Soviet rubles and Polish zlotys and U.S. dollars and Swiss francs.

Just before his inauguration as president, Gannett News Service carried the following item about Obama's employment for BIC: "1983-84: Works for Business International Corp., a firm helping American business abroad." [295] Gannett failed to do its homework on the firm's links to the CIA.

Australian author John Pilger stated that BIC specialized in infiltrating foreign labor unions with the goal of promoting disruptions in targeted economies. Pilger stated that BIC, as a CIA front, engaged in such actions in Australia. More recently, the CIA has used labor disruptions in pre-coup attempts in Venezuela and Bolivia. Labor strife was also used by the CIA to cause problems for Bachelet's government in Chile, as well as the husband and wife Kirchner presidencies in Argentina.

Although BIC had its headquarters in New York, near the United Nations, in 1984, while Obama worked for the firm, it leased an office in downtown Washington at 815 15th St. NW, near what would eventually become Obama's home, the White House. While Obama was with BIC, the firm closely monitored the burgeoning foreign debts of Latin American nations, thanks primarily to high U.S. interest rates. The Sandinista government in Nicaragua was also high on BIC's watch list, something that may have colored Obama's reaction to the military coup against Zelaya in Honduras and the opposition to that coup from Sandinista President Daniel Ortega in Nicaragua. As a CIA employee from 1983 and 1984, Obama would have been indoctrinated into the entire U.S. propaganda effort aimed at convincing the American people that there was a "communist threat" to the United States in Central America.

The tilting of the Obama administration to Pinera raised eyebrows all over Latin America, which has, after

---

[295] Gannett News Service, Obama Inauguration: Barack Obama Timeline, January 18, 2009.

310

the support of the Obama administration for the military coup against President Manuel Zelaya in Honduras, taken a jaundiced view of the intentions of Obama in Latin America.

The use of Colombia as an American "aircraft" carrier in Latin America also reminded Latin Americans, especially Chileans, of the actions of the Nixon administration. Declassified Nixon administration documents indicated that the Nixon administration used Brazil as a base for overthrowing Allende in Chile. The use of Colombia by the Obama administration had many Latin American countries recalling the worst excesses of the Nixon administration in the region. According to documents obtained by the National Security Archive, a Nixon conversation with Brazil's President Emilio Medici in 1971 stated, "The president [Nixon] said that it was very important that Brazil and the United States work closely in this field. . . . If money were required or other discreet aid, we might be able to make it available." Medici, Brazil's military dictator, told Nixon that Brazilian military officers were working with Chilean officers to overthrow Allende. Nixon designated Kissinger, who later served as Obama's special envoy to Moscow, as his back channel liaison to Medici to discuss the overthrow of Allende and the use of a sex scandal involving an affair and a love child with Miss Peru to embarrass left-wing Peruvian President Juan Velasco Alvarado of Peru.

Given the policies of the Obama administration toward Latin America, Colombia's President Alvaro Uribe replaced Emilio Medici as America's willing "dirty tricks" operative in Latin America. In fact, when it came to Latin America, Barry Obama began looking more and more like "Tricky Dick" Nixon, every day.

In a practical carbon copy of Ronald Reagan's covert policies in Latin America, President Obama not only authorized CIA-planned coups in Honduras and Ecuador, but, according to sources in Costa Rica, re-launched a new generation of Contras to destabilize the Sandinista government of President Daniel Ortega in Nicaragua.

As in the 1980s, the Contras were operating from Honduras, which, after the CIA's and Mossad's ouster of President Manuel Zelaya, became a safe operating base for the Nicaraguan rightists, and Costa Rica. Costa Rica was governed by a right-wing administration, including a pro-Israeli Vice President, Luis Lieberman Ginsburg, who authorized the Costa Rican Intelligence and Security Directorate (DIS) to work with Mossad to wiretap phone lines, emails, and web sites to ensure the success of the Contra activities being directed against Ortega.

The pro-U.S. docile governments of Costa Rican President Laura Chinchilla, Honduran President Porfirio Lobo, and Panamanian President Ricardo Martinelli were reportedly supporting the CIA and Mossad operations in Nicaragua. Martinelli was one of Israel's few allies in Latin America and he condemned the UN's Goldstone Report on Israel's invasion and genocide in Gaza. Under Martinelli, Israeli training programs for the Panamanian National Police increased substantially.

Nicaragua saw a surge in "civil society" activity, most notably operated by the CIA-connected USAID, the National Endowment for Democracy (NED) and its components, and George Soros's various non-governmental organization (NGO) contrivances, including the Movement for Nicaragua. Costa Rican sources pointed to two USAID-linked contractors being involved in the covert activities in Costa Rica, Tetra

Tech International, which had a substantial historical link to the CIA, particularly in the Middle East, and DPK Consulting, which was not only active in Costa Rica but also in Honduras, El Salvador, Guatemala, Dominican Republic, Ecuador, and Venezuela.

Ortega, who was barred from running for re-election in 2011 before waiving the constitutional prohibition, faced the same CIA, Mossad, and NGO construct that forced Zelaya from office in Honduras. Ortega reinstated a 1987 constitutional provision, known as Law 201, that permitted judges and other government officials to stay in office beyond their terms until replacements could be appointed. The U.S.-backed opposition cried foul in a manner similar to the proposed constitutional referendum that was used to force Zelaya from office in Honduras.

U.S. ambassador to Honduras Hugo Llorens was the key player in providing support to the neo-Contras and to ensure that the Honduran resistance movement to the Lobo regime did not receive assistance from the Ortega government across the border in Nicaragua. Lloren's role was similar to that of John Negroponte during the Reagan administration, complete with CIA-backed death squads in Honduras resuming assassinations of student, labor leaders, and journalists.

U.S. covert activities in Honduras and Nicaragua were staged out of the Palmerola airbase in Honduras and were coordinated largely by Col. Robert W. Swisher, the U.S. Defense Attaché at the U.S. embassy in Tegucigalpa. Williams Brands was the USAID coordinator who provided U.S. funds from the Office of Transition Initiatives to NGOs acting on behalf of U.S. intelligence. Silvia Eiriz, the political officer, was also reportedly the CIA station chief who coordinated the anti-Ortega activity with her counterpart in Managua.

The anti-Ortega operation in Nicaragua was the primary responsibility of U.S. ambassador Robert Callahan, an old CIA hand who went back to the days of assisting Negroponte with the running of the death squads in Tegucigalpa in the 1980s.

The Sandinsta movement was split, thanks to CIA and NGO interference, into pro-Ortega and anti-Ortega factions.

The Nicaraguan opposition became engaged in "false flag" street violence using bogus Sandinistas in classic "false flag" action carried out on behalf of the CIA and Mossad stations in Managua.

Similar activities on the Colombian-Venezuelan border were carried out against civilian targets in Colombia and then blamed on Revolutionary Armed Forces of Colombia (FARC) working with Venezuela's President Hugo Chavez. In fact, the attacks were carried out by Israeli and British commandos dressed in FARC uniforms, according to Latin American sources. The operation was designed to force Chavez from office by tying him to terrorists. The Venezuelan Directorate of Intelligence and Prevention Services (DISIP) linked the phony FARC attacks in Colombia to media propaganda operations orchestrated by Venezuela's Jewish community leaders working closely with opposition-controlled media in Venezuela, as well as media in the United States and Europe.

The CIA and Mossad were funding their neo-Contras with proceeds from the growing drug trade in Honduras and Costa Rica. As a result, drug-related murders were increasing on both sides of the Nicaraguan-Costa Rican and Nicaraguan-Honduran borders. When he was in power in Honduras, Zelaya drastically reduced the drug trade.

In Honduras and Costa Rica, customs officials looked the other way as Israeli private security personnel, mostly ex-Israeli commandos, guarded half-length trucks without license plates that were moving drugs and weapons from Honduras and Costa Rica into Nicaragua to support the new Contras gearing up to fight the Sandinistas prior to the 2011 election.

Key border crossing points for the Israelis were in the Peñas Blancas National Park of Costa Rica and Cardenas, Nicaragua on Lake Nicaragua. The Penas Blancas area was a hotbed of Contra activity during the Reagan administration's secret war against Nicaragua. Old CIA bases in Honduras that once supported the Contras in the 1980s were also reportedly being reactivated.

Costa Rican police and DIS personnel were allegedly involved in the cross-border drugs and weapons trafficking. A Colombian bank was being used to buy up land along the Costa Rican-Nicaraguan border ostensibly for "tourist" purposes but the $2 billion project was designed to establish staging areas for renewed Contra warfare in Nicaragua with the expectation that the Sandinistas would remain in power beyond the 2011 election. The U.S. private military contractor Dyncorp also provided assistance to the Contras using the cover of "humanitarian assistance."

After conducting its successful coup d'etat in Honduras against President Manuel Zelaya, the neo-imperialistic Barack Obama administration became bent on ousting Nicaraguan President Daniel Ortega by massing a huge U.S. Coast Guard and Marine Corps presence in neighboring Costa Rica, a base of operations for Reagan administration-backed CIA operations in the 1980s in support of the Nicaraguan contras.

Costa Rican government officials, including President Laura Chinchilla, Vice President Luis Liberman Ginsburg, Security Minister Jose Maria Tijerino, counter-narcotics commissioner Mauricio Boraschi, and the Costa Rican Congress agreed to Operation Joint Patrol, which saw U.S. Marines, U.S. Coast Guard vessels, and helicopters and combat aircraft descend on Costa Rica, which maintained no military forces of its own.

Not only was Obama expanding the U.S. military presence in Central America; the Caribbean (where a U.S. Cooperative Security Location [CSL] was being built in the Dominican Republic to complement other expanded U.S. Forward Operating Locations (FOLs) in Aruba, Curacao, and Panama; and Colombia, but the Obama administration also inked base agreements with countries in southern South America, including an agreement to establish a Military Operations on Urban Terrain (MOUT) base at the Fort Aguayo naval base in Chile and an air facility in Resistencia in Chaco province in Argentina.

For Latin America, ex-CIA employee Barack Obama, Jr. was as much an interventionist as George H. W. Bush. One could expect nothing else from a CIA-bred president in a part of the world the CIA always considered to be its personal "backyard." The CIA coursed through their veins. The venom that Obama spat forth when dealing with Ortega in Nicaragua and Qaddafi in Libya made it appear that he was "finishing the job" started by Reagan and G. H. W. Bush. It was "back to the future."

Afterword

Barack Obama and his family, while vacationing in Hawaii for the Christmas and New Year's holiday prior to the 2012 Republican presidential caucuses in Iowa, visited the East-West Center and an exhibit honoring Ann Dunham's anthropological work in Indonesia. Obama and his family visited the less-than-inclusive photographic exhibit, titled "Through Her Eyes: Ann Dunham's Field Work in Indonesia." Not mentioned in the exhibit were the details of Ann Dunham Soetoro's work on behalf of the CIA in Indonesia and the complicity of her husband, Lolo, in the massacre of some one million Indonesians.

The Obamas also visited the National Memorial Cemetery of the Pacific at Punchbowl to pay their respects to Stanley Armour Dunham. The Obama visit to the East-West Center and the Punchbowl helped to cement the false history of Obama's family developed over the decades by their true employers, the CIA. A complicit corporate media merely helped to reinforce the fairy tale story of the "rags-to-riches" Obama, Jr. prior to the beginning of the actual presidential campaign, mere hours before the Iowa caucuses.

It also helped that Obama, working with Hawaii Senator Daniel Inouye, managed to restore $16.7 million for the East-West Center originally cut by the Republican-controlled House of Representatives. The money for the East-West Center was embedded in the Consolidated Appropriations Act of 2012, which consisted mostly of military construction programs for Hawaii, including an aviation combat installation at

Schofield Barracks and a Readiness Center at Kalaeloa, formerly Barber's Point.[296]

Washington Post columnist David Ignatius, whose own connections to the CIA have been on the lips of many Washington observers and pundits over the years, penned an unusual op-ed column in *The Washington Post* on the tenth anniversary of the 9/11 terrorist attack. Ignatius wrote that Obama, the anti-war candidate of 2008, disappeared into a presidency marked by secret wars. Ignatius wrote that Obama "is opaque, sometimes maddeningly so, in the way of an intelligence agent." Ignatius quoted National Intelligence Director James Clapper as stating that Obama was "a phenomenal user and understander of intelligence" who hungered for extra intelligence material during the President's Daily Brief.

Ignatius also wrote that Obama did not like to "leave fingerprints" in making decisions in private and after receiving intelligence in the rawest form as possible.[297] Ignatius was either speculating about Obama's CIA agent-like behavior or had been passed some inside information about Obama's previous work by numerous sources inside the intelligence community who had shared information with Ignatius in the past.

Exposing Obama's and his family's ties to the CIA was not without heavy criticism from certain sectors of the American right-wing, elements that had long enjoyed a close relationship with the CIA through political and financial links. For example, Accuracy in Media, a right-wing "media watchdog" operation

---

[296] Chad Blair, "Inouye Still Brings Home the Bacon," *Honolulu Civil Beat*, December 20, 2011.

[297] David Ignatius, "The covert commander in chief," *The Washington Post,* September 10, 2011.

established by Reed Irvine, an apologist for past CIA outrages in El Salvador and the Unification Church, itself having ample links to the CIA, and its stewardship of the right-wing *Washington Times*, took to task anyone who would dare report on Obama's CIA links. Recalling the CIA's past use of the Mellon Foundation as a financial conduit to various political groups, it should be noted that AIM enjoyed the financial backing of right-wing philanthropist Richard Mellon Scaife

In a November 18, 2011, screed on the website of Accuracy in Media, the group's chief polemicist, Cliff Kincaid, attacked those reporting on Obama's CIA connections:

"Tabloids sometimes get the story right, such as when the *National Enquirer* exposed the love child of former Democratic presidential candidate John Edwards. But its sister publication, the *National Examiner* (also published by American Media Inc.) has a real dud on its hands in the case of Mondo Frazier's new book, *The Secret Life of Barack Hussein Obama*, which is promoted on the cover of the November 21 issue that is screaming at people in the supermarket check-out lines.

This 'scrupulously researched' book, according to the book flap, includes such 'eye-opening' revelations as that of a female 'Obama associate,' who allegedly spent a night with Obama and then 'moved to the Caribbean, where it was whispered that she was involved in overseeing a mysterious fund-raising apparatus.'

Frazier's bio says he has 'written and edited for a variety of publications, including the Official Racing Program & News,' and is the 'founder/editor/writer of DeathBy1000Papercuts.com.' It is not clear what the 'Official Racing Program & News' is all about.

One thing is certain: his own website describes itself as 'The WORLDWIDE LEADER in WEIRD,' which is certainly true. The book is also weird. Underneath photos of 'Stars Without Makeup!,' the cover of the Frazier book is featured on the *National Examiner* and trumpets 'news' about Obama's alleged arrest in Russia, 'his strange CIA cover-up,' and his 'sinister Pakistan ties' going back 30 years. But a quick look finds that Frazier relies on Wayne Madsen for the claims of Obama's CIA ties. Madsen is the propagandist for Russian TV who has been making the rounds alleging that Obama may be a secret CIA operative. Such fanciful and easily discounted claims have the effect of diverting attention away from Obama's communist and socialist connections, which is where the scrutiny should be applied."[298]

It stands to reason that the CIA would pull out all the stops to ensure the "plausible deniability" of Obama's links to the CIA remained ironclad. The ludicrous notion that the CIA or any other part of America's secret power structures would permit a Communist sympathizer to become President of the United States is laughable on its face. However, as long as there was a notion that Obama was some sort of "Manchurian Candidate," a product of a secret Kremlin cabal, attention was taken off Obama's irrefutable links to Langley.

Barack Hussein Obama. Jr. was elected as the result of charismatic speeches and simple catchy phrases like "Hope," "Change," and "Yes we can." The CIA pioneered in the use of political psychology in pre- and post-coup d'etat engineering and election tampering in

---

[293] Cliff Kincaid, "The Secret Life of Barack Obama," Accuracy in Media, November 18, 2011.

nations around the world. For the American people in 2008, the CIA chickens, indeed, came home to roost.

322

Appendix

MIDDLE EAST – AFRICA – SOUTH ASIA

This publication is prepared for regional specialists in the Washington community by the Middle East - Africa Division, Office of Current Intelligence, with occasional contributions from other offices within the Directorate of Intelligence. Comments and queries are welcome. They should be directed to the authors of the individual articles.

CONTENTS

Saudi Arabia: Structural Changes Being Considered. .1

Kenya: Uneasy Stalemate. 3

25X1D

Pakistan-Afghanistan: Afghan Troop Movements a Response to Tribal Clashes in Pakistan. 7

June 24, 1975

TOP SECRET UMBRA

SECRET

COPY NO. 71
OCI NO. 0403/62

9 February 1962

Current Intelligence Weekly Summary

DIA and DOS review(s) completed.

CENTRAL INTELLIGENCE AGENCY
OFFICE OF CURRENT INTELLIGENCE

SECRET

SECRET

CURRENT INTELLIGENCE WEEKLY SUMMARY

9 February 1962

SOVIET-TURKISH RELATIONS . . . . Page 14

The USSR is engaged in a new effort to weaken Ankara's ties with the West and to encourage neutralism both within the government and among political leaders outside the ruling party. The Turkish Government has publicly rejected recent Soviet offers of financial and technical assistance, but Moscow probably continues to hope that economic problems will lead Turkey in the future to look to the USSR for economic aid.

KENYA CONSTITUTIONAL CONFERENCE . . . . Page 15

The conference on Kenya's constitution scheduled to open in London on 14 February is likely to produce a timetable for the final stages of the colony's transition to independence. British and Kenya leaders expect establishment some time this summer of a government headed by an African chief minister, with independence likely early next year. The chances are fairly good that Jomo Kenyatta and his extremist associates can be isolated at the conference and a "national government" of moderate elements formed to lead Kenya into independence.

CONFERENCE OF INDEPENDENT AFRICAN STATES . . . . Page 16

The 20 moderate African states which participated in the pan-African conference held in Lagos, Nigeria, between 22 and 30 January achieved some progress toward closer economic and technical cooperation. However, the boycott of the meeting by the five radical Casablanca group states and by Tunisia and Libya, plus the Sudan's early withdrawal, damaged the prestige of the conference and wrecked Nigeria's hopes of presiding over a rapprochement between the moderate and radical groupings.

FOREIGN POLICY DEVELOPMENTS IN THE ASIAN COMMUNIST SATELLITES . . . . Page 17

Mongolia, having gained UN membership, has renewed its attempts to secure recognition from numerous countries and has been recognized by three in the past week. North Korea's and North Vietnam's efforts in this regard have been less successful. In intrabloc affairs, Mongolia alone of the three has given the USSR strong support on

SECRET

5

Secret

DIRECTORATE OF
INTELLIGENCE

WEEKLY SUMMARY
Special Report

The New Order in Indonesia

Secret
45
11 August 1967
No. 0303/67A

6

☐ are Celebrating
Gil's ACS Award
and
30th Anniversary of Teaching
University of Hawaii 1948 - 1978 University of Illinois
at the
East-West Center, University of Hawaii
STAT   Tuesday, April 3, 1979 at 10 PM
following the
Division of Chemical Education Dinner

Join Us!

Send your "yes"
Before March 28th

7

8

Approved For Release 2004/10/13 : CIA-RDP88-01315R000100520001-9

⊕ BUSINESS INTERNATIONAL'S EXECUTIVE BRIEFING ⊕

LATEST FROM CANBERRA . . .

LATIN AMERICA

ASIA

WESTERN EUROPE

EASTERN ECONOMIC REVIEW AND BUSINESS INTERNATIONAL
STAFFS, FINALLY ... CONSIDERATION WAS FURTHER VISIT TO TOKYO AND SIDE TRIP
TO SINGAPOREFOR INTERVIEWS WITH U.S. OIL AND MINING
COMPANIES ON ACTUAL OR POTENTIAL TRADE RELATIONS WITH PRC.
MEANWHILE, GAO ENQUIRY IN U.S. WILL INCLUDE DISCUSSIONS
WITH USG AGENCIES, U.S. COMPANIES HEADQUARTERS AND TRADE
ASSOCIATIONS.

8. OUR INITIALCONCERN ABOUT GAO INSISTENCE ON CONTACTING
PRC AGENCIES-- CHINA RESOURCES AND BANK OF CHINA, -- WAS
DISSIPATED WITH TEAM SENSIBLY TOOK OUR ADVICE THAT COM-
PLICATIONS ANDPOSSIBLE MISUNDERSTANDINGS WOULD NOT BE
WORTH SMALL AMOUNT OF INFORMATION LIKELY TO BE OBTAINED.
PROBLEMS OF ACCESS TO FILES WAS NOT SO EASILY RESOLVED.
HERE TEAM SEEMEDTO WANT TO TESTUS TO SEE HOW FAR THEY
COULD GAIN ACCESS WHEN THERE WAS CLEARLY ALREADY NOT
ENOUGH TIME TO ACTUALLY READ INTO THE VOLUME OF FILES
THEY WERE REQUESTING. THEY ASKED TO EXAMINE FILES ON
R2 SUBJECT HEADING WITHPRIORITY TO 19 IN PRC ECONOMIC
AFFAIRS (GENERAL), FOREIGN TRADE AND TRADE PROMOTION
(WHICH INCLUDES OUR FILES ON THE CANTON TRADE FAIR).
WE SCREENED THE 19 IN ACCORDANCE WITH 4 FAM 934. THE
TEAMINITIALLY CLAIMED WE WERE NOT SUPPOSED TO DO THAT;
THEN, UPON ... 4 FAM 934, ASSERTED WE WERE
OBLIGED TO PROVIDE A LIST OF ANYTHING REMOVED FROM THE

#7 EAST EUROPE BRANCH NOTES February 5, 1974 25X1

EAST GERMANY

Trade Conference with Westerners Opens

A three-day roundtable conference █████ Business International and East German officials concerned with the promotion of trade opened in East Berlin on February 4. Orville Freeman, President of Business International, heads the foreign participants, comprising presidents, vice presidents, and board members of important US and West European enterprises. GDR Premier Sindermann told the group further steps toward detente have a favorable effect on the expansion of foreign economic activities. He also said that East Germany plans to expand substantially its economic relations with non-socialist countries.

25X1

APPROVED FOR RELEASE 1993
CIA HISTORICAL REVIEW PROGRAM

11 May 1965

MEMORANDUM FOR THE RECORD

SUBJECT: ████████, Conversation with

1. The writer had a short discussion this morning with ████ ██y concerning the involvement of A. Philip RANDOLPH, the distinguished Negro leader, in the so-called "Declaration of Conscience" against participation in the war in Vietnam. In fact, this Declaration of Conscience goes so far as to attempt to get Negroes to refuse to register for the draft which is, in effect, illegal activity and against Federal law.

2. In summarizing ████████ point of view, the problem appears to be something like this. The Communist left is making an all out drive to get into the Negro movement. If through any mechanism they can link prominent Negro leaders to illegal activities and activity which is against President Johnson's policy, this may cause a serious break between Johnson and the Negro leadership which in turn, may create a violent disruption in the Negro Civil Rights Movement which would give the Communists an opportunity to cause chaos and disruption.

3. Furthermore, if the above is coupled with an exposure of Martin Luther KING, Jr. by other than members of his own race, the damage to the Negro movement would be impossible to estimate. ████████ is gravely concerned that KING may be exposed by white sources, official or otherwise, which would have no good effect and would probably only make KING a martyr. ████████ was also concerned that KING might possibly be assassinated before his exposure which would have the effect of making him a martyr and would not be at all helpful to the Negro movement. It is ████████ belief that some new or other Martin Luther KING must be removed from the leadership of the Negro movement, and his removal must come from within not from without. ████████ feels that somewhere in the Negro movement, at the top, there must be a Negro leader who is "clean" who could step into the vacuum and chaos if Martin Luther KING were either exposed or assassinated.

4. In summary, ████ feels that unless the Negro leaders, other than KING, are informed and are capable of intelligent maneuvering, the Communists or Negro elements who will be directed by the Communists may be in a position to, if not take over the Negro movement, completely disrupt it and hence cause extremely critical problems for the Government of the United States.

James Allen

14

UNCLASSIFIED

OFFICIAL ROUTING SLIP

	TO	NAME AND ADDRESS	DATE	INITIALS
1		Mr. Tweedy, D/DCI/IC		
2				
3				
4				
5				
6				

ACTION	DIRECT REPLY	PREPARE REPLY
APPROVAL	DISPATCH	RECOMMENDATION
COMMENT	FILE	RETURN
CONCURRENCE	INFORMATION	SIGNATURE

Remarks:

PENDING YOUR APPROVAL, I HAVE NOT COORDINATED THIS PROJECT OUTSIDE PRG

FOLD HERE TO RETURN TO SENDER

FROM: NAME, ADDRESS AND PHONE NO.   DATE 5/18/72

Chief, PRG

15

THE DIRECTOR OF CENTRAL INTELLIGENCE
WASHINGTON, D. C. 20505

MEMORANDUM FOR: Director, Bureau of Intelligence and Research,
                Department of State
                Director, Defense Intelligence Agency
                Deputy Director for Intelligence
                Deputy Director for Science & Technology
                Director of National Estimates

SUBJECT: ARPA Sponsored Research Relating to Intelligence
          Production

1. In furtherance of the responsibilities assigned to me by the President to improve the intelligence product, I am interested in working with the Advanced Research Projects Agency of the Defense Department to identify research which ARPA could sponsor with the object of providing better analytic methodologies for use in the production of intelligence.

2. I am advised that the ARPA Director of Behavioral Sciences intends to engage a contractor for six months to develop a typology of basic and applied research needs, with particular attention to political science. This project will cover more than the interests of the intelligence production organizations, but I am assured that participation of the intelligence community would be both welcome and important.

3. We have an opportunity to identify our research needs and to work with the ARPA contractor in developing a program which, hopefully, will have both near term and long term benefits for the intelligence community.

4. The ARPA survey is expected to get underway in July or August. In the meantime, it is requested that each addressee prepare a list of the types of basic and applied research projects which his organization considers would be most useful as a means of improving analytic methodologies or of making available analytic tools which could be used in the production of intelligence. Suggestions as to areas in which exploratory research might prove profitable should be included.

335

CONFIDENTIAL

25X1A

5. These lists should be submitted to [ ] Chief, PRG/IC, not later than 15 June 1972, along with nomination of a member to the ad hoc group which will review the submissions from all addressees and formulate a program for my review and submission to ARPA.

6. Once the ARPA contractor has been selected, members of the ad hoc group will serve as points of contact in the intelligence production community. In order for the contractor to prepare his recommendations as to the types of projects which ARPA should finance, and to insure that he has translated the intelligence proposals into researchable issues, it will be necessary for him to be able to interview appropriate members of the intelligence production community. This is to insure that he understands what is involved in the production process and the problems concerning which research in the behavioral sciences should be able to make a contribution. Security clearances for the contractor will be handled by ARPA.

7. It is expected the contractor will submit a report before the end of 1972.

8. ARPA has been supporting research in the behavioral sciences for a number of years and considerable work, which is potentially related to intelligence production, has been conducted at M.I.T., Yale, the University of Michigan, U.C.L.A., the University of Hawaii, and other institutions as well as in corporate research facilities. I look on this proposed survey as an opportunity to relate ARPA supported research more directly to the needs of the intelligence production community.

Richard Helms
Director

DO/A Registry
File

6 1 APR 1977

MEMORANDUM FOR: Director of Central Intelligence

FROM: John F. Blake
Deputy Director for Administration

SUBJECT: Introduction of The Honorable Harlan
Cleveland - CIA Guest Speaker on
10 May 1977

1. Action requested: It is requested that you introduce the CIA Guest Speaker, Ambassador Harlan Cleveland, on 10 May 1977, at 3 p.m. in the Headquarters Auditorium.

2. Background: The CIA Guest Speaker on Tuesday, 10 May 1977, will be Ambassador Harlan Cleveland, Director of the Program in International Affairs of the Aspen Institute, who will speak on "The Ethics of Public Service in Foreign Affairs." Mr. Cleveland was U.S. Ambassador to NATO under President Johnson and President of the University of Hawaii from 1969-1974. He is also a former Dean of Syracuse University's Maxwell Graduate School of Citizenship and Public Affairs. He has written and lectured on the subject of ethics. A biography of Ambassador Cleveland and a copy of our invitation to him are attached.

3. Recommendation: It is recommended that you introduce Ambassador Cleveland at the CIA Guest Speaker Program. Your association with this first major presentation to a CIA and Intelligence Community audience on the subject of ethics in public affairs will indicate your interest in the question and help encourage our efforts to stimulate discussion within the Agency concerning it.

/s/ John F. Blake

John F. Blake

Attachments:
1 - Biography of Ambassador Cleveland
2 - Copy of Invitation

ADMINISTRATIVE - INTERNAL USE ONLY

ADMINISTRATIVE - INTERNAL USE ONLY

(This Notice Expires 31 October 1984)

DOI CHRONO
18 April 84

STAT

18 April 1984

ORGANIZATIONAL CHANGE

POLITICAL PSYCHOLOGY DIVISION

OFFICE OF GLOBAL ISSUES

Effective 16 April 1984, the Political Psychology Division (FPD) is renamed the ███████ Psychology Center and transferred from the Office of Global Issues (OGI) to the Office of Scientific and Weapons Research (OSWR).

STAT

Robert M. Gates
Deputy Director for Intelligence

Distribution "A" (1-6)

ADMINISTRATIVE - INTERNAL USE ONLY

SECRET/SENSITIVE

Agenda for Meeting on Political Action
August 5, 1982

I. Concept and Current Capabilities

A. Foreign policy and national security role of political
   action (Secretary Shultz and Secretary Weinberger)

B. Case history of what can be done by private and government
   efforts--Portugal (Deputy Secretary Carlucci)

C. Need for comprehensive capabilities--covert action but also
   U.S. trade unions, political parties, foundations, government
   initiatives and programs to do campaigns, infrastructure
   building, etc. (Director Casey)

D. Information programs (Director Wick and Chairman Shakespeare)

E. President's perspective and role (Judge Clark)

II. The Future

A. Priority to be given political action

B. Near-term needs

   1. FY '83 funding for radios

   2. Moving bipartisan foundation ahead

   3. USG organizational structure (USICA keeps lead on
      information and NSPG remains intact; NSC leads on
      overall political action; all agencies examine
      internal structures/capabilities for giving high
      priority to political action.)

C. Long-term needs

   1. NSSD on political action (policy strategy and
      permanent solution to funding).

SECRET/SENSITIVE
RDS 7/30/02

20

21

22

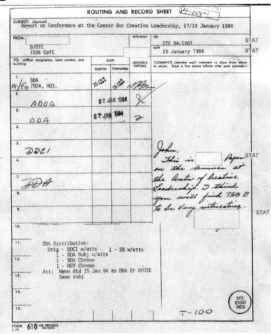

SECRET/NOFORN

SAIC/CW DC: 92-017
COPY NUMBER 2

**Phenomenological Research
and
Analysis
Technical Proposal (U)**

27 August 1992

SAIC

Science Applications International Corporation
An Employee-Owned Company
Authors:

Edwin C. May, Ph.D. and Wanda L. W. Luke

Presented to:

U. S. Government

RFP MDA908-92-R-0164

Submitted by:

Science Applications International Corporation
Cognitive Sciences Laboratory
1010 El Camino Real, Suite 330
Menlo Park, California 94025

Classify by: Contractor Security Procedures Guide
DT-S-1040-S
Declassify on: OADR

1010 El Camino Real, Suite 330, P.O. Box 1412, Menlo Park, CA 94025 • (415) 325-8292

SECRET/NOFORN

24

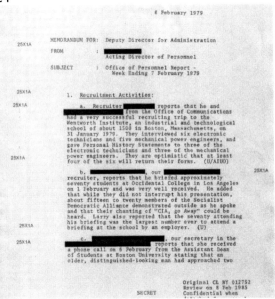

25

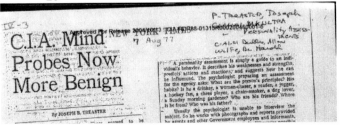

26

8 February 1979

25X1A MEMORANDUM FOR: Deputy Director for Administration

FROM : ▓▓▓▓▓▓
Acting Director of Personnel

SUBJECT : Office of Personnel Report -
Week Ending 7 February 1979

25X1A

1. Recruitment Activities:

25X1A

a. Recruiter ▓▓▓▓▓ reports that he and
▓▓▓▓▓▓ from the Office of Communications
had a very successful recruiting trip to the
Wentworth Institute, an industrial and technological
school of about 1500 in Boston, Massachusetts, on
31 January 1979. They interviewed six electronic
technicians and five mechanical power engineers, and
gave Personal History Statements to three of the
electronic technicians and three of the mechanical
power engineers. They are optimistic that at least
four of the six will return their forms. (U/AIUO)

b. ▓▓▓▓▓▓▓, our ▓▓▓▓▓▓ 25X1A
recruiter, reports that he briefed approximately
seventy students at Occidental College in Los Angeles
on 1 February and was very well received. He added
that while they did not interrupt his presentation,
about fifteen to twenty members of the Socialist
Democratic Alliance demonstrated outside as he spoke
and that their chanting of "CIA, go Away" could be
heard. Larry also reported that the seventy attending
his briefing was the largest number ever to attend a
briefing at the school by an employer. (U)

25X1A

c. ▓▓▓▓▓▓▓▓, our secretary in the
▓▓▓▓▓▓▓ reports that she received
a phone call on 6 February from the Assistant Dean
of Students at Boston University stating that an
older, distinguished-looking man had approached two

Original CL BY 012752
Review on 8 Feb 1985
Confidential when

SECRET

345

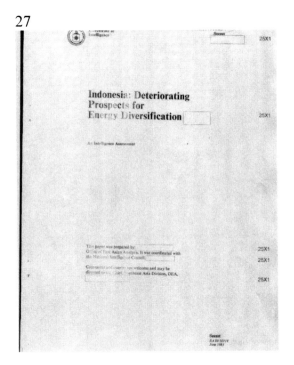

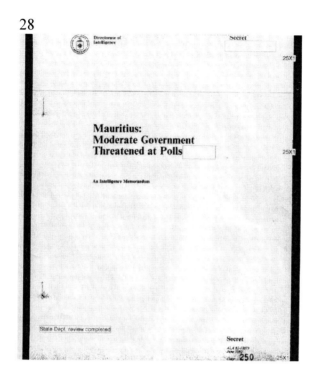

30

THE DIRECTOR OF CENTRAL INTELLIGENCE

WASHINGTON, D. C. 20505

National Intelligence Officers

DDI-6224-82/1
29 July 1982

MEMORANDUM FOR: See Distribution

FROM   : National Intelligence Officer for Latin America

SUBJECT   : Monthly Warning Assessment: Latin America

1. Attached is a copy of the Latin America Warning Assessment based on our discussion of 21 July 1982.

2. The next warning meeting will be held on 18 August 1982 at 1015 hours in room 7064 CIA headquarters with the following tentative agenda and requested brief oral presentations (2-3 minutes) by department/agency and individual as indicated:

Nicaragua

-- Military buildup--troops vs weapons; Soviet and Cuban presence/activities (CIA, ____)   25X1

-- Internal political situation; Directorate politics; anti-Sandinista threat (INR, Patterson)

Honduras

-- Terrorist activity; Nicaraguan threats (CIA, ____)   25X1

El Salvador

-- Guerrilla/military balance; plans and intentions (DIA ____)   25X1

-- Coalition politics; implications for reforms, certification; potential for negotiations (INR, Tomchik)

Suriname

-- Political situation; Cuban involvement (CIA, ____)   25X1

Guyana

-- Prospects for Burnham regime (INR, DuBose)
                                                                 25X1

SECRET   25X1

349

31

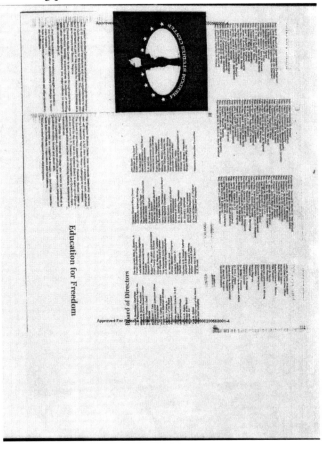

32

P 1

FORM APPROVED
BUDGET BUREAU NO. 47-R117.4

DEPARTMENT OF STATE
FOREIGN SERVICE OF THE UNITED STATES OF AMERICA

APPLICATION FOR

☑ RENEWAL ☐ AMENDMENT ☐ EXTENSION
OF

☑ PASSPORT ☐ CARD OF IDENTITY
☐ REGISTRATION ☐ CERTIFICATE OF IDENTITY

Document No. F-777788 Date Issued July 19, 1965

POST Djakarta, Indonesia

☐ REFERRED TO DEPARTMENT FOR ACTION
☑ RENEWED (EXPIRES) to 21, 18, 1970
☑ AMENDED AS REQUESTED

$ 5.00 FEE COLLECTED
☐ NO FEE COLLECTED

(PLEASE PRINT NAME IN FULL)
(FIRST NAME) (MIDDLE NAME) (LAST NAME)
I, Stanley Ann Dunham Soetoro, a citizen of the United States, do hereby apply for the service indicated above. (If amendment, set forth details on REVERSE.)

DATE OF BIRTH (Month, day, year) PLACE OF BIRTH
Nov. 29, 1942 Wichita, Kansas

NOW RESIDING AT
Djakarta, Indonesia

UNITED STATES RESIDENCE (Street address, city, county, state)

IN THE EVENT OF DEATH OR ACCIDENT NOTIFY (Name in full, relationship, street address, city, state)
Stanley Armour Dunham, Bank of Hawaii, Honolulu

HAVE YOU EVER BEEN REFUSED A PASSPORT OR REGISTRATION AS A CITIZEN OF THE UNITED STATES?
IF THE ANSWER IS YES, EXPLAIN WHEN AND WHY

NO

PROPOSED TRAVEL PLANS

I INTEND TO RETURN TO THE UNITED STATES PERMANENTLY TO
RESIDE WITHIN indefinite MONTHS

I INTEND TO CONTINUE TO RESIDE ABROAD FOR THE FOLLOWING
PERIOD AND PURPOSE INDEFINATE - MARRIED
TO AN INDONESIAN CITIZEN

IF RETURNING TO U.S. COMPLETE THE FOLLOWING

POST OF DEPARTURE

NAME OF SHIP OR AIRLINE

DATE OF DEPARTURE

I have and (and no other person included or to be included in the passport or documentation has), since acquiring United States citizenship, been naturalized as a citizen of a foreign state; taken an oath or made an affirmation or other formal declaration of allegiance to a foreign state; entered or served in the armed forces of a foreign state; accepted or performed the duties of any office, post, or employment under the government of a foreign state or political subdivision thereof; voted in a political election in a foreign state or participated in an election or plebiscite to determine the sovereignty over foreign territory; made a formal renunciation of nationality either in the United States or before a diplomatic or consular officer of the United States in a foreign state; ever sought or claimed the benefits of the nationality of any foreign state; or been convicted by a court or court martial of competent jurisdiction of committing any act of treason against, or attempting to overthrow, or bearing arms against, the United States, or conspiring to overthrow, put down or to destroy by force, the Government of the United States.

(If any of the above-mentioned acts or conditions have been performed by or apply to the applicant, or to any other person included in the passport or documentation, the portion which applies should be struck out, and a supplementary explanatory statement under oath (or affirmation) by the person to whom the portion is applicable should be attached and made a part of this application.)

Stanley Ann Dunham Soetoro
(To be signed by Applicant)

Subscribed and Sworn to(affirmed) before me this 13th day of August 13, 1968
(SEAL)
Signed ___ Consul ___ of the United States at Djakarta, Indonesia

(The Department will assume that the consular officer, in executing the application for the Department's decision, is fully satisfied as to the applicant's identity unless a notation to the contrary appears.)

FORM FS-299
1-64

351

352

Index

100 Universities Program, 192, 226
30 September Movement, 60
303 Committee, 234
Abercrombie, Neil, 11
Academi Inc., 257
Accuracy in Media, 318, 319, 320
Afghanistan, 21, 27, 86, 89, 99, 100, 101, 146, 147, 148, 152, 174, 177, 184, 225, 228, 279, 280, 285
Africa Bureau, 238
African American Labor Center, 236
African National Congress (ANC), 238, 274
African-American Institute, 236, 238, 240
Agnew, Spiro, 135, 246, 270
Aidit, D. N., 49
Air America, 28, 90, 138, 149, 254
Air Asia, 28, 149
Airlift Africa, 4, 10, 11, 16, 19, 23, 34, 154, 210, 235, 239, 240

Albania, 228
Albright, Jr., Harry W., 247
Albright, Madeleine, 308
Algeria, 2, 7, 277
All-African People's Conference (AAPC), 6
Allen, Morse, 286
Allende, Salvador, 108, 300, 307
Al-Mansour, Dr. Khalid, 290
Altgeld Gardens, 284
AMAX, Inc., 241
American Anthropological Association (AAA), 93
American Committee on Africa, 14
American Metal Climax Corporation, 241
American Samoa, 149, 231
American Society of African Culture (AMSAC), 236
Anderson, Jack, 190
Andrew Hamilton Fund, 237

353

Angola, 2, 7, 13, 14, 127, 139
Appalachian Fund, 237
Aristide, Jean-Bertrand, 255
Asia Foundation, 91, 92, 127, 140, 162, 233, 259, 260
Asian Development Bank, 88, 105, 135, 136, 147, 151, 152, 164, 209
Asian Foundation, 240
Atlantic Richfield Company (ARCO), 88
Australia, xvi, 46, 76, 87, 92, 110, 112, 139, 144, 148, 149, 211, 220, 263, 277, 309
Australian Secret Intelligence Service (ASIS), 110, 201
Australian Security Intelligence Organization, 201
Bandaranaike, Solomon, 106
Bank of Credit and Commerce International (BCCI), 143, 148
Bank of Hawaii, 34, 37, 138, 142, 143, 148, 149, 150, 249, 271
Bank Rakyat, 88, 284

Barbados, 279, 289
Basutoland, 7
Batista, Fulgencio, 216
Bavadra, Timoci, 211
Beacon Fund, 236
Beals Report, 98, 107, 108, 114, 116, 117, 120, 121, 123, 133, *See* Beals, Dr.Ralph
Beals, Dr.Ralph, 93, 95
Beck, George, 249
Beech, Keyes, 282
Belafonte, Harry, 14
Bell, David E., 210
Benjamin Rosenthal Foundation, 237
Berenger, Paul, 265
Berkeley mafia, 254
BIC. *See* Business International Corporation
Business International Corporation, 119, 146, 163, 164, 175, 176, 177, 178, 179, 199, 200, 202, 203, 204, 205, 206, 207, 208, 209, 210, 211, 212, 213, 214, 215, 216, 217, 218, 219, 220, 222, 223, 225, 227, 229, 230, 233, 241, 272, 275, 276, 280, 282, 283, 284,

285, 289, 306, 309, 310
Bishop Museum, 127
Bissell, Richard, 109, 164, 234
Black Panthers, 212, 269, 280, 284, 285, 287, 289, 291
Blackwater, 257
Blagojevich, Rod, 295
Blake, John F., 174, 219
Bloodworth, Dennis, 282
Bloomberg, Michael, 248
Bolivia, 118, 156, 228, 257, 279, 299, 302, 307, 310
Borden Trust, 236
Bourne, Dr. Peter, 188
Bourne,Sir Geoffrey, 189
Bouterse, Desi, 153, 301
Brennan, John O., xii, 81, 202
Brezhnev, Leonid, 202
British North Borneo, 89
Broad-High Foundation, 237
Brown, H. Rap, 285
Brzezinski, Zbigniew, 146, 181, 183, 193, 232
Budjiardjo, Carmel, 189

Bundy, McGeorge, 102, 113, 234, 245
Burke, John, 189
Burkina Faso, 153, 154, 155, 156
Burma, 27, 45, 92, 233, 277
Bush, George H. W., xiii, xv, xvi, 125, 169, 214, 247, 291, 316
Bush, George W., x, 41, 169, 174, 183, 197, 248
Bush, Jeb, xv
Business International Corporation (BIC), 209
Business International Roundtables, 210
Caltex, 58, 87
Cambodia, 27, 46, 65, 91, 92, 150, 254, 271, 277
Cameroun, 7, 277
Campaore, Blaise, 157, 158
Carlucci, Frank, 33, 176, 274
Carmichael, Stokely, 273, 285
Catherwood Foundation, 237
Celebes, 109, 110, 111, 218

Center for Creative Leadership (CCL), 178
Center for the Study of Democratic Institutions, 217
Central Intelligence Agency (CIA), i, v, ix, x, xi, xii, xiii, xiv, xv, xvi, xvii, 1, 2, 3, 4, 5, 6, 7, 8, 10, 11, 12, 13, 14, 15, 16, 18, 19, 20, 21, 22, 23, 24, 25, 26, 27, 28, 29, 30, 31, 32, 33, 34, 35, 36, 37, 38, 39, 41, 42, 43, 44, 45, 46, 47, 48, 49, 50, 51, 52, 53, 54, 55, 56, 57, 58, 59, 60, 61, 62, 63, 64, 65, 66, 67, 68, 72, 76, 77, 78, 79, 81, 85, 86, 87, 88, 89, 90, 91, 92, 93, 94, 95, 97, 98, 99, 100, 101, 102, 103, 106, 107, 108, 109, 110, 111, 112, 113, 114, 115, 116, 117, 118, 119, 120, 121, 122, 123, 125, 126, 127, 128, 129, 130, 131, 132, 133, 134, 135, 136, 137, 138, 139, 140, 141, 142, 143, 144, 145, 146, 147, 148, 149, 150, 151, 152, 153, 154, 155, 156, 157, 159, 161, 162, 163, 164, 165, 166, 167, 168, 169, 170, 171, 172, 173, 174, 175, 176, 177, 178, 179, 180, 181, 182, 183, 184, 185, 186, 187, 188, 189, 190, 191, 192, 193, 194, 195, 196, 197, 199, 200, 201, 202, 203, 204, 205, 206, 207, 208, 209, 210, 211, 212, 214, 215, 216, 217, 218, 219, 220, 223, 225, 226, 227, 228, 229, 230, 231, 232, 233, 234, 235, 236, 237, 238, 239, 240, 241, 242, 243, 244, 245, 248, 250, 253, 254, 255, 256, 257, 258, 259, 260, 261, 262, 263, 264, 265, 266, 267, 269, 270, 271, 272, 273, 274, 275, 280, 281, 282, 283, 284, 285, 286, 287, 288, 289, 290, 291, 292, 294, 295, 296, 299, 300, 301, 302, 303, 304, 305, 306, 308, 309, 310, 311, 312, 313,

314, 315, 316, 317, 318, 319, 320, 321
Chamoun, Camille, 38
Chavez, Hugo, 163, 255, 299, 300, 304, 314
Cheney, Dick, 171, 197, 206
Chesapeake Foundation, 237
Chiang Kai-shek, 150, 271
Chicago, v, 29, 31, 39, 58, 142, 144, 164, 176, 183, 199, 207, 211, 212, 217, 229, 270, 271, 272, 280, 282, 283, 284, 285, 286, 287, 288, 289, 290, 291, 292, 293, 295, 296, 297
Child, Julia, 32
Chile, 32, 103, 108, 118, 123, 135, 279, 300, 307, 308, 309, 310, 316
China, 3, 7, 13, 16, 21, 29, 32, 42, 45, 46, 47, 76, 87, 88, 109, 112, 114, 130, 137, 203, 213, 242, 262, 304
Chou En-lai, 45
Church of Scientology, 188
Church, Frank, 94, 109, 229

Civil Operations and Revolutionary Development Support (CORDS), 86, 90, 100
Cleveland, Harlan, 174
Climax Molybdenum, 241
Clinton, Hillary, ix, xi, 86, 231, 302
Cohn-Bendit, Daniel, 227
Colby, William, 33, 100, 116, 138, 166, 171, 206, 208, 218
Cold War College, 269, 270, 280
Colombia, xvi, 117, 124, 165, 220, 221, 279, 307, 308, 310, 311, 314, 316
Columbia University, xii, 13, 83, 115, 121, 131, 146, 153, 179, 181, 183, 186, 193, 209, 210, 217, 218, 225, 228, 232, 272, 306
Committee for a Free Asia, 92
Congo (Leopoldville), 7
Congress for Cultural Freedom (CCF), 238
Congress of Cultural Freedom, 233

Conlon, Richard P., 205, 206
Cook County, 270, 296
Cook, Genevieve, 200, 201
Cook, Michael J., 200, 201
Coombs, Walter P., 239
Copeland, Miles, 188, 203
Corporate Data Exchange. Inc., 230
Correa, Rafael, 299
Corsi, Jerome, 29
Costa Rica, 260, 279, 307, 311, 312, 314, 315
Council on Foreign Relations, 33, 99, 164, 213, 226, 234, 236, 249
Covert Action Division Number Five, 244
Cowan, L. Gray, 12
Craig, Greg, 246, 250
Crane, Kent B., 135
Cuban-American National Foundation, 255
Cyprus Amax Minerals Company, 241
Daley, Jr., Richard, 296
David, Joseph, and Winfield Baird Foundation, 237
Davis, Artur, 249

Defense Intelligence Agency (DIA), 172, 184, 187, 195, 196
Defense Signals Directorate (DSD), 201
Desai, Morarji, 202
Development Alternatives, Inc., 126, 129, 131, 163, 254
Development Communities Project (DCP), 283
DeVore, Dr. Irven, 133
Dewey, Alice, 96
Diego Garcia, 265, 266
Dillon, Douglas, 164, 243
Doces Majestic Furniture Company, 34
Dodge Foundation, 237
Doktor, Robert, 172
Dole Corporation, 241
Dole, Bob, 247
Dominican Republic, 27, 279, 312, 315
Drake, Thomas, xiv
du Berrier, Hilaire, 13
Duckett, Carl, 171
Dukakis, Michael, 291
Dulles, Allen, 30, 54, 102, 110, 111, 114, 164, 216, 234, 243, 270

Dulles, John Foster,
111, 243
Dunham, Ann
also Stanley Ann
Obama/Soetoro/Sut
oro, v, xi, xvii, 2,
4, 11, 24, 26, 27,
31, 32, 34, 36, 41,
42, 43, 44, 47, 50,
51, 53, 54, 56, 72,
89, 92, 95, 96, 99,
105, 107, 114, 123,
125, 129, 130, 132,
137, 151, 154, 161,
165, 168, 201, 209,
216, 225, 228, 232,
241, 244, 253, 255,
256, 258, 271,
273, 값275, 280,
284, 306, 317
Dunham, Madelyn, x,
26, 31, 34, 37, 72,
125, 138, 143, 148,
149, 150, 250, 271
Dunham, Stanley
Armour, x, xvii, 12,
23, 31, 32, 33, 34, 36,
37, 39, 72, 169, 271,
317
DuPont, Elise R. W.,
215
Durkin, John, 213
Dwyer, Richard, 189

East African Institute of
Social and Cultural
Affairs, 236
East African Publishing
House, 236
East Germany, 203, 217
East Timor, 41, 128,
130, 162, 168, 245
East-West Center, 22,
34, 46, 47, 48, 52, 56,
67, 86, 89, 91, 104,
116, 126, 128, 132,
136, 137, 162, 170,
243, 244, 260, 264,
269, 317
Economist Intelligence
Unit, 212, 263
Ecuador, 279, 300, 301,
302, 311, 312
Edbrook, C. D., 126
Educational Testing
Service (ETS), 193
Eisenhower, Dwight,
38, 243
Eisenstat, Stuart, 263
El Pyramid Real Estate
and Maintenance
Corporation, 287
El Rukn gang, 212, 280,
284
Emanuel, Rahm, 244,
295
Engberg, Edward, 217
Equator Bank, 256
Erikson Institute, 295
Ethel, Willis G., 166

Ethiopia, 2, 13, 134, 242, 261, 278

Evans, Ben, 171

Evidence-Based Research (EBR), 263

Fairfield Foundation, 238

Faleomavaega, Eni, 231

Family Jewels, 171

Farsight Institute, 187

FBI (Federal Bureau of Investigation), xiv, 24, 35, 36, 98, 229, 230, 269, 272, 273, 283, 286, 287, 288, 289, 290, 291

Fiji, 148, 211

Findlay, Paul, 203

Fisher, John, 272

Fitzgerald, Patrick, 295

Fitzgerald, Peter, 294

Florence Foundation, 237

Food for Peace, 91, 254

Ford Foundation, 4, 12, 14, 43, 50, 59, 63, 67, 88, 93, 94, 95, 97, 102, 104, 113, 120, 130, 135, 136, 151, 152, 154, 162, 164, 168, 209, 210, 218, 225, 232, 233, 234, 236, 238, 253, 306

Ford, Gerald, 171, 246, 262

Fort, Jeff

aka, Abdullah Malik, 287

Fourth World Conference on Women, 256

Franchon, Benoit, 228

Franco, Francisco, 222, 223, 224

Fraser, Donald, 189

Frazier, Mondo, 319

Freedom Studies Center, 269, 270, 272

Freeman, Orville, 173, 203, 217, 243

Freeport McMoran, 241, 245

Gairy, Eric, 188

Gandhi, Indira, 143

Gandhi, Rajiv, 143

Gannett Newspaper Foundation, 282

Gates, Robert, x, xii, 175, 302

Gayler, Noel, 178

Geertz, Dr. Clifford, 58, 95

Geithner, Peter, 43, 55, 232

Geithner, Timothy, 43

Georgia Republic of, 46, 71, 260

Ghana, 6, 7, 92, 114, 134, 151, 153, 154, 155, 156, 278

Gilchrist memo, 57

Gilchrist, Andrew, 57
Gilman, Richard C., 225
Giuliani, Rudolph, 246
Gizenga, Antoine, 20
Gonzalez, Henry, 144
Goodyear Tire and
   Rubber, 58
Gothan Fund, 237
Gottlieb, Dr. Sidney, 60,
   115, 171, 180
Grameen Bank, 256,
   257
Green, Marshall, 167
Grenada, 29, 188, 189,
   190, 302, 303, 305
Guantanamo Bay, xvi,
   116, 184
Guatemala, 29, 109,
   117, 118, 229, 279,
   307, 312
Guinea, 2, 7, 13, 64,
   112, 114, 134, 167,
   208, 245, 278
Gurirab, Theo-Ben, 274
Guyana, 189, 190, 280,
   289
Haig, Alexander, 193
Haile Selassie, 13, 220
Haley, John, 204
Halloran, Richard, 282
Halperin, Morton, 281
Hamilton, Lee, 144
Hammer,Armand, 226
Hampton, Fred, 287,
   288, 291

Harding, Murray Glenn,
   242
Harris, Fred, 117
Harvard University, 94,
   102, 107, 152, 274
Hastert, Dennis, 294
Hawaiian Sumatra. *See*
   Sumatra
Hayakawa, S. I., 215
Haynes, Eldridge, 202,
   205, 209
Haynes, Elliott, 204,
   205, 209
Heights Fund, 237
Helms, Richard, 116,
   170, 178
Ho Chi Minh, 29
Hoffman, Abbie, 285
Holder, Eric, 249
Holdridge, John, 136
Holsinger, Joe, 190
Honduras, 118, 280,
   300, 301, 302, 307,
   310, 311, 312, 313,
   314, 315
Hong Kong, 28, 134,
   138, 140, 144, 207,
   213, 214, 277
Hoover, J. Edgar, 24,
   35, 272, 287
Hudson Institute, 304
Huffco, 264
Huffington, Arianna,
   264

Huffington, Michael, 264
Huffington, Roy M., 264
Hugh Tovar, Bernardo, 165
Hughes, Thomas L., 95
Huizenga, John, 171
Hull, Blair, 292
Human Ecology Fund, 114, 115, 116
Human Terrain System, 86, 100, 101
Hume, Cameron, 78
Humphrey, Hubert, 14, 206
Hungary, 221, 228, 276
Hunt, Richard M., 240
Ibbitson, Helen, 200, 201
Ignatius, David, 318
Independent Research Foundation, 229
Indonesia, v, xi, 7, 25, 26, 27, 37, 41, 42, 46, 47, 49, 50, 51, 52, 53, 55, 56, 57, 58, 59, 60, 61, 62, 63, 64, 65, 68, 69, 71, 73, 75, 76, 77, 78, 79, 81, 82, 83, 84, 85, 86, 87, 88, 89, 90, 91, 92, 94, 95, 96, 97, 99, 101, 102, 104, 105, 106, 108, 109, 110, 111, 몘112, 113,

114, 116, 119, 120, 123, 126, 128, 130, 131, 132, 133, 134, 135, 136, 138, 143, 146, 147, 151, 152, 153, 154, 155, 161, 162, 165, 166, 167, 168, 189, 194, 196, 201, 202, 209, 215, 218, 221, 224, 229, 231, 232, 235, 244, 245, 253, 254, 258, 260, 263, 264, 269, 271, 277, 284, 285, 296, 306, 317
Indonesian Biodiversity Foundation, 258
Indonesian Environmental Forum, 258
Indonesian Heritage Society, 126
Indonesian National Development Planning Agency (BAPPENAS), 128
Inouye, Daniel, 140, 317
Institute for Defense Analysis (IDA), 229
Institute for Management and Education and Development, 104
InterMatrix, 215

International
Association of
Cultural Freedom
(IACF), 233
International
Cooperation Agency
(ICA), 295
International Labor
Organization, 129,
152, 163
International Monetary
Fund (IMF), 50, 156
International
Republican Institute
(IRI), 307
International Subud
Center, 104
Israel, 158, 214, 236,
260, 279, 301, 312
J. Frederick Brown
Foundation, 237
J. M. Kaplan Fund, 236
J. Walter Thompson
advertising agency,
259
Jackson, Jr., Jesse, 293
Jamaica, 280, 289
Japan, 27, 37, 76, 85,
87, 134, 140, 166,
221, 277
Jarrett, Valerie, 295
Java, 25, 43, 50, 51, 56,
64, 75, 76, 80, 87, 94,
95, 101, 104, 107,
109, 110, 111, 128,

129, 130, 132, 151,
163, 165, 218, 306
Johnson, Lyndon B., 46,
243
Jones, Howard P., 47,
48
Jones-O'Donnell
Foundation, 237
Joseph P. Kennedy
Foundation, 2
Juan Carlos, King, 222,
223, 224
Kariuki, Josiah, 8
Kellman, Jerry, 283
Kempton, Murray, 233,
234
Kennedy, Edward, xiii,
115, 116
Kennedy, John F., 22,
66, 199, 210, 216,
227
Kenneth Kaunda
Foundation, 236
Kentfield Fund, 236
Kenya, 1, 3, 4, 6, 8, 9,
10, 11, 13, 15, 16, 17,
18, 19, 23, 26, 29, 33,
43, 64, 73, 84, 91, 92,
104, 129, 151, 152,
153, 154, 235, 239,
241, 244, 278, 291
Kenyan African
Democratic Union
(KADU), 3

Kenyan African National Union (KANU), 3
Kenyatta, Jomo, 7, 236
Kerr, Sir John, 91, 144
Khrushchev, Nikita, 202
Kibler, Austin, 171
Kim, Stephen, xiv
King, Jr., Martin Luther, 78
Kiriakou, John, xiv
Kissinger, Henry, 92, 136, 162, 163, 167, 193, 204, 245, 246, 281, 307, 311
Kizito, Renato, 244
Koinonia. *See* Koinonia Foundation
Koinonia Foundation, 242
Konrad Adenauer Stiftung, 255
KOPASSUS, 41, 135
Kosygin, Aleksei, 202
Kunen, James, 210, 211
Kyrgyzstan, 260, 261
LaHood, Ray, 294
Lake Arrowhead, 239
LaMacchia, Frank, 239
Lansdale, Edward, 112, 270
Laos, 21, 27, 65, 77, 88, 91, 129, 155, 254, 260, 277

LaRouche, Lyndon, 180, 207
Lashbrook, Dr. Robert, 115
Lebanon, 24, 25, 27, 31, 32, 37, 72, 139, 176, 279
Lederer, Jr., William (Bill), 29
Lederer's Bar, 29, 271
Leibowitz, Shamai, xiv
Liberia, 7, 134, 156, 256, 278
Linowitz, Sol M., 205
Lippo Group, 86, 136, 148
Littauer Foundation, 237
Llorens, Hugo, 313
Lobo, Porfirio, 312
Lon Nol, 150, 271, 272
Lowenstein, Allard K., 273
Luce, Clare Boothe, 269, 272
Lucidity Institute, 185
Ludlum, Robert, 189
Lumumba, Patrice, 19, 20, 60, 210, 240
Lydman, Jack, 167
Macapagal-Arroyo, Gloria, 259
Machel, Samora, 220
Malaysia, 87, 89, 90, 92, 139, 165, 186, 260, 277

Mali, 7, 89, 278
Malik, Adam, 50, 87
Manchurian candidate,
xi, 116, 194
Manning, Bradley, xiv,
116
Mansur Medeiros,
Mohammad, 107
Maraniss, David, 200,
201
Marcos, Ferdinand, 142,
143, 259, 271
Marcuse, Herbert, 227
Marshall Foundation,
237
Martens, Robert J., 165
Masood, Ahmad Shah,
145
Masters, Edward, 165
Matthias, Willard, 12
Mauritius, 264, 265,
266, 278
Mboya, Tom, 3, 6, 8,
15, 18, 154, 235
McCain, John, xi, 204,
307
McCone, John, 226
McGehee, Ralph, 62
McGregor Fund, 237
Mead, Margaret, 41, 97
Mellon Foundation, 319
Menges, Constantine,
304
Menteng, 36, 64, 67, 68,
69, 75, 76, 77, 78, 79,
80, 82

Menteng State
Elementary School,
64
Mercer Island,
Washington, 14, 26,
37, 38, 77
Methven, Stuart E., 127
Mexico, 27, 117, 135,
202, 207, 211, 221,
224, 255, 280, 307,
308
Military Professional
Resources, Inc.
(MPRI), 263
Millikan, Max, 94, 102,
196
Milton Obote
Foundation, 236
Mitrione, Dan, 137, 260
Mobil Oil, 5, 43, 58, 65,
263, 264
Mobutu, Joseph, 19
Mombasa, 26, 84
Mondale, Walter, 206
Mondlane, Eduardo, 14
Mongolia, 21
Monroe Fund, 237
Monroe Institute, 187
Monroe, James L., 195
Montesinos, Vladimiro,
257
Morales, Evo, 257, 299
Morocco, 7, 28, 278
Morse, Wayne, 134

365

Mossad, 154, 155, 157, 259, 301, 311, 312, 313, 314
Mossadeq, Mohammed, 296
Mozambique, 2, 14, 220, 278
Mugabe, Robert, 300
Muliro, Masinda, 3
Musharraf, Pervez, 146
Nasakom, 61
Nasution, 48, 53, 60, 61
Nation of Islam, 212, 285, 289
National Democratic Institute for International Affairs (NDIIA), 308
National Endowment for Democracy (NED), 163, 238, 262, 307, 312
National Security Agency (NSA), 8, 178, 201
National Student Association, 228, 235, 273
Natomas Oil Company, 87
Ne Win, 233
Nehru, Jawaharlal, 202
Netherlands New Guinea, 245
New Order

Post-CIA coup Indonesian government policy, 50, 85, 96, 162, 254
New Zealand, 87, 110, 148, 277
Nicaragua, 119, 155, 157, 204, 242, 260, 280, 299, 302, 307, 310, 311, 312, 313, 314, 315, 316
Nielsen, Waldemar A., 234
Niger, 7
Nigeria, 2, 7, 89, 114, 134, 263, 278
Nixon, Richard, 1, 150, 203, 213, 243, 246, 283, 299, 307
Nkrumah, Kwame, 6, 154
Norman Fund, 237
North American Congress on Latin America (NACLA), 230
Nugan Hand Bank, 138, 139, 148, 149
Nyasaland, 4, 7
Nyerere, Julius, 262
Obama, Barrack. *See* Obama, Sr., Barack H.

Obama, Jr., Barack, vii,
ix, 3, 15, 31, 43, 119,
150, 153, 192, 216,
218, 225, 226, 258,
274, 275, 280, 316
Obama, Michelle, xvi,
158, 222, 296, 307
Obama, Sr., Barack H.,
xvii, 73, 210, 216,
280
Occidental College, 83,
145, 146, 150, 153,
163, 183, 191, 192,
194, 200, 212, 219,
225, 226, 228, 239,
272, 274, 280, 281
Odinga, Oginga, 8, 10,
11, 15, 241
Odinga, Raila, 10, 11,
241
Office of Strategic
Services (OSS), x, 1,
31, 137, 194
Office of Transition
Initiatives, 255, 313
OPERATION BLUE
BAT, 38
Operation
Cenderawasih, 64
Operation CHAOS, 285
OPERATION
MIDNIGHT
CLIMAX, 181
Ortega, Daniel, 155,
257, 310, 311, 315

OSS. *See* Office of
Strategic Services
Ouko, Robert, 5
Paisley, John, 139, 206
Pakistan, 27, 28, 56, 82,
86, 87, 88, 90, 99,
101, 116, 119, 126,
131, 136, 145, 146,
147, 148, 151, 152,
153, 201, 218, 253,
257, 258, 279, 285,
288, 320
Pakistan Agricultural
Development Bank,
151
Palau, 149, 260
Palmer, Alice, 293
Panama, 134, 205, 280,
307, 308, 316
Pappas Charitable Trust,
237
Papua New Guinea, 64,
149
Park Chung Hee, 271
Parsons, Richard, 244,
250
Patman, Wright, 213
Peace Corps, 55, 59,
117, 120, 130
People's Temple, 187,
188
Peru, 32, 118, 124, 280,
307, 311
Pherson, Ann, 243
Pherson, John R., 243

367

Philippines, 27, 37, 46, 54, 55, 87, 91, 110, 112, 139, 142, 152, 165, 167, 259, 260, 271, 277
Pickering, Thomas, 263
Pike, Otis, 229
Pilger, John, 309
Pinck, Dan, 25, 134
Pinera, Sebastian, 308
PKI
  Communist Party of Indonesia, 8, 47, 48, 49, 50, 51, 53, 55, 57, 60, 61, 62, 63, 86, 97, 106, 161, 162, 165, 166, 167, 168, 189, 190
Poitier, Sidney, 14
Pratt Furniture, 34, 37, 271
Price Fund, 236, 237, 238
Princeton University, 281
Project ART, 65
Project ARTICHOKE, 169, 171, 180, 197
Project BLUEBIRD, 180
Project CAMELOT, 100, 101, 108
Project CENTER LANE, 196
Project Democracy, 132, 255

Project GONDOLA WISH, 196
Project GRILL FLAME, 172, 196
Project LOOKING GLASS, 177, 197
Project MK-DELTA, 114
Project MK-NAOMI, 114
Project MK-ULTRA, v, 60, 103, 114, 115, 169, 170, 173, 180, 181, 187, 188, 194, 197, 286
Project MOCKINGBIRD, 176
Project Modjokuto, 96, 102
Project PANDORA, 187, 197
Project PHOENIX, 62, 68, 100, 101
Project PROSYMS, 56, 57, 64, 68, 86
Project Simpatico, 117, 118
PROJECT SLEEPING BEAUTY, 188
Project STAR GATE, 186, 187, 196, 197
Project SUN STREAK, 196
Punahou High School, 150

Qaddafi, Muammar, 156, 157, 212, 286, 287, 316
Radio Free Europe, 228
Ramgoolam, Seewoosagur, 265
Ramon Magsaysay Foundation, 259
Rand Corporation, 28, 52, 101, 174
Rawlings, Jerry, 153
Reagan, Ronald, xii, 135, 247, 299, 311
Remnick, David, 102
Rewald, Ron, 140, 141
Reynolds, Mel, 260, 293
Rhee, Syngman, 272
Rice, Condoleezza, 263
Rice, Susan, 263
Richardson, Bill, 189, 255
Riley, Bob, 249
Risen, James, xiv
Robert E. Smith Fund, 237
Robinson, Gerold T., 228
Robinson, Jackie, 14
Rockefeller Family Fund, 230
Rockefeller Foundation, 117, 225
Rockefeller, David, 193, 248
Rockefeller, Happy, 246

Rockefeller, Laurance, 248
Rockefeller, Michael, 245
Rockefeller, Nelson, 207, 245, 246, 247, 248
Romney, George, 270
Roosevelt, Eleanor, 14
Rositzke, Harry, 2
Rostow, Walt W., 102, 243
Rove, Karl, 183, 248
Rumsfeld, Donald, 171, 262
Russian Institute, 228, 232
Ryan, George, 295
Ryan, Jack, 292, 293, 294
Ryan, Leo, 189
Ryan, William Fitts, 234
San Jacinto Foundation, 238
San Miguel Fund, 237
Sankara, Thomas, 153, 157
Santo Fransiskus Assisi Catholic school, 64
Satterthwaite, Joseph C., 239
Scheper-Hughes, Nancy, 98
Schlesinger, James, 171
Schnider, Robert, 293

School of International Affairs (SIA), 229
Schultz, George, 176
Science Applications International Corporation (SAIC), 184
Scientific Intelligence Committee (STIC) CIA, 190
Scott, Janny, 11, 38, 39, 46, 47, 51, 64, 66, 77, 82, 88, 89, 104, 128, 130, 164, 284
Scott, Michael, 296
Scott, Peter Dale, 96, 97
Sears, Roebuck & Company, 272
Senegal, 7, 278
Siegelman, Don, 248
Sigmund, Paul, 274
Sindermann, Horst, 217
Sirleaf-Johnson, Ellen, 256
Society for the Anthropology of Consciousness (SAC), 195
Society for the Investigation of Human Ecology, 114, 116, 195
Socony (Standard Oil of New York), 5
Soebarkah, 43, 81, 82, 83, 105, 145

Soetoro, Lia, 73, 74, 75
Soetoro, Lolo, xvii, 26, 36, 42, 47, 49, 51, 53, 56, 57, 58, 59, 64, 65, 66, 67, 68, 69, 72, 82, 83, 94, 114, 125, 129, 132, 146, 154, 161, 163, 166, 167, 200, 224, 231, 269, 273, 280
Soetoro-Ng, Maya, 72, 76
Sokoine, Edward, 262
Somalia, 2, 7, 86, 101, 278
Soomro, Muhammadmian, 146
Soros Foundation, 261
Soros, George, 11, 256, 260, 308, 312
South Africa, 2, 7, 238, 262, 266, 274, 278, 291
South East Asia Treaty Organization (SEATO), 111
South Korea, 28, 37, 91, 254, 271, 272
South Vietnam, 27, 68, 77, 86, 89, 90, 91, 97, 100, 134, 166, 217, 228, 254, 260
South West Africa People's Organization (SWAPO), 274

Southern Air Transport, 149

Southern Rhodesia, 4, 7, 104, 239

Soviet Union, 3, 76, 87, 109, 203, 210, 215, 240, 262

Spain, 91, 148, 222, 223, 224, 254, 276, 280

Spanish Republic, 223

Sprague, Mansfield D., 234

Standard Oil of California, 5

Standard-Grunbaum Furniture, 34

Stanford Research Institute (SRI), 172, 175, 180

Steinem, Gloria, 229, 275

Sterling, Jeffrey, xiv

Stevenson, Adlai, 14, 243

Stone, Shepherd, 232

Student Nonviolent Coordinating Committee, 289

Students for Democratic Society (SDS), 210, 272, 273

Subuh Sumohadiwidjojo, Muhammad (Bapak), 104

Suharto, 42, 47, 48, 49, 50, 52, 53, 55, 56, 57, 58, 60, 61, 63, 66, 68, 71, 85, 87, 89, 94, 96, 97, 106, 113, 120, 128, 129, 130, 135, 136, 143, 150, 154, 162, 164, 165, 166, 167, 189, 218, 221, 224, 245, 253, 254, 264, 269, 271

Sukarno, 7, 41, 42, 44, 45, 47, 48, 49, 51, 52, 54, 55, 56, 58, 59, 60, 61, 62, 64, 76, 85, 86, 93, 97, 101, 106, 108, 109, 110, 111, 112, 113, 131, 135, 136, 151, 154, 162, 165, 189, 245, 269, 271, 296, 300

Sumatra, 50, 51, 58, 59, 76, 109, 110, 111, 112, 130

Suriname, 153, 154, 156, 299, 301, 302, 304, 305, 306

Sutton, Percy, 290

Sydney and Esther Rabb Charitable Foundation, 237

Taiwan, 21, 27, 37, 91, 139, 140, 142, 150, 254, 271

Tavistock Institute, 179, 180, 186

Taylor, Robert, 285
Tempelsman, Maurice, 243
Thailand, 27, 28, 46, 55, 65, 77, 89, 90, 91, 92, 97, 105, 134, 138, 139, 152, 165, 166, 215, 228, 254, 260, 277
The Analysis Corporation, xii, 81, 202
Tito, Josip, 222
Tower Fund, 237
Treaster, Joseph, 194, 195
Trilateral Commission, 247
Trinidad and Tobago, 289
Trowbridge, Alexander B., 215
Tshombe, Moise, 20
Tsvangirai, Morgan, 261
Tsvangirai, Susan, 261
Tudjman, Franjo, 261
Turdi, 36, 77, 80
Turner, Stansfield, 126, 129, 150, 152, 170
Tutu, Desmond, 78
Tweedy, Bronson, 170
U.S. Africa Command (AFRICOM), 100
U.S. Agency for International

Development (USAID), 25, 43, 55, 67, 134, 209
U.S. Information Agency (USIA), 30, 77, 123, 176
U.S. Rubber Company, 58
Ukraine, 260
Union Oil of California (UNOCAL), 58
United Arab Republic, 7, 38
United Nations, 55, 209, 222, 310
University of Hawaii, 2, 3, 4, 6, 10, 11, 23, 27, 34, 36, 42, 44, 46, 52, 53, 54, 56, 86, 87, 94, 96, 104, 107, 116, 126, 127, 132, 137, 142, 151, 152, 162, 169, 170, 172, 174, 175, 178, 186, 188, 191, 210, 232, 235, 236, 244, 260, 269, 273, 280, 281, 282
Untung, 48, 49, 50
Venezuela, 124, 134, 163, 222, 254, 255, 280, 299, 300, 304, 307, 309, 312, 314
Verity, Jr., William, 178
Vernon Fund, 237
Vignola Furniture Company, 271

Village Community
Development Bureau,
232
Virgin Islands
Economic
Development Bank,
204
Walters, Vernon, 13
Warden Trust, 237
Wazed, Sheikh Hasina,
257
Webber, Dan, 190
Weinberger,Caspar, 176
West Papua, 114, 168,
231
Whitlam, Gough, 92,
139, 144, 205
WikiLeaks, xiv, 85, 145
Williams, Edward
Bennett, 250
Williford-Telford Fund,
237
Wisner, Jr., Frank, 132
Wisner, Sr., Frank, 93,
108, 132
Wolfowitz, Paul, 136
Women's World
Banking, 255
World Affairs Council,
226, 239

World Bank, 50, 55, 59,
88, 105, 119, 152,
154, 156, 186, 241,
254, 264, 267
World Youth Festival,
274
Xe Services, 257
Yapex Union Oil
Company, 88
Yemen, 91, 101, 228,
279
Young Obama
movie, 77, 78, 79
Yudhoyono, Susilo
Bambang, 52, 231
Yugoslavia, 76, 222,
224, 276
Yunus, Muhammad,
256
Zaire, 127, 150, 262
Zelaya, Manuel, 299,
310, 311, 315
Zhukov, Yuri, 227
Zia-ul Haq,
Muhammad, 258
Zimbabwe, 262, 300,
301
Zimbabwe African
National Union-
Patriotic Front, 262
Zobel, Enrique, 143

Wayne Madsen's book *The Manufacturing of a President* is the number one authoritative book on the origins of President Barack Hussein Obama, Jr. At once provocative, profound and contrary to every other account written on the past and present life of Obama, it is also the best resource for journalists daring to go beyond "news conference journalism" and a unique historical account in it's own right.

Applying his talents as a former U.S. Navy intelligence officer, Madsen dissects, catalogues and exposes Obama and his regime for what they really are, traveling to Jakarta, Indonesia to interview former school authorities and individuals associated with Obama during his early life there.

One of the best minds in journalism and one of the last of a dying breed of true investigative journalists, Madsen's magnificent contribution to literature will stand as a penetrating look into the falsehoods and outright lies put forth by the Obama administration in response to less the informed and "balanced" media in America, and is a primer for investigative journalism, journalists, and news media professionals that live and breathe journalism - and insist on the truth.

- Robert S. Finnegan, former editor of the *Jakarta Post*

Madsen at the Jakarta Menteng school, attended by Obama as a child. (Photo by Robert S. Finnegan)

This enquiry into Obama's formative years in Indonesia shows how his administration is largely modeled after the Suharto regime – with the 2008 bailout of banks and major industries running parallel to the crony capitalism that reigned in Jakarta, extrajudicial killings by drones and U.S. special forces identical to the murderous methods of the Kopassus death squads, and a blatant disregard for constitutional guarantees similar to the illegal repression during and after the Indonesian military coup of the 1960s. Obama's boyhood dream of becoming the supreme leader of a militarist state has been realized – not in Indonesia but in the United States of America.

- Yoichi Shimatsu, former editor of the *Japan Times Weekly* and founding lecturer at the journalism schools in Tsinghua University and the University of Hong Kong

About the Author

Wayne Madsen is a Washington, DC-based investigative journalist, author and syndicated columnist. He has written for *The Village Voice, The Progressive, Counterpunch, In These Times,* and *The American Conservative*. His columns have appeared in *The Miami Herald, Houston Chronicle, Philadelphia Inquirer, Columbus Dispatch, Sacramento Bee,* and *Atlanta Journal-Constitution,* among others.

Madsen is the author of *The Handbook of Personal Data Protection* (London: Macmillan, 1992), an acclaimed reference book on international data protection law; *Genocide and Covert Operations in Africa 1993-1999* (Edwin Mellen Press, 1999); co-author of *America's Nightmare: The Presidency of George Bush II* (Dandelion, 2003); author of *Jaded Tasks: Big Oil, Black Ops & Brass Plates* and *Overthrow a Fascist Regime on $15 a Day.* (Trine Day).

Madsen has been a regular contributor on RT. He has also been a frequent political and national security commentator on Fox News and has also appeared on ABC, NBC, CBS, PBS, CNN, BBC, Al Jazeera, and MS-NBC. Madsen has taken on Bill O'Reilly and Sean Hannity on their television shows. He has been invited to testify as a witness before the US House of Representatives, the UN Criminal Tribunal for Rwanda, and a terrorism investigation panel of the French government.

As a U.S. Naval Officer, he served in anti-submarine warfare, telecommunications, and computer security positions. He subsequently was assigned to the National Security Agency. Madsen was a Senior Fellow for the Electronic Privacy Information Center (EPIC), a privacy advocacy organization.

Madsen is a member of the Society of Professional Journalists (SPJ) and the National Press Club.

Lightning Source UK Ltd.
Milton Keynes UK
UKOW01f2017060417

298543UK00001B/31/P